The Emotional Life of the Toddler

The Emotional Life of the Toddler

ALICIA F. LIEBERMAN

THE FREE PRESS

NEW YORK

The Free Press
A Division of Simon & Schuster Inc.
866 Third Avenue
New York, New York 10022

First Free Press Paperback Edition 1995

Book design by Maura Fadden Rosenthal

Printed in the United States of America

printing number

17 19 20 18 16

Library of Congress Cataloging-in-Publication Data

Lieberman, Alicia F.
    The emotional life of the toddler / Alicia F. Lieberman.
        p.   cm.
    Includes bibliographical references and index.
    ISBN 0–02–874017–3
    1. Toddlers.   2. Toddlers—Psychology.   3. Child
rearing.   I. Title.
    HQ774.5.L54   1993
    649'.122—dc20   93-8018
                                                        CIP

Photographs by Eytan Avital except where noted.

To my parents,
Dr. Manuel Fridman
Dr. Rosa Asrilevich de Fridman

and to my son,
Michael Morris Lieberman

Roots and fruit

Contents

Acknowledgments

EVERY BOOK IS A TRIBUTE TO THOSE WHO MADE IT POSSIBLE. Many people accompanied me in the writing of this book, and their voices are often intertwined with my own.

Three extraordinary women were my early teachers and helped me to discover who I wanted to be.

Mary Ainsworth took me on as a graduate student when I was a newcomer in this country. She introduced me to research, taught me how to observe babies and parents, and gave me the vocabulary of attachment theory, which grows ever more useful with the years. She provided guidance through my doctoral thesis and helped to unlock the pleasures of writing in a new language. She equipped me for the journey ahead, and has remained a trusted and reliable secure base.

From Selma Fraiberg I learned about healing. She knew how pain can be transmitted from generation to generation, from parent to child, and she knew how to speak sensibly, openly and tactfully to break the cycle of alienation and restore intimacy and love. She taught with joy, and her teachings live on as a result.

Marjorie Harley showed me the world beyond infancy. She gave much and expected much, and I am richer for it.

Two superb supervisors pointed me on my current course. Joseph Adelson encouraged me to write and, even more to the point, challenged me to think. Peter Blos, Jr. showed by example. His clinical skills are an ongoing reminder of what is possible when we know how to listen.

I had the good fortune of finding my first job under the direction of Stanley Greenspan, whose ebullient pursuit of knowlege is matched only by his enthusiasm in sharing it. His understanding of constitutional sensitivities in infants ushered important advances in preventive intervention, and it was a privilege to work with him at the cutting edge of this field.

The present deserves as much appreciation as the past. The Infant-Parent Program, where I now work, is my second home in every sense of the word. I owe Jeree Pawl, its Director, a debt of gratitude for many years of inspired and inspiring leadership. This book carries the imprint of many happy hours spent together musing over, discussing, reconstructing, remembering and sometimes simply imagining the inner world of the toddler.

I am fortunate to work with colleagues who are also dear friends. I wish to thank Judith Pekarsky, Graeme Hanson, Barbara Kalmanson, and Stephen Seligman for infusing the activities of teaching, clinical work, and even administration with a spirit of camaraderie and intellectual curiosity that enlivens the daily routine.

Cherished colleagues read earlier versions of this book and were generous with their advice. I want to thank Mary Ainsworth, Berry Brazelton, Emily Fenichel, Jeanne Miranda, and Arietta Slade for their careful reading and their thoughtful comments.

My editor, Susan Arellano, was unstinting in her support and unerring in the clarity of her vision. Herself the mother of a toddler, she knew when refocusing was needed. The book profited greatly from her input.

The vignettes and case examples given in the book involve real life toddlers and their families. I am grateful to them for allowing me to come close and to work with them. This book could not exist without their cooperation.

Stephanie Berg typed this book's manuscript heroically and was my most immediate editor. Her smile or soberness as she gave me back a newly typed chapter gave me either encouragment or early warning, and she was usually right. Anne Cleary, our Administrative Assistant, makes me feel that no goal is out of reach and that she is there as a partner in the reaching.

Most of this book was written at home, after hours, in the sustaining company of my husband, David N. Richman, whose depth of thought and feeling enriches my own. He taught me what it means to be accompanied while in solitude, and I thank him for that and for much more.

The Emotional Importance of Early Relationships

LIVING WITH A CHILD BETWEEN 1 AND 3 YEARS OLD IS AN EXHILARATING experience. Who else could show us so convincingly that a wet, muddy leaf lying on the ground is actually a hidden marvel, or that splashing in the bathtub can bring ultimate joy? Toddlers have the gift of living in the moment and finding wonder in the ordinary. They share those gifts by helping the adults they love to reconnect with the simple pleasures of life.

But toddlers have dark moments too. They are notoriously willful and unpredictable, and their behavior can be difficult to understand and strenuous to handle. At times parents find themselves caught in a contest of wills, vaguely embarrassed at being unable to win more handily at this uneven match. Other times they are simply at a loss. It is hard to fathom what the child is asking for, and the child cannot explain. He or she can only act, repeating the same behavior again and again until the parent finally deciphers the message and comes up with an appropriate response.

The examples of toddler behavior begging for an explanation are multiple.

- Blair hits his head against the wall if he is angry or frustrated.
- Eddy cries with hunger but rejects every choice his mother offers him for dinner.
- Sandra screams and tries to hide when she sees the picture of an elephant in a children's book.
- Lenya lets go of her father's hand and runs toward a horse galloping in the field next to her house.
- Mary looks for her mother all over the house only to run out of the room as soon as she finds her.
- Marty goes back and forth between crying to be held and demanding to be put down.

These and many other behaviors defy adult logic. Why would a child seek pain, choose to stay hungry, become terrified of a harmless picture, rush into danger, search for her mother only to run away from her, or want comforting while rejecting it at the same time?

While inexplicable from the perspective of grownups, these reactions make perfect sense from the viewpoint of a child who is 1, 2, or 3 years old. This book tries to explain why this is so. The ideas presented are my personal synthesis of child observation, clinical work with toddlers and their families, theories of development, and current research findings. The organizing themes come from attachment theory, which was developed by psychoanalyst John Bowlby and psychologist Mary Ainsworth to explain the intense need that all children in the first three years of life have for a close relationship with the mother and a small number of cherished adults. The basic premise of attachment theory is that toddlers can grow into autonomous and competent children only if they can rely on an adult who makes them feel safe and protected. From this basic feeling of security grows the impetus to try out new skills and learn how things work in the world.

The most important emotional accomplishment of the toddler years is reconciling the urge to become competent and self-reliant with the longing for parental love and protection. This process is apparent in the behavior of toddlers who have just mastered walking on their own. The child moves back and forth between staying close to the parent, moving away to do things on his own, and going back to the parent to share discoveries, to be comforted, or simply to "recharge batteries" with a hug or a cuddle before going off yet again for another bout of autonomous activity.

Parents serve as the home base for the toddler's explorations. When they respond to the child's experiences with encouragement and understanding, this home base becomes a *secure base*. The child derives a feeling of security from the parent's support, and this security generates the self-confidence to seek larger horizons.

Different toddlers use the secure base provided by the parents in different ways. Some children are by temperament shy and retiring, and they need more time close to the parents before they are ready to explore on their own. Other children can hardly be held back because they are very active and enthralled by novelty. The temperamental tendencies of toddlers put their own individual stamp on how they use their parents as a secure base for their explorations.

Yet most parents are neither fixed in one place nor infinitely available. The secure base is human, and the parent has to attend to aspects of life other than being responsive to the child. The separate needs and wishes of parents and toddlers have to be negotiated and balanced in a mutually satisfactory way, and what "satisfactory" means changes in the course of development.

When the child first begins to walk, parents postpone or adjust many of their own wishes and plans because the new physical and emotional demands of locomotion often call for immediate and sustained attention. As toddlers get firmer on their feet and acquire greater self-control between about 18 and 24 months, parents are under less pressure to defer to the child. They increasingly expect the toddler to adjust to their plans and wishes rather than the other way around.

This is the time when many of the socialization pressures begin. Older toddlers are asked to learn many new things in a relatively short period of time. They are expected to relinquish the satisfactions of being a baby and trade them in for the more ambiguous pleasures of growing up. Many a toddler feels that toilet training, giving up the bottle, and complying with the rules of the household are more trouble than they were worth. They respond by refusing to do things before they are ready and by throwing a tantrum if all else fails. Yet these protests come at an emotional cost. Toddlers are scared that displeasing their parents will result in losing their love, and this fear finds expression in the common difficulties of toddlerhood, such as separation anxiety, sleep disturbances, and inexplicable fears.

In responding to the needs of the older toddler, the function of parents as protectors undergoes a transformation. They can no longer serve primarily as an external secure base that anchors the child's comings and goings. They must now help the child become a partner in sorting out disagreements and finding solutions that will preserve mutual good will. This partnership leads to a more complex feeling of security that is based on the child's growing feeling of competence in conflict resolution.

Partnership is a reliable ally for the child in times of grief, anger, and frustration because it serves as a protection from despair and emotional collapse. The child learns that he or she can go through difficult times and recover from them. Through the emotional partnership between parent and child, the supportive function of the parent becomes a part of the child. What at first was an external secure base becomes internal. The child comes to carry the parents' care and protectiveness inside of him wherever he goes.

Partnerships are not always harmonious, because disagreements cannot be invariably worked out to both partners' satisfaction. This is probably more true of the toddler years than of any other age until adolescence. Temper tantrums, screaming, defiance, physical aggression, sulking, and alienation are frequent components of family life in raising a toddler. This is as it needs to be. It is neither possible nor desirable to be always attuned to the moods of children because this thwarts their need to test and enrich their individuality by standing up to adult authority. What is possible and

desirable is to cultivate an *attitude* of partnership: to be willing to listen, acknowledge that parents and children at times have different goals, try to reconcile the differences, and agree to disagree if this is not possible.

The partnership between parent and child by necessity has to remain unequal for a long time. The child may feel strongly about his or her goals, but it is the parent who is raising the child and not vice versa. While retaining their empathy, adults need to achieve the self-confidence to have the last word when they are not being cruel or unreasonably arbitrary. Parental firmness reassures the child that the grownups he or she loves know what they are doing and can be trusted to do the right thing.

Every aspect of the toddler's development is influenced by the presence or absence of a secure base and a partnership between parent and child. Milestones like toilet training and common anxieties like fear of separation and sleep disturbances can be understood better from this perspective. Even the child's responses to external events like the beginning of child care or parental divorce become clearer and easier to manage in light of these concepts. The chapters that follow describe how toddlers think, feel, and respond to the challenges of growing up, and how parents can help them meet these challenges with greater self-confidence and joy.

Parents and children help each other to grow. In raising their children, parents are also raising themselves. Child rearing gives parents the chance to redo their own childhood and to improve on it. This book will do its job if it helps parents to raise their toddlers in the way they wish they had been raised.

CHAPTER TWO

Who Is the Toddler?

The loving mother teaches the child to walk alone. She is far enough from him so that she cannot actually support him, but she holds out her arms to him. She imitates his movements, and if he totters, she swiftly bends as if to seize him, so that the child might believe he is not walking alone. . . . And yet, she does more. Her face beckons like a reward, an encouragement. Thus, the child walks alone with his eyes fixed on his mother's face, not on the difficulties in his way. He supports himself by the arms that do not hold him and constantly strives towards the refuge in his mother's embrace, little suspecting that in the very same moment that he is emphasizing his need for her, he is proving that he can do without her, because he is walking alone.[1]

As if echoing the scene described above, 2½-year-old Linda whispers to her mother: "I am a baby and a big girl both." (Her mother, moved to tears, thinks to herself, "So am I.")

THESE TWO VIGNETTES CONVEY THE ESSENCE OF THE SECOND YEAR OF life. Toddlers are defined by their capacity to walk without assistance. The ability to walk alone, which develops and consolidates between about 12 and 30 months of age, is a dramatic change, for both parents and child, from the physical closeness of the first year. As little Linda knows, there is continuity as well: as in infancy, the child has an ongoing need to be in frequent contact with the parents. However, with independent movement, the toddler herself can now determine when and where to go, without having to rely on the parent as the necessary (and sometimes unwilling) means of transportation.

This new autonomy brings about a revolution in the toddler's self-concept. Her major emotional task is to integrate the excitement of exploring away from the parents with the feeling of safety that she gets from their ongoing presence. The parents' job (not an easy one) is to protect their child tactfully from the new and unexpected dangers posed by locomotion, and to do so again and again while the child gradually becomes more able to protect herself.

In many settings and under many different circumstances, the parents and the toddler need to negotiate a mutually satisfying balance between the safety of closeness and the excitement of exploration and discovery.

In this sense, childhood is an early laboratory for the challenges and dilemmas of adult life. Perhaps more dramatically than any other age, this period brings us face to face with two powerful yet contradictory impulses: the longing to feel safe in the protective sphere of intimate relationships, and the exhilarating thrust of carefree, unrestricted, uninhibited exploration, where one can soar free without looking back at those who are left behind.

Toddlers feel this duality with passion, and their specific experiences with closeness and exploration have long-term implications. Much of our individual style through life is determined by our unique way of expressing, balancing, and integrating these two impulses. We might experiment with different possibilities at different junctions in our lives, alternating periods of giddy adventure with times of reflective holding back. Ultimately, however, we tend to re-create again and again the unique balance between caution and daring, familiarity and novelty, intimacy and autonomy that in some intangible way feels most like "us."

The question Who is a toddler? can be answered briefly by saying that the toddler is a young human being who is emerging from a year-long initial period of almost total reliance on the parents and is now eager to discover the world and his or her place in it. The impetus to explore propels the toddler forward, but the ability to rely on supportive relationships is still at the core of the child's capacity to learn.

This chapter is an elaboration of that short answer. It focuses on the two major settings for the toddler's explorations: the world outside, where the child exercises the new skills of walking and talking, and the inside world of the body, which is the site of new sensations and feelings that need to be understood and mastered so that the child can become a full member of the social world.

Discovering the World

Toddlerhood brings about a restructuring of the relationship between two basic human motivations: attachment and exploration. Each of these motivations is expressed through specific behaviors that enable parents to understand what the child wants or needs at any given time. Attachment behaviors bring the child close to the parent through approaching, following, searching for the absent parent, reaching for pick-up, hugging, cuddling, and clinging. These behaviors indicate that the toddler feels a need for closeness and reassurance. Exploratory behaviors take the child away from the parent in order to walk, climb, run, jump, and inspect the world around. Here, the child's predominant motive is to learn about the world.

As the toddler experiments with attachment and exploration, the par-

ent, in turn, must become comfortable with two complementary sets of caregiving behaviors: protective behaviors that provide the child with nurturance and safety through proximity and closeness, and letting go behaviors that encourage him to explore without fear.

Jeannie, 20 months old, is going to her first party. When she and her parents arrive, Jeannie is confronted with a crowd of strangers in a new house. Jeannie holds on to her mother's skirt and hides her face in it, looking out periodically with a worried expression. The hostess tries to entice her with alluring toys, but for the first 15 minutes Jeannie seems to be glued to her parents. It is clear that she needs close contact with them to feel safe in this unfamiliar situation. Her parents recognize this and do not pressure her. Instead, they point to familiar people and nice features of the room to help her feel at ease. Gradually, as she sees a 9-year-old boy she knows and likes, she relaxes and accepts his offer to play but keeps visual tabs on her parents, who make encouraging comments. Soon Jeannie tags along happily after the other children, although she returns periodically for a cuddle or to show her parents a toy.

Harry, 18 months old, has been asking the whole morning to go to the "pak" (park). It is only 9 o'clock, but this Sunday morning, Harry has been awake since 6:30. Cuddling with him in bed, his father keeps him at bay with short-term promises: "After we finish breakfast, Harry. First I'll get up, and then I'll shower, then we'll go to the park." This litany satisfies Harry for a while. He goes back and forth from the parental bedroom to his own room and brings toys to play with by his father's side. He asks periodically: "Daddy up now? Pak now?" By the time they finally arrive at the playground, Harry lets go of his father's hand and runs joyously ahead to the slide. He is eager to explore and he knows that his father is following close behind. For a while Harry climbs on the slide by himself, a favorite and well-practiced activity. His father watches him with pleasure, commenting every once in a while on his son's feats. After a while Harry decides to move on to the swings. He turns to his father, takes his hand, and starts walking in that direction, saying "Daddy swing." Harry knows that now he needs his father's help, and turns to him trustingly with the expectation of getting it.

A Secure Base

These two examples show that the balance between attachment and exploration in the child is mirrored by the balance between protectiveness and encouragement of exploration in the parent. When things go well enough, the parent serves as a secure base from which the child sets forth to explore and to which he can trustingly return for solace before moving off yet again.

Because of this parental role, the balance between attachment and exploratory behaviors in the child has been aptly named "secure base behavior."[2] The toddler, absorbed in the challenges of learning and exploration, uses the parent as a haven of comfort and security when something is scary or when he is tired or in need.

Adults often feel irritated when toddlers become clingy or ask to be held in situations that to grown-up eyes appear perfectly safe. For example, they may feel impatient when their child wants to follow them into the bathroom, cries when a stranger pats his head, clings desperately at the sight of the meekest of dogs, or calls out for company instead of falling asleep at night.

Although these behaviors can be quite trying for parents, it is actually adaptive for a young child to be scared of common situations such as the dark, being left alone or with strangers, and unfamiliar or intense stimuli like loud noises or sudden movement. In the course of human evolution, these situations became associated with an increased risk of danger in the forms, for example, of accidents or predator attacks. Humans (including children) are biologically equipped to recognize cues to danger, and we respond with built-in behavioral mechanisms that maximize safety and enhance survival.[3,4] These mechanisms include moving closer to people we trust in search of protection—the very behaviors that toddlers instinctively rely on when they are upset.

Locomotion is an eloquent preverbal indicator of what the child is feeling. Seeking proximity and contact (attachment behavior) indicates that the child needs help to feel more secure. Moving away from the parents (exploratory behavior) suggests that the child feels safe enough and is eager to seek novelty rather than security. The child's development is enhanced when parents are able to recognize the meaning of these behaviors and respond appropriately to them.

The Toddler's Need for Protection

The ability to engage in secure base behavior makes the toddler an active partner in contributing to his own protection. This is not always understood: one textbook on child development, for example, maintains that "babies creep and toddle right into danger" and that "there would be no more babies" unless parents set limits on infant behavior.[5] In fact, toddlers seem to be equipped with an internal monitor system that enables them to scan the environment and to keep track of conditions that make them feel endangered or secure.

Actually, toddlers often take the initiative in taking care of themselves by remaining relatively close to their mothers. A British investigator tape-recorded 15-minute descriptions of individual toddlers' behavior as they moved about in a London park while the mother remained seated on a bench or on the grass. The results showed that, with a few exceptions, the toddlers seemed to determine their own boundaries and stayed within about 200 feet from the mother.[6]

This perimeter happened to coincide with the mother's own judgment of what constituted a safe distance. The mothers did not retrieve their children if they remained within this boundary, but did so if the toddlers strayed beyond it. However, nearly 70 percent of the children never went far enough to warrant retrieval. These toddlers had the opportunity to wander off if they wished to, but they managed their exploration in a way that kept them within a safe distance but also blissfully free from the mother's direct physical control.

The intricacies of secure base behavior are beautifully illustrated by the details of this study. The toddlers moved in "bouts" that either increased their distance from the mother or brought them closer to her. These bouts accounted for most of the children's locomotion: the mother served as the center for the child's activities and they organized their comings and goings in relation to where she was. It is particularly telling that the children were most likely to stay in one place when they were close to the mother (within three feet); playing at a distance from the mother tended to be brief. In other words, the children felt most secure where it was actually safest and preferred to spend more time there.

When they were away from the mother, the toddlers kept track of her whereabouts through quick visual checks and pointing at interesting sights. The mother routinely ignored these behaviors, with one major exception: if her toddler pointed at a potential source of danger such as a dog on the loose, the mother called out for the child to come closer and picked him up if he did not comply. This suggests that pointing helps the child to learn what is safe and what is dangerous through the mother's response. When the object pointed at is safe, the mother pays no attention or may express mild interest; when it is threatening, she takes definite action.

The mothers' behavior in this study illustrates how parents can help their children to be safe and to feel secure. The mothers did not interfere with exploration and did not feel the need to be by their child's side constantly. They took their cues from the child, and were available but not intrusive. On the other hand, they moved in instantly when action was needed.

The parent's readiness for action is essential because the toddler's ability to cooperate in her own protection is by no means foolproof. The young child's mechanisms for monitoring the environment remain immature for a long time. For example, toddlers do not have fully developed distance vision and cannot appraise accurately whether a somewhat distant object may pose a threat. Moreover, in a highly technological society, the biologically based cues to danger (darkness, sudden loud noises, animals, being alone) are only a subsample of the myriad threats to a child's safety. Dangers may lurk in speeding cars, seemingly friendly strangers, stairs, elevators. The list is endless, and the toddler is equipped neither through biology nor experience to anticipate these dangers.

This means that, in spite of their innate competence in seeking protection, children's safety depends largely on the adult's more developed capacity to anticipate danger. Accidents are the leading cause of death in early childhood, a chilling reminder of the toddler's vulnerability. In many circumstances, the adult needs to provide protection unilaterally, often in spite of the child's energetic protest.

Secure Base as Metaphor for Inner Balance

Children do not encounter danger only while moving. They may ingest harmful substances, play with matches and sharp objects, or pull heavy objects on themselves. In fact, every one of the child's encounters with the world may elicit fear or danger and lead to the need for reassurance or protection. In every autonomous action, the toddler comes face to face with the paradox of being free to explore yet held hostage to internal limitations (such as fear) as well as external constraints (such as the parents' prohibitions).

The concept of secure base is a useful metaphor for the push and pull of emotion that the toddler experiences in this new stage. Parents help the child to sort out when to explore and when to come near. In this process, toddlers gradually develop an inner trust in the possibility of feeling safe and protected while also being outgoing, competent, and independent. The secure base initially represented by the parents becomes internalized as a stable component of the child's personality.

In learning to balance closeness and exploration, the toddler encounters other emotional dualities. Depending on what happens in each situation, coming close to the parent and moving away can represent intimacy versus autonomy; social belonging versus individual fulfillment; being tied down and held captive by others versus soaring free; subservience and humiliation versus personal power; love versus hate and alienation.

The toddler experiences every one of these states because she is constantly facing circumstances that make her feel either powerful and strong or small and helpless. In one moment she can dart off and be reckless, and minutes later become clingy and whiny and want everything done for her.

When Johnny can walk from one end of the living room to the other without falling even once, he feels invincible. When his

JOHN ARMS

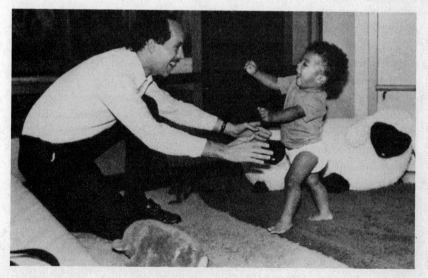

older brother intercepts him and pushes him to the floor, he feels he has collapsed in shame and wants to bite his attacker (if only he could catch up with him!). When Johnny's father rescues him, scolds the brother, and helps Johnny on his way, hope and triumph rise up again in Johnny's heart: everything he wants seems within reach. When exhaustion overwhelms him a few minutes later, he worries that he will never again be able to go that far and bursts into tears.

From the parents' perspective, this is a bewildering state of affairs. If adults experienced and enacted the full range of feelings available to an average toddler in the course of a day, they would collapse from emotional exhaustion or be diagnosed with the weighty psychiatric label of "emotionally labile." As it is, living with a toddler demands that parents be ready for anything. Gradually, however, the child will come to an increasingly modulated experience and expression of emotions, and the turmoil of toddlerhood will subside into the relative harmony of the preschool years.

The English language has many expressions that convey the high regard we have for those who can move on their own: "that person will go far"; "she can stand on her own two feet"; "he is an upright person."[7] While accurate, these accolades play down the hidden liabilities of autonomy. Going far on one's own two feet has its dangers: unprotected aloneness and the possibility of falling and getting hurt. Toddlers' play with blocks, which consists of building towers and then making them fall, is a good symbol of the sudden collapses that often follow new feats of locomotion. By engineering the fall of the tower, the child makes happen what usually happens to him. In other words, he takes control of the situation and acquires mastery over it.

Playing can occur only when the child feels safe: the sequence of building towers and making them fall is a form of remembering hard times from a position of strength (i.e., sitting down). When the child is actually falling, she does not play. She turns to mommy. But this welcome rescue has its own inherent danger because mommy may worry about another fall and forbid further forays. It is no wonder that many toddlers rush off from the mother's arms the very moment they can get back on their feet. Children often recover from their mishaps far more quickly than their parents do, and are eager to take off again. Being held back is one of the great frustrations of this age.

Developmental Changes in Secure Base Behavior

Toddlers' balance between attachment and exploratory behavior is never static: it fluctuates depending on many factors, including the specific situation, the parent's mood and the child's mood. Sometimes the child's impulse to explore predominates for weeks at a time, only to be replaced by a period of intense clinginess that makes the parents worry that their child has seriously regressed. Other times the reverse is true. Weeks of clinginess are superseded by a powerful thrust towards exploration, and the parents find themselves longing for a little more of the very dependence they had so recently worried about. In spite of these fluctuations, some broad developmental trends do emerge and are outlined below.[8]

The "Junior Toddler": Walking and Talking

Between about 12 and 18 months of age, most toddlers are elated by their newfound ability to move around in the world. In the upright position, things can be seen from new visual angles and different perspectives, and the child practices again and again his emerging locomotion skills. Returns to the mother are often brief and may consist of no more than a touch; it is the forays into the world that hold the greatest thrill. So absorbed can the toddler become in his new achievements that for a while he may be quite oblivious to knocks and falls. The important thing is to keep on practicing, discovering, mastering.

Exhilaration is a key mood of this period. The toddler loves to run off again and again, only to squeal in delight on being pursued and scooped up by the mother. This game is of great symbolic importance for the junior toddler. It reassures him that mobility need not mean alienation or abandonment, and that the mother will not leave him to his own (fledgling) devices but will *want* to retrieve him again and again. For a worn-out parent, this game may seem like an endless tease. For the toddler, it is a crucial reassurance that independence and togetherness can go hand in hand.

The best evidence of the toddler's wish and need to be retrieved is what happens when the parent does not do it: the toddler falls down or gets hurt, and the episode ends in tears instead of giggles. In such a situation, the implicit parental message to the child is: "You are on your own, and going off in a giddy spree will get you into trouble." The range of experience and feeling the toddler learns to perceive as safe is prematurely narrowed down.

Locomotion puts the junior toddler's body at the center of her experience. Her legs can accomplish wonders: walk, climb, jump, run. And the legs, in turn, are in the service of eager little hands. She can now climb on the dresser to reach that colorful porcelain doll that had always beckoned to her. She can drag all the stuffed animals from her room to join Mom in the kitchen. She can squeeze herself under a cabinet to find a long-lost marble and put it in her mouth. She can be silent and out of sight for a long time, only to be found carefully tearing the pages of a book that she found by climbing on mommy's desk.

The body is the riveting agent of all these pursuits. At this age children first learn to recognize themselves in the mirror, and delight in pointing to and naming their own and everybody else's eyes, nose, mouth, ears, hair, hands, feet. They find new interest in their genitals, which they explore attentively and learn a name for. They experience an irresistible urge to bite as new baby teeth erupt in rapid succession. Many moments of intense absorption are spent poking at the belly button, fingering the genitals, looking in the mirror, biting and chewing, examining toes.

Finding names for the important things of the world is as momentous an achievement as walking. There is a marvelous symmetry in the fact

JACK GALLAGHER

that the abilities to name and to walk occur at about the same time. The great myths of creation describe the world as coming into being through the Word. The human child, too, creates meaning through naming the world she is discovering. Some of the names coincide, exactly or approximately, with the labels adopted by the culture at large: "mamma," "daddy," "wow-wow" (for dog), "ba-ba" (for bottle). Others are totally idiosyncratic, magically created by the child for his own personal use. Language opens new vistas, just as walking does. The joy of creating meaning through words can be as exhilarating as the joy of creating new horizons through motion.

Walking and talking come together in ways that give toddlers a new confidence in their ability to make themselves feel secure.

Ari, 18 months, runs after a kitten, thoroughly intoxicated by the pleasure of the pursuit. As he turns around, he sees that his mother is not close at hand but has stayed behind, at a greater distance from him than ever before. His face registers momentary shock and disbelief, but he quickly recovers and runs back to her, yelling: "Who coming to me? Who coming to me?" This is the call his mother uses (in the adult version) to entice him back when he strays too far, and he has now made it his own to support himself in a moment of need.

The fear of losing the parent. When the preferred parent or a trusted caregiver is present, toddlers feel elated with their new skills. When he or she leaves, the child often cries and protests by clinging and trying to stop his or her departure. During the parent's absence, the child's mood can become sober and low-keyed. Activity level often slows down and interest in exploration diminishes. The toddler seems to turn inward, as if holding on to the reassuring memory of the absent parent. When the external secure base is absent, the young child needs to work hard to evoke it internally through memory and imagination. The junior toddler has not yet learned that "out of sight" need not mean "out of mind."

The low-keyed mood comes to an end when the parent returns. The toddler's response to the reunion is a subtle indicator of her personal style and of the way she is experiencing her relationship with the parent.[3] Some children may burst into tears on first seeing the parent as a way of relieving pent-up tension. Others may "pick a fight" by becoming provocative or defiant. Ambivalence may be expressed by simultaneously clambering up on the parent and pushing away from her or giving little kicks against her side. Sometimes the child's low-keyed mood persists in the form of avoidance after the parent's return: looking away or even moving away from rather than towards the parent. Some toddlers continue to play as if nothing had happened, totally ignoring the parent's greeting.

These various responses reflect the child's unique style of showing anger and distress about the parent's absence. The child may worry that the parent is not truly back and may leave soon again, either physically or emotionally. The child's ambivalent greeting is an effort to protect himself from yet another experience of disappointment through renewed separation. Parents can help alleviate this anxiety by being emotionally available when they spend time with the child, by saying good-bye before leaving, by promising to return, and by greeting the child with pleasure and affection even if the child rebuffs them at first. Chapters 7 and 8 focus at length on separation difficulties and what parents can do to help.

Most frequently, however, toddlers greet their parents joyfully after a manageable separation. Here, too, the specific responses are quite varied and reflect the child's individual style. One toddler may smile or greet the parents from a distance; another may show them a toy; a third may come close to them and insist on being picked up. All these are attachment-promoting rather than exploratory/distancing behaviors. These unambivalent responses indicate that the child trusts the parent's ongoing availability even during a temporary absence. The child's inner sense of a secure base helps him bridge the gap until the parent returns.

Sometimes there can be too much togetherness, and the child rebels by becoming testy and uncooperative, as the example below illustrates.

Natalia, 14 months, and her mother attend a weekly swimming lesson for toddlers. For 45 minutes Natalia holds on to her mother as they both splash about the swimming pool together. Although she loves these sessions, Natalia invariably becomes angry, moody, and negativistic afterwards, when her mother tries to shower and dress her after the swim. Natalia's mother realizes that the child needs a respite from the intense reliance on her that is needed in the swimming pool. She lets Natalia run around on her own after the swimming lesson until the child spontaneously approaches her again. Once Natalia shows that she is ready for more togetherness, the mother tells her that it is time to get showered and dressed. Now Natalia complies happily because, after having a chance to explore on her own, she no longer feels engulfed by her dependency on her mother.

This example shows how a sensitive parent can use a toddler's unspoken cues to understand what is needed. This mother was serving as a secure base for Natalia by recognizing when it was time to hold back and waiting patiently for the child to return.

A Transitional Phase: Heightened Insecurity

By about 18 months, locomotion has been perfected and is no longer the driving obsession of the child's life. Instead of being a goal in itself, walking becomes the means to an end. The effort at mastery shifts from locomotion per se to the goals that can be achieved through it.

This evolution contains a psychological paradox. For many children, separation anxiety is at its highest at about 18 months. Longitudinal studies of children's responses to brief separations from the mother show that crying peaks then and declines gradually thereafter.[9] Similarly, Mahler and her colleagues describe the onset at this age of a behavior they call "shadowing," which refers to the child's incessant monitoring of the mother's every move.[10]

Children also become more demanding of the mother's attention during this period. Dinah, at 22 months, began to yell "talk only with me" whenever her mother tried to maintain a conversation with others. Michael, 24 months, agreed to go on family outings only if his mother promised to sit next to him and speak to him alone during the car ride. Some toddlers want to drink from the mother's glass and eat from her plate. They may also offer the mother bits of their food and bring her interesting objects, which they pile on her lap. A combination of escalating demands, screaming, and tears often results when the wishes to have mommy all to oneself are not granted. The child often becomes very sensitive to minor cuts or hurts and may be unusually distressed when things are broken or disappear.

Why would the toddler become more clingy and needy just when she is also more competent at being on her own? It makes sense to think that following a period of absorption in locomotion and exploration between 12 and 18 months, the toddler needs to rediscover the mother as the ongoing provider of protection and emotional support. Once she has mastered mobility, she is also more aware of the troubles it can bring. Precisely because she feels better able to stand on her own, the toddler can now indulge the wishes for protective closeness with mother that were put on the back burner while she was learning to walk.

Again the metaphor of a secure base helps to explain this process. Just as moment to moment and day to day the toddler alternates between moving away to explore and then coming back close to the parent, so the growing child goes through extended periods where he is more intensely invested either in exploration or in intimacy. Much of toddlerhood can be understood in terms of the child's gradually coming to grips with the two motives of attachment and exploration, integrating them into a unique individual style that becomes relatively stable through life.

The Senior Toddler: Inner Awareness and Socialization

Around the time of the second birthday, the child's inner life becomes increasingly more accessible to the parent through language and symbolic play. He learns to label feelings as well as physical objects and is quite proud to announce that he is glad, or sad, or mad. "Me" and "mine" become talismans against a world only too ready to take his treasures away. It is not unusual for a 2-year-old to use the word "mine" to greet another child, while a favored toy is clutched firmly in hand. Such a toddler already knows that prevention is the best cure.

Feelings that cannot be talked about often find expression in symbolic play or in reenactment through action. Acting, for the child, is a form of remembering.

A little girl, Rhonda, who had lost her mother at age 2, carried socks from the laundry basket and spread them all over the house. Her mother had used old socks to dust the furniture. The nanny asked Rhonda to put the socks back in the basket. The child dutifully obeyed, but kept one sock. When the nanny insisted that all socks be put back, Rhonda retreated to a corner with a sad expression, hugging the sock to her chest. This sequence expressed what she could not articulate: that she missed her mommy and wanted to hold on to her.

The fear of losing the parent's love. The new ability to imagine and fantasize enriches the child's inner life. One consequence is that the older toddler acquires a more sophisticated sense of what to fear. While the younger child worries primarily about the mother's actual whereabouts and is afraid of separation and loss, the older toddler contends with a subtler but equally chilling dread: the parents' disapproval, which he equates (quite understandably) with losing their love. Some of the most meaningful dialogues of this age unfold around the parent's message: "even when I am angry at you, I still love you." This unbelievably good news is assimilated only gradually by the toddler, who needs to perform a veritable cognitive feat to understand it. He has to counterbalance the immediate and powerfully concrete experience of a parent's angry face and booming voice (or, in the case of more controlled types, an uncharacteristically cold demeanor) with the accumulated memory of past loving exchanges, which at the moment may seem too distant to be relied upon.

It is hard to remember a reassuring past while facing a frightening present, and even some adults have been known to lose faith when faced with this ordeal. In all truth, parents often have to remind themselves that they can love and be angry at the same time. Some parents even learn this for the first time in the process of reassuring their child.

The toddler's wish to please. The fear of losing a parent's love has a beneficial side: the toddler is willing to do almost anything in order to preserve it. This is a powerful aid in helping the child to develop a social awareness and, eventually, a moral conscience. The child's love for the parent is so strong (even when not so visible) that it causes him to change his behavior: to refrain from hitting and biting, to share toys with a peer, to become toilet trained. This wish for approval is the parent's most reliable ally in the process of socializing the child. Appealing to it is far more effective and much healthier than threats of punishment.

Emma, 22 months, has acquired an annoying habit of screeching whenever she does not get what she wants. Every time this occurs, her parents say firmly: "Stop it, Emma. It hurts my ears." If she does not stop, they put their hands over their ears and say: "Now I can't hear you." After about a week, the screeching declines markedly and by the third week it disappears completely.

David, 28 months, has bitten his baby brother. His mother scolds him: "I told you not to do that, David. I am very angry at you." David comes close to his mother and cries his heart out while burying his head on her lap. His mother has her hands full calming down the baby, who is still screaming from the bite. At first she has no patience or resources for David's distress, but then she caresses his head and says, "I don't like it when I'm angry at you, but you can't bite. It's a no-no." David looks at her very seriously, nods his head from side to side, and says, "no-no." His mother repeats "no-no," now in a softer tone, and helps him get back to play. In the following days, David is seen making

pretend biting movements while nodding his head and saying to himself "no-no."

These children are complying with their parents' expectations because they want to please them. Toddlers who are growing well seek approval but are not obsessed with it. They can tolerate reasonable amounts of frustration, and they can go back and forth flexibly between asserting their will and complying with the will of others. The healthy child also feels comfortable with a full range of emotions. Michael, 3 years old, was asked by his solicitous mother if he was happy. His answer: "I am happy *and* sad *and* angry *and* bitey *and* clingy." He refused to be seduced into acknowledging only his happy side.

Parents need to be careful not to squander the gift of their child's innate wish to please them. Toddlers whose parents are too critical can experience difficulties in their emotional development. Such toddlers can be excessively worried about losing love and may become overly compliant. At the other extreme, the child may use defiance as the only way to pursue his agenda, because he anticipates parental opposition and gears himself to fight back. Either reaction—excessive submission or persistent nega-tivism—signals a restriction in the capacity for give-and-take available to the child.

Parents whose children are showing either of those patterns will do well to examine carefully their attitudes, expectations, and responses to their child. It is likely that becoming less demanding and more reassuring will quickly alleviate their child's difficulties. Chapters 3, 7, and 8 examine common struggles and anxieties of this period and suggest specific steps for coping with them.

The urge to assert one's will. Paradoxically, the toddler wants to please but also needs to risk parental anger and disappointment again and again. This is because being true to oneself becomes a compelling motive at this age. The cycle of disagreement–resolution–reconciliation, occurring with greater or lesser intensity throughout the day, is a cornerstone of the toddler's psychological growth. It allows her to know that she is not a clone of the parent but has an autonomous will, that disagreements with loved ones are inevitable, and that anger can be experienced and survived. As Berry Brazelton points out, toddlerhood is at its essence a (sometimes ambivalent) declaration of independence.[10]

Discovering the Body

The healthy toddler's curiosity knows no bounds. When not in motion, he is deeply absorbed in discovering the mysteries of the body. He touches, pokes and pulls at himself, learns to recognize himself in the mirror, delights in finding the names for different body parts, and is entranced by the discovery of gender differences. The child's unfolding sense of who he is and his feelings of security or anxiety are powerfully shaped by the body experience.

Self-recognition

Babies show interest in their mirror reflections early in the first year. At about 4 months they smile at themselves; between 8 and 12 months they show active excitement—laughing, babbling, and jiggling with delight. These happy responses are not altered if the mirror is distorted. The babies

seem primarily interested in how their movements change the mirror image, much as if they were squeezing a toy to make noise or shaking a mobile. The question of Who is the baby in the mirror? does not seem to enter their minds.

These responses change noticeably in the second year. Between 13 and 15 months, toddlers become serious and subdued when looking at themselves in the mirror. If the mirror is distorted, they stare at it intently, as if trying to understand what they are seeing. When someone surreptitiously places a smudge on the child's face, the junior toddler may tentatively touch the smudge *in the mirror*. There is no recognition that the child in the mirror is a reflection of the self.

At about 18 months, toddlers begin to show that they recognize themselves in the mirror. The clearest evidence for this conclusion is an experiment in which toddlers' faces are surreptitiously marked with lipstick. Younger infants point to their image in the mirror rather than to themselves. After 18 months, they touch the mark on their own faces rather than pointing to the mirror.[11] At about the same time, toddlers begin to use the pronouns "I," "me," and "mine," and even proper names, to refer to themselves.

These observations suggest that the toddlers are now able to experience themselves objectively, as people who can be seen from the outside as well as felt from the inside. This important development makes them more self-aware and more interested in their own appearance. Parents report that at about this time the toddler begins to have strong opinions about what to wear and how to look.

In its beginnings, the child's ability to see herself from the outside can be easily disrupted by unusual departures from her customary appearance.

At 22 months, Jessica was bitten in the face by another child and had a swollen lip for a few days afterwards. During that period, she repeatedly went to the mirror and looked worriedly at herself, repeating softly: "Jessica?" She seemed to be asking whether she had remained herself in spite of her changed looks.

It is a common observation that toddlers are also quite distressed when their parents wear masks, even if the child watched them putting those masks on. The visual immediacy of the change is so compelling that it overrides the child's emerging ability to identify internal continuity in spite of differences in external appearance. This is why Halloween can become disconcerting and even frightening for some toddlers; the people surrounding them change too radically from the way they look in everyday life. Knowing this can help parents to help their child by choosing costumes that do not drastically alter the appearance and by opting for small settings rather than trick-or-treating in the street, which may be too frightening for the child.

After their second birthday, toddlers become more confident and self-assured in their response to the mirror. Now, if a smudge of lipstick is placed on their faces, they may wipe it off or look around for the lipstick and try to apply it on themselves. However, distorted mirrors still elicit worried looks. The children are still evolving a sense of how they look in the mirror, and any dramatic changes are interpreted as changes in themselves. It does not occur to them that the mirror would play tricks on them. In that sense, toddlers are already partaking of the adult preoccupation with how they look and the relationship between "outer look" and "inner feel."

Gender Awareness and Sexual Curiosity

The interest in how the inside and the outside fit together leads quite naturally to renewed attention to the genitals. Infants of all ages like to touch themselves, but toddlers do so with a new purposefulness. In the second year of life there is an increased capacity for urethral and anal control. As a result, toddlers become more aware of their genitals and more capable of differentiating between anal and genital sensations. Their scrutiny of their bodies helps them find out how they are made. Also, they associate their actions directly with the different kinds of pleasure they feel as a result.

The discovery of the genitals and the pleasure they give are a source of tremendous pride and exuberance. Toddlers love to run around naked, to show off and to be admired. The body with all its wonders has center stage.

Ira, 30 months, holds his penis while peeing and proclaims: "This is the Empire State." (His father, an architect, had just shown him a picture of that building and told him what a big, beautiful structure it was).

The future of the toddler's pleasure in herself depends largely on the parents' reaction to it. Responding to pleasure with pleasure put the child's experience on the firm, reliable base of parental acceptance.

This does not mean that a parent should feel compelled to celebrate and admire all of the child's self-displays. Personal standards and cultural norms are important, and it is up to the individual parents and their social circle to judge which behaviors are publicly appropriate and which are not acceptable in their household and their milieu.

It is the parents' tone and attitude, rather than the specific content of their teaching, that help to socialize the child without squashing pleasure or engendering shame. Giving a toddler something other than his genitals to occupy himself with works smoothly in most situations. When a child is overly self-absorbed in a setting that the parent finds inappropriate, it may help to say something along the lines of: "I know it feels good when you touch yourself. You can do that in your room or when you take a bath, because it is something private."

Having a penis or a vagina not only gives pleasure but allows for comparisons with other boys and girls. By about 18 months, children have acquired a deeply ingrained sense of their gender and identify themselves as a boy who belongs with other boys or a girl who belongs with other girls. Mutual comparisons are rampant and go on unabated until the child is 5 or 6 years old. These comparisons can bring pleasure in oneself and the other but also some anxiety.

Lori, in the bathtub with her friend Nick, tells him: "Yours is gorgeous, Nick." Nick smiles in agreement but does not return the compliment. After a pause, Lori says: "Tell me that mine is gorgeous too." Children may indeed need reassurance that they are "gorgeous" just the way they are made.

Knowing that one is a boy or a girl and liking one's gender do not imply that the toddler has given up the notion of being both genders at the same time. Many toddlers who can put their fantasies into words declare emphatically that they have both a penis *and* a vagina. Boys are convinced for the longest time that they can get pregnant, give birth, and be both a mommy and a daddy to their baby. Girls make plans for marrying their mothers as well as their fathers. Boys want to grow breasts and suckle their babies. Everybody wants to have everything. Here again, as in many other settings, toddlers refuse to accept the constraints imposed on them by outside rules—including those of biology.

The emerging awareness that one is a boy or a girl but cannot be both is accompanied by a sense of loss that is often expressed symbolically in children's play. Below is Lori's expression that she is missing something as she plays it out with her mother:

Lori: (As she undresses her doll) Let's see what's happening to this girl.

Mother: What happened?

Lori: She has to go to the hospital.

Mother: Why does she have to go to the hospital?

Lori: She lost her tail.

Mother: What is going to happen at the hospital?

Lori: She'll get an injection.

Mother: What about the tail? Will she get it back?

Lori: No. A frog bit my tail. (Pause)

Lori: Do you have a tail?

Mother: No.

Lori: Get one, from a dog. (Laughs, and rides off on her play horse, which, by the way, has a very notable tail).

On another occasion Lori asks her mother to tape a carrot between her legs and then runs all over the house with the dangling carrot, giggling with excitement. Another time her father sees her standing by the toilet, trying to pee like a boy.

It is generally accepted that girls wish they had a penis and express this wish in many overt and covert ways. It is less widely acknowledged that boys wish they had breasts and carried babies. Ari's version of these wishes as they unfold between 28 and 34 months is described below. This period coincides with his mother's second pregnancy.

Ari is carrying a doll held tightly in his arms. He says: "Don't cry, baby. I will give you milk." He pretends to breast-feed the doll.

Ari stuffs a small pillow under his sweater, and parades around the house saying: "I am having a baby."

> Ari is on the potty, quite constipated. He pushes to evacuate and is in some pain. He says: "Maybe I am having a baby."

> Ari looks at himself in the mirror with a serious expression. He says: "Look at my big stomach. Everybody will think that I am pregnant. Nobody will believe it is because I ate so much."

Perhaps the best approach to toddlers' wish to partake of the gifts of both genders is to sympathize with it and to provide corrective information only when the child asks for it directly. Far from being harmful, wishful thinking and fantasy play such as Lori's and Ari's provide the child with a safe setting to explore reality at her or his own pace. As they experiment, children come up with their own explanations for things. Parents do best not to correct these explanations unless the child asks directly for their input. The child's fanciful ideas will be useful temporarily and will be replaced by increasingly more accurate versions of reality when the child is ready. The parent's role is to be close at hand to provide the facts that the child wants without adding more information than the child is asking for.

> Martin, 36 months, asks his pregnant mother: "Mom, do you love the baby?" Martin's mother tells him she loves the baby very much. Martin now wants to know: "Then why did you eat him?"
> A mother could be forgiven for giving her child a long explanation about how babies are made and born. Instead, Martin's mother wisely chooses to answer only what Martin asked. She says: "I didn't eat him, Martin. My tummy is very big because babies grow inside their mommies' tummies." Martin listens wide-eyed but says nothing. Two days later, after having digested this information, Martin asks the next logical question: "Did I grow in your tummy too?" He smiles with pleasure as his mother tells him how he grew and grew until he was ready to be born. Not until four months later, after his sister is born, does it occur to Martin to ask: "How did she come out?"

Children ask questions piecemeal because they take their time to make sense of the information they receive. They know what they can manage and stop asking when they had enough. It is a good idea to respect this signal and not to worry that the child has not learned as much as we imagine she should.

Learning About Body Products

Just as the toddler loves to experiment with body parts, he is deeply interested in what the body can produce.

Max, 19 months, sits in his little rocking chair with a far-gone expression on his face. He has his finger in his right nostril and is slowly bringing out a long string of thick mucus, the product of a protracted cold.

Monica, 20 months, has just begun to use the potty. She sits on it with her legs wide open and lets her warm pee dribble over her hand.

Andrés, 28 months, refuses to have his hair cut. "It's my hair. I made it," he wails. His parents resort to a hair clip to keep it in place.

Sandra, 19 months, is found methodically smearing her feces on the bathroom wall.

Tobias, 30 months, moves his penis in different directions as he urinates. "I can make drawings with my pee," he exclaims.

Tina, 18 months, has just emerged from a prolonged tantrum. She slowly touches the tears still on her face and licks her fingers thoughtfully.

Sofia, 15 months, refuses to have her nails clipped. "Mine, mine," she cries.

Sammy, 28 months, makes careful little mounds of spit on the kitchen table.

Leticia, 30 months, passes gas noisily as she and her mother are in line at the grocery store. "I farted!" she announces gleefully.

These experiences are the building blocks of the child's familiarity with what her body can create. Urine, feces, nails, hair, tears, mucus, saliva, gas—all these are fascinating areas of exploration.

These children do not know that from an adult perspective their behavior is unacceptable. The process of socializing the body is slow and arduous. Toddlers (not unlike most adults) would much prefer celebrating the body to disciplining it.

A child can learn about his body and its products with interest and joy or with embarrassment and shame. Much depends on the parent's response. Rejoicing in the body can go hand in hand with learning that some things are private, no matter how pleasurable they are or how natural they seem. When parents can support the child's interest in the body while teaching about private and public domains, they are bringing physical sensations into the sphere of a secure base for exploring oneself.

CHAPTER THREE

The Challenges of Being (and Raising) a Toddler

THERE IS A WIDESPREAD BELIEF THAT IT IS IN THE VERY ESSENCE OF toddlers to be stubborn, defiant, and negativistic. In some ways, this is a useful belief. When an exhausted parent emerges from a seemingly endless battle with her toddler, she may worry that she's raising an irredeemable monster who will go through life antagonizing friend and foe alike. At those times, one consoles oneself by thinking that the real culprit is the child's age rather than the child's nature. We know that age changes; we are not so sure that nature does.

It is true that raising young children is a stressful activity. Home observations of mothers and their preschoolers show that mild to moderate conflicts take place once every three minutes, and major conflicts occur at the rate of three per hour.[1,2,3,4] The younger the child, the more frequent these disturbances. Conflicts between 2- and 3-year-olds and their mothers occur twice as often as for 4- and 5-year-olds.[2] As a result, mothers of toddlers often experience such tension and fatigue that one author was moved to describe them as "the unacknowledged victims."[1]

This chapter is based on the premise that not every problem of this age has a clear and immediate solution. There are conflicts that will be revisited again and again. There are areas of irritation, dissatisfaction, or regret that will resurface at different times with more or less intensity.

The goal of this chapter is not to provide quick fixes but to describe the emotional experience of toddlers and parents, offering an attitude for understanding the trials and tribulations of this age. The challenges of toddlerhood—negativism, defiance, temper tantrums, no-win situations, and parental frustration, anger, and fatigue—are described as necessary, inevitable, and indeed valuable hurdles as toddlers learn to become individuals aware of their own needs and wishes but also mindful of the needs and wishes of others. To help their child in this process, parents need to cultivate an attitude of partnership with the child in which the give-and-take is guided by the parent's awareness of the age-appropriate rights and responsibilities of each partner. How a secure base evolves into a partnership, how this partnership develops, and the upheavals that accompany its formation are the main topics of this chapter.

The Parents' Experience

What makes childrearing so emotionally charged? For one, it is often lonely. Without the support provided in the past by extended families, stay-at-home mothers find themselves having to run a household *and* be reliably attentive to their children without the assistance and companionship of other adults. Lack of recognition and appreciation adds to the burden, since housewives are traditionally considered "non-working mothers" although they clean, mend, cook, wash clothes, iron, shop, do errands, manage money, pay bills, drive, coordinate the family's activities, and find time and energy to nurture, stimulate, and socialize the children.

For mothers holding a job, the pressures are compounded even further. Women with children under 3 years of age work an average of 90 hours per week when the demands of the job, household chores, and child care are counted in. This is 24 hours longer than the average week of the working father.[5] In fact, it seems that the fathers' principal role in the average family with preschoolers consists of providing emotional support for the mother and playing with the children rather than sharing equally in the household and caregiving chores.[1,6] This more marginal paternal role in the day-to-day management of child rearing and household chores remains the norm in spite of a social trend towards greater father participation.

When we introduce into this picture the figures indicating a high frequency of mother–child conflicts, all of which need to be negotiated and resolved, it becomes clear that mothers have a lot to do. It is not surprising that as a group they report relatively high rates of tension, depression, and dissatisfaction with their everyday lives. This maternal experience affects fathers as well because it colors the emotional atmosphere of the family. Many fathers feel guilty about being less involved in child care than mothers but find it difficult to change this state of affairs.

When stressed and overburdened, parents are less likely to muster the patience and resilience that would help them to cope with the boundless determination of a healthy toddler. The very energy of the child may seem at times like an assault on their frazzled nerves and weary bones. The child's resolute defiance may look every bit like a personal attack. Advocating an attitude of partnership would seem in such a situation like the invention of an ivory tower professor. At these times, it might be useful to withdraw from the conflict, take a little "time out," and reflect on one's own experience and that of the child.

Obstacles to a Secure Base

The previous chapter described the toddler's use of the parent as a secure base from which to learn about himself and about the world. This works well when parent and child are relaxed and getting along. In the midst of conflict, finding a rewarding balance between closeness and exploration can be a taxing process for all involved.

Four different factors contribute to the upheavals between parents and toddlers: disagreements about what is safe and what is not; the toddler's desire to "have it all"; the opposition and negativism that accompany this new sense of a personal will; and the temper tantrums that may follow when the parent says no. Each of these factors becomes easier to handle when parents can understand the cognitive and emotional challenges facing the child in the second and third year of life.

Discrepancies in Toddlers' and Parents' Perceptions

Toddlers and parents often have sharply opposing views of what is safe. These disagreements often result from a different understanding of what constitutes danger.

At 22 months, David refuses to hold his mother's hand while crossing the street. Cars and busy roads are a familiar feature of this urban child's life, and he sees adults using them with equanimity. He cannot understand that they pose a threat to his well-being. Why can't *he* cross the street on his own, like everybody else?

Beth, 24 months, cannot fall asleep at night. "The monster will come," she says. Her parents know that monsters will not come in the dark, but they cannot persuade Beth of this fact. Leaving a night light on reassures her.

Nathaniel, aged 30 months, is found playing with matches. His father scolds him roundly. Nathaniel replies indignantly: "But you do it!"

Seth, 15 months, is mesmerized by the glowing embers in his family's fireplace. He lurches forward and his mother barely manages to retrieve him in time. He screams: "Shiny! Shiny!"

Amy, 28 months old, screams and insists on leaving when the lights go off during her first visit to a movie theatre. All efforts at reassurance are useless.

Andy, 30 months old, cries every time he sees an African mask in his uncle's house. "Bad man," he says. Reassurances that the mask is not real are only marginally helpful in calming him down.

These examples illustrate toddlers' often puzzling fear reactions to situations the adults find commonplace, and their breezy confidence in tackling on their own enterprises that make their parents tremble with fear.

Clearly, the toddler and the adult do not see the world in the same way. Selma Fraiberg,[7] in her classic description of early childhood, speaks about the magical quality of young children's thinking. They reach their own personal conclusions about the relation between cause and effect, they have their own ideas about the magnitude and limitations of their own and their parents' power, and they develop unique theories about what is real and what is pretend, what is safe and what is scary, what is alive and what is inanimate.

Toddlers are always trying to make sense of what happens to them and around them. When their theories seem to work, they derive a strong feeling of pride in their emerging reasoning powers.

Marc, 30 months old, wakes up with conjunctivitis. His mother tells him: "You have a red eye." Marc looks at himself in the mirror and says pensively: "Because I looked at too many red things." That day, he carefully avoids looking at red objects, seeming quite confident of his approach to treatment. (In fact, it seems to work. The red eye is gone a day later).

Sometimes things are not resolved so smoothly. Toddlers can get quite unsettled by their fantasies of how the world works. Many of the seemingly bizarre fears of this age are based on faulty causal reasoning that goes undetected because the child does not yet have the language skills to explain what she is thinking.

Cynthia, 18 months old, has been screaming loudly for a week every time she needs to take a bath. She loves the swimming pool, so her parents know that she is not afraid of the water. On close observation it emerges that Cynthia eventually relaxes when she can hold on to her mother while in the bathtub, but screams and clings to the mother when the water bubbles down the drain at the end of the bath. Cynthia's mother suddenly remembers that a small toy animal went down the drain the week before. The child's fear then becomes clear: if her toy could disappear with the water, what would stop her from disappearing too?

Adults often laugh at these irrational terrors, or feel impatience at the inconvenience they cause. Yet the simplest way of relieving these fears is to take them seriously. Listening attentively, asking questions to clarify what the child believes, and offering a reassuring explanation as well as the promise of protection ("I won't let you get hurt") are good ways of letting the toddler know that this perceptions are being respected and that the parent will make sure he is safe.

The Toddler's Wish To Have It All

The mastery of locomotion develops hand in hand with a new sense of personal will. The toddler desires things with a passion that the more jaded adults might well envy. "I wannit, I needit," says Jessica, fearful that her merely wanting something may not fully convey the urgency of her inner state. For a while, this formula is applied to everything she wants: her mother's new necklace, a doll in her aunt's house, toys in a store window, the cookies carefully set aside for after dinner. Her "I want it, (ergo) I need it" equation is not manipulative. It is her best effort at expressing the longing to own whatever it is she likes, to enhance herself through her possessions.

Fulfilled desire brings the toddler ecstatic pleasure and an inner experience of fullness and completion. We are all familiar with the sublime expression of joy in the face of a toddler who just got what he wanted (such as a balloon). However, the child is often faced with the need to choose between mutually exclusive sources of pleasure. He wants everything, but he usually cannot have everything at once. He cannot be close to mommy while running free. He cannot stay at grandma's house but also go somewhere with mom and dad. He cannot go down the slide and be on the swing at the same time. But he wants to, because everything is so full of wonder and possibility.

Choosing means having something, but also giving something up. The toddler's puzzled expression as he learns this bitter truth is the best barometer of his confusion. The world he discovers is not made quite the way he would have it, and its rules fly in the face of the way things ought to be.

The toddler responds to such a displeasing state of affairs with characteristic bluntness: she refuses to accept it and learns to say no. Sometimes the no is said primarily for the sweet pleasure of savoring its possibilities. "No," says Lucy quite placidly when her mother announces that they will go to the park, then cheerfully takes her mother's hand and trots along. Other times the refusal is fiercely, deeply felt: "No, no, no, no," clamors the same easygoing Lucy as her mother makes one suggestion after another regarding her outfit for the day. Exhausted, the mother narrows the list to two choices: the red or green sundress? "The green," answers Lucy, proud of having the power to decide.

Opposition and Negativism

The toddler encounters a world full of no's, and for better or for worse, it falls on the parent to be the primary naysayer. "No, you can't climb on the record player. No, you can't put your fingers in the electric outlets. No, not in the VCR either. No, you can't eat the dirt from the plants, no matter how yummy it tastes. You can't bite your sister and you can't pull the dog's tail. And you can't hit me when I tell you no."

The list of prohibitions is nobody's fault. It is part of the long and often tedious process of converting a toddler into a person who will gradually learn to live according to the values and rules of his culture. No matter how thoughtfully parents childproof the house or how tactfully they divert a child to acceptable pursuits, there are still many "no's" that need to be said fair and square. It is small wonder that the toddler (being a fast learner) also feels compelled to announce his personal list of "no's," for the sake of fairness if nothing else. The underlying theme of the child's

FLORENCE SHARP

negativism is, "No, I am not your clone, and I will not relinquish my sense of myself to do what you want me to do and to be who you want me to be." From this perspective, we have to admit that toddlers are quite easy to understand and not so terrible after all.

Still, the child's passion in enforcing her message can make parenting challenging at best. Some parents feel angry and discouraged in the face of relentless opposition. They miss the earlier months when their baby was cuddly, complacent, and compliant and they knew how to read and respond to her signals in a way that brought mutual solace. As the toddler becomes assertively independent, even imperiously demanding, many parents long for the lost intimacy of babyhood, with its shared agendas and its physical closeness.

Parent and toddler often stare at each other across a gulf of mutually opposing expectations, and hugs alone can no longer restore the pleasure of the bond. Nothing but learning to accept, respect, and even love their differences will do. Only then can the old intimacy of the first year survive and be weaved into the new order of things.

Toddlerhood is also a fertile ground for the emergence of negativism because the child's immature language skills leave much room for miscommunication with the adults. Toddlers' curiosity about the world, their intense feelings about themselves and their body and their increasing autonomy and will power would best be served by the ability to talk well. But language is slow in coming and painstaking in evolving. As a result, toddlers encounter many frustrating situations. They want to express something but do not have the words to say it. They do not know, want to learn, but are unable to ask. They find that they cannot understand what others say, and others cannot understand them.

When toddlers are unable to speak about urgent matters, they must resort to crying or screaming. This happens even with adults. The voice is the carrier of emotion, and when speech fails us, we need to cry out in whatever form we can to convey our meaning. Often, what passes for negativism is really the toddler's desperate effort to make herself understood.

Temper Tantrums

When the "no" does not do its job and the child finds his will thwarted by higher powers, he may have little choice other than a temper tantrum. What else could a toddler do? His language skills are not developed enough to articulate his case persuasively. His access to the family resources is minimal, so he cannot get his way by threatening to withhold an allowance or to take the car keys away. Offended emotional withdrawal requires too much self-control for such a passionate creature. The temper tantrum— throwing oneself on the floor with a mixture of heart-rending crying and angry screaming—is a wonderfully eloquent if seldom appreciated expression of the toddler's inner experience. It represents his inner collapse as well as his proud protest at finding out that his will does not reign supreme.

Much of the emotional turmoil in the second year revolves around the difficult task of integrating the child's will into the family constellation. The child learns that her personal wishes (so cherished, seemingly so right) need to fit reasonably well with what others want. The parents learn that they, too, have to say "no" with firmness and conviction but hopefully without harshness.

This is why temper tantrums are so important for healthy development. Tantrums take a child to the very bottom of his being, helping him to learn that anger and despair are part of the human experience and need not lead to lasting emotional collapse. If the parents can remain emotionally available even while firm in their position of denying something, tantrums also teach a child that he will not be left alone in his "dark night of the soul."

Helena, 13 months, likes to career down the hall pushing a toy chicken that moves smoothly on wheels. On this particular day she wants to expand her horizons and pushes the toy through the door to her father's study. One wheel gets stuck and the chicken won't budge. Helena throws herself on the floor sobbing and hitting the floor with her head. Her father is not happy to be interrupted, but he picks her up and says: "I'll help you." Helena continues sobbing. The father repeats "I'll help you," and puts Helena's hand on the stuck wheel. He then guides her hand until the toy gets unstuck. Giddy with pleasure, Helena pushes her chicken into the study.

Tommy, 18 months, wants his older brother's shiny new tricycle. He cries and screams. His mother talks to him soothingly, saying: "You can have one when you are big like Daniel." She takes him outside to look for bugs, an activity he loves. When they return, the mother coaxes Daniel into letting his little brother have a "turn."

Sandra, 24 months, has a tantrum when her mother tells her she cannot have cookies until after dinner. She bangs her fist on the floor. Her mother says firmly: "I am sorry, Sandra, but dinner first, then cookies." Sandra cries for a while lying on the floor. Her mother continues cooking, saying: "It is not too long to wait, and dinner is simply yummy."

Jerry, 28 months old, hits his mother when she tells him that they cannot go to the park at night. She holds his hand and says sternly "I know you don't like it, but you cannot hit me." Jerry kicks her. Mom picks Jerry up and carries the child to his room while he screams loudly. She says: "You have to stay here until you are ready to be with me again."

Managing a tantrum involves nothing less than the formation of character. Even the parent's capacity to cope well with conflict can improve with this experience. When a parent knows he is right and does not give in for the sake of temporary peace, everybody wins. The parent learns that denying some pleasure does not create a neurotic child and the child learns that she can survive momentary frustration.

The child's insistence on having his way confronts the family with

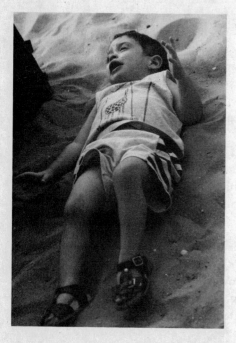

important issues in communal living. Everybody, parents and child, must at some time or another delay gratification and tolerate the resulting frustration with some grace. We all need to channel anger and even flashes of temporary hatred in acceptable ways and we also have to maintain a tolerable balance between exercising power and yielding it. The lessons derived from managing tantrums are valuable not only within the family but extend to other social situations as well.

When anger and frustration prevail over closeness and reconciliation, a child may become precociously hopeless about the fate of human relations. Gabriel, 3½ years old, whose parents had recently separated, observed: "Grown-ups live together, then they fight, then they can't live together any more." His comment related only to adults and reflected an unconscious assumption, based on the good parenting he continued to receive, that this did not happen to children. However, it was clear that Gabriel's experience of his parents' separation had led him to conclude that adult anger is conducive to alienation rather than to repair.

Gabriel has, of course, expressed a profound truth. Anger is difficult to manage, and expressing it in inappropriate ways can spell disaster. In the raising of every toddler, society recapitulates its own development. When a child is caught between the impulse to strike out (i.e., bite, hit, kick) and the fear of its consequences, conscience begins to be formed and civilization begins. Under the best circumstances, physical aggression is gradually replaced by the ability to verbalize anger and to find a negotiated solution to intense disagreements.

Parents represent for the child a secure base to explore not only the external environment but also the wide range of feelings that emerge in the course of growing up. The parent's ability to guide the child through episodes of anger and despair helps toddlers learn that the parent is a reliable ally in time of need. The sections that follow discuss how the experience of a secure base can be transformed into a rewarding partnership between parents and child.

From Secure Base to Partnership

Ari's mother is 8 months pregnant and feeling it. Faced with a living room strewn with toys just before Ari's bedtime, she says: "Ari, you need to put the toys away." Ari answers, "You do it, mommy. I'm too tired." The mother replies, "I am tired too,

Ari. Let's do it together." Ari retorts, "OK, together. You pick them up and I watch you."

It is hard to know how Ari arrived at his definition of "together." Did he really believe that his watching his mother pick up the toys was a legitimate part of the task? (This is possible. After all, he had done precisely that many times before.) Or did he pretend to believe that watching was a form of helping, hoping to fool his mother into agreeing with him?

No matter how he arrived at his suggestion, Ari was engaged in an active negotiation with his mother. He knew that she had a goal (getting him to put the toys away) that differed from his own (not doing it). He first invoked a reason for his goal—being tired—that had served him well in the past. When his mother not only dismissed this defense but even took it over for herself, Ari had to think fast for another avenue to reach his aim. His mother provided the perfect entry by suggesting that they do the dreaded task together. Instantly, Ari allotted himself the only part of the job that was to his liking: watching it be done. The fact that his offer was not accepted does not detract from his brilliant if somewhat transparent negotiating skills.

In this exchange, Ari was practicing the nuts and bolts of goal-corrected partnership,[8] a concept awkwardly named, but very useful for understanding how children become social partners with their parents. When toddlers insist on carrying out their personal agendas, they come to realize that their mothers and fathers have their own plans and that these plans may be quite different from what the child had in mind. When the competing goals of parents and child can be accommodated or reconciled through negotiation, their relationship is characterized by flexible give-and-take, and it becomes a partnership where the parties work together to readjust their goals in order to arrive at a mutually agreeable course of action.

Children begin to learn about partnerships from their parents' example, and it can take a long time (sometimes a lifetime) to become adept at being a true partner. Toddlers are like other people at trying first and foremost to further their own goals, which can remain quite stable over time. Three months after the incident described above, in almost identical circumstances, Ari came up with yet another compelling reason for not picking up his toys: "I can't now, mommy. I only have two hands and I am doing something else." Children's resourcefulness in furthering their interests calls for ever-increasing creativity on the parents' part to protect *their* goals. In this case, Ari's mother lived up to the challenge. She said:

"Your hands have been doing the same thing for too long, Ari. They need to learn something new right now."

Upheavals in the Road to Partnership

In secure base behavior the child finds a comfortable balance between two opposing goals: proximity to the mother and exploration away from her. When the parent is physically and emotionally available, the toddler can decide freely when to leave and when to return to her side. This is when we see toddlers at their happiest and most charming. To move away and discover new vistas when one wants to, and to be welcomed back warmly by the loved one whenever one chooses to return—that is the definition of happiness for an active young child.

When the child can come and go at will and the parent is always present and receptive, the parent's goals coincide with those of the toddler and there is no clash between the parent's and the child's plans. Harmony prevails because the parent is willing and able to be totally available, just as the child wants her to be.

Many factors interfere with this ideal state of affairs. Most poignantly, the child often wants to be close to the parent when he or she cannot be present for him, be it physically or emotionally. She may need to go to work, or she may wish time for herself or for other important people in her life. The toddler may not be able to simply let her go. The mother is the center of his universe, and he feels the need for her too strongly to be capable of such equanimity. The child clamors for her and clings to her, and she needs to peel him off and remove herself from his reach. Sometimes she does this with anguish and guilt; other times she feels irritation or annoyance. When a parent and child cannot meet each other emotionally at a time of strong need, the result is often mutual estrangement, anger and frustration.

Other times the child is eager to move away, and the parents cannot let him do it. They may want to protect him from a realistic source of danger, or they may disapprove of what he is about to do, or they may simply want him by their side to enjoy his company. At these times it is the child who pushes away, feeling engulfed by the parent's presence and constricted by the parental demands. The parent, in turn, may feel rejected, unneeded, and unloved.

It is in these situations of strong competing needs that a goal-corrected partnership becomes most critical to a resolution of the conflict. Parent and child have to find a way of moving away from a confrontation where one rigid "no" is pitted against another, with escalating anger and impotence on both sides.

Negotiating Disagreements

What are some of the obstacles to a negotiated solution? Sometimes the parents fear that giving way will spoil the child. They believe that, once having said no, they need to stick to it in order to be consistent.

> **Mary, 18 months, starts playing with a golf ball that is reserved for playing "catch" with the family dog. She throws it and then runs to retrieve it, in almost perfect imitation of the dog. She giggles with excitement and delight. Her father tells her that the ball is dirty, and she can't play with it. Mary cries bitterly as her father takes the ball away. Mary's brother sticks up for his sister, saying, "But we all play with the ball, and she's not putting it in her mouth." The father feels a little foolish, but he has his honor to maintain. He announces: "I said no, and that's that."**

> **Stefan, 3 years old, is splashing with his bare feet on the puddles left by the garden hose as his mother waters the plants. It is a hot summer day and the mother is tired and irritable. "Stop it, Stefan," she says. Stefan replies: "But I like it." "No!" says his mother. "Why?" says Stefan. "Because I said so," replies his mother, unwilling to reverse herself.**

Many parents are haunted by inner and outer demands to respond always in the same way and not give in to the child. They cling to every inch of their wavering will power in confrontations with the child because being "consistent" has acquired for them the aura of a transcendental virtue.

We have to acknowledge, however, that all of us make decisions in the spur of the moment that seem silly or unnecessary on further reflection. Insisting on that course of action against our better judgment smacks of rigidity rather than consistency. If another adult pointed this out to us, we would agree with relief and change our minds. Why not do the same when it is our child who protests one of our less inspired edicts?

Toddlers can be remarkably perceptive when it comes to parental shortcomings. At 34 months, little Josh said to his screaming mother, tears streaming down his cheeks: "That is not fair, mommy. You should do better than that." His mother heard him and did do better. She stopped screaming, put herself together, and explained: "Let me tell you why I got so mad, Josh. I don't like it when you don't do what I say." This mother's willingness to change her behavior led to a very fruitful conversation with her child about what each of them was supposed to do to get along with the other.

Willingness to change our minds in the face of persuasive evidence teaches the child a higher form of consistency: the readiness to engage in dialogue about differing points of view.

There are many times, of course, when the parent's goals need to take precedence over the child's and when the adult's "no" has to prevail.

Let's think of a common occurrence: parents who are getting ready to go out for the evening, leaving their toddler with a baby-sitter. The child clings to the mother's neck, screaming "Don't leave me!" The mother feels torn between empathy for her child's distress and irritation, between the lure of a night out and the impulse to stay home. No compromise seems possible in such a situation. Is there any room for partnership?

To do justice to the situation, we need to look first at its background. What are the child's motives? Has she had some satisfying times with the parents during the day, or does this outing add insult to injury because the child had no opportunity to fulfill her attachment needs? Does she know and like the baby-sitter, or is this a new person who cannot yet inspire trust as a temporary replacement for the parents? The child's protest may serve as useful incentive to evaluate whether perhaps we are expecting too much from her and not giving her enough support to cope with our absences.

Well, the parent may answer, it is true that the day was harried, and our regular baby-sitter cancelled at the last minute, and we had to find a replacement our child barely knows. What are we supposed to do now?

Paying Attention to Feelings

Understanding how the child may be feeling and how we may have contributed to it need not change our actual decision (in this case, going out). It does change the tone with which we explain the decision to the child. Toddlers find it very reassuring to hear a sympathetic description of what they are feeling but cannot put into words. The toddler is relieved to hear us say that we know he is upset, that mommy and daddy were busy today and had no time to play, that here they are, going out yet again, and that is not fair. We can tell him that he doesn't like to stay with this new lady because he doesn't know her, but that *we* know her and chose her because she is nice with children. We can assure him that we will come back and kiss him on his cheek while he is asleep and make sure he is all cuddled up and warm under his blanket. We can promise him that tomorrow we will make a special time to be together to make up for the little time we had today. We can say all this, a little at a time, or focus only on what seems most relevant for the child. And then we can say that now we need to go.

Sometimes, of course, our children cling to us before we leave even if we spent the whole day with them and their favorite baby-sitter is available. Here too there is room to talk. We can tell them that it was wonderful to do all the things we did together during the day, and that it is hard to stop. We can say that their baby-sitter will help them have a good time even while we are gone. And then we tell them that we need to go now. As Stanley Greenspan has pointed out, "setting firm limits" (that magic formula handed down from generation to generation as a panacea to the complexities of childrearing) need not preclude appropriate empathy for the child's feelings about the experience.[9]

Putting Feelings into Words

Children understand language much earlier than they can speak it. When the parent is able to translate the toddler's experience into words of understanding, this helps to contain the child's negative feelings and makes them bearable. In this sense, talking can represent relief from amorphous feelings because it puts some order into chaos.

The preverbal child is at the mercy of rages and anxieties centered in the body and experienced viscerally: hunger pangs, teething pains, the abdominal urges of defecation, the sudden shocks of falling, the stabs of ear infections. (It is said that Martin Luther first understood the devil during a bout with constipation.)

Loneliness, too, although not originating in the body, is experienced through it. Longing for the mother takes the form of inner emptiness and of undefined hungers and thirsts. All these can only be expressed at first through sounds of anger and distress: whining, crying, and screaming.

A parent (most often the mother) tries to find meaning in these noises, searches for their origins, and ministers to their causes. When she is successful and can make a difference, the child is soothed. When she is not successful, the child remains in the clutches of unnameable pain. This is why the mother and father are at the center of the young child's sense of well-being or despair: they are the ones in charge of understanding the child's experience and attending to it, and they are also the ones who find a substitute to act for them when they are not there.

With the acquisition of language, toddlers acquire a new tool for communicating with the parents and the other important people in their world. They can now describe experiences that could not be talked about before. Even before this happens, toddlers learn from listening to their parents that language is a vehicle for sharing emotions.

Reggie, 14 months, has been moved from a loving but temporary foster home where he has been since birth to an adoptive family. He has not yet started to talk. During the first two weeks in his new home, he screams almost continuously, hardly sleeps, and throws himself on the floor sobbing hopelessly at the slightest frustration. His adoptive mother begins to have serious doubts about keeping him; she worries that he is not a normal child. In consultation, she is advised to respond to every episode of screaming by holding him very tightly and saying repeatedly: "You are staying here with me. No more bye-byes. I am your mommy now." This incantation serves to contain her own fear and distress as well as the child's. The message is received. Reggie's tantrums soon decline and eventually disappear.

His new mother's empathy and her ability to name his fear enabled Reggie to transform his lonely rage and despair into a trust that someone heard him and understood. This trust will help him in time to use words to express what he feels. Reggie's experience, although painful, is more hopeful than that of a child who has nobody to translate his feelings into words of caring and support.

Using language enables toddlers to become more equal partners in their interpersonal relations. They now have a richer behavioral repertoire to which they can resort in their negotiations with others. Language provides the child with a practical set of symbols that can be used as a concise way of representing complex experiences. The word "mommy," for example, can evoke major portions of the child's experience with the mother, such as the loving looks, the comforting smell, the soothing voice, the warm touch, the cherished games. One word captures the emotional flavor of thousands of exchanges. As a result, each word is an economic way of encoding meaning and helping the child to remember. Words enhance the child's memory, the capacity to understand how things work, and the understanding of cause and effect. Words also allow the child to think about different alternatives and to decide what course of action to take.

Because of all this, toddlers can use language to put into words feelings that previously could only be expressed through action. They can say: "Go away" instead of pushing someone off, or "mine" instead of grabbing another child's toy, or "me mad" instead of hitting. It follows that the ability to use words can serve as a protection against being overwhelmed by anxiety, rage, and fear.

When Words Are Not Enough

Language opens new vistas for communication, but it also has its limitations. Precisely because of the conciseness of language, subjective experiences are seldom captured completely, in all their multiple and subtle nuances. Words can address aspects of an experience, but not the whole experience in its global multisensory texture. The word "mommy" may evoke only the positive feelings the child has for the mother. The struggles, ambivalence, anger, and fear that form a part of the relationship may remain outside of the realm of speech.

In this sense, putting things into words has an inherent alienating effect because the part of the experience that remains unnamed is cut off and fragmented from the portion that is given official existence through language.[10]

This applies also to the child's emotional life. Because the young child feels with such intensity, he experiences sorrows that seem inconsolable and losses that feel unbearable. A precious toy gets broken or a good-bye cannot be endured. When this happens, words like "sad" or "disappointed" seem a travesty because they cannot possibly capture the enormity of the child's loss. He needs a loving adult presence to support him in his pain but he does not want to be talked out of it. As Kevin Frank puts it:

> The impulse is to calm the child, to make things better. But the scream comes back, "Don't even try to calm me down!" whether in words or equivalent. Why is this so unnerving? Doesn't it evoke all the fear, resentment, frustration, which hasn't really changed at all since our

own childhood? And isn't the impulse to get the child calmed down, by any means possible, an impulse to stifle this Pandora's box? It's an enormous challenge to really be with the child in its inconsolable state.[11]

At these times, only staying near wordlessly does honor to the child's experience. Hugging and holding if the child allows it can convey feeling much better than words. In fact, to use language in these conditions is necessarily to misuse it. There will be time for words later, when the parent is helping the child to reflect on what she just went through. Coaxing children to bind their feelings to words before they are ready alienates them from access to the unspeakable realms of experience and teaches them wrongly that talking is equivalent to feeling.

Collapses in the Sense of Partnership

There are times when the parents cannot be emotionally available or helpful because the child's anger and pain touch too deeply into their own buried emotions. Instead of staying near, or offering support, or putting feelings into words, the parents may find themselves screaming out or withdrawing into an icy silence. Whatever sense of partnership has been built between parent and child comes tumbling down and seems irretrievably lost. Hatred replaces love. Neither the relationship nor one's inner space offer a secure base for immediate retreat.

Without necessarily advocating such loss of control, we can take some consolation in its being only too human. It may even have some advantages. If not overdone, it may help the child to appreciate that his parents also, and not only himself have (sometimes unwanted) access to a full range of feeling.

Parents are under much pressure nowadays to be unfailingly empathic and supportive. They are asked to cultivate conscientiously their children's optimal mental health, cognitive development, creativity. This is a tall order and may actually have some serious costs. In an atmosphere where parents are always trying to be attuned to the child, the toddler is deprived of important opportunities to learn about deep, spontaneous emotion. When a parent is overly solicitous, the toddler gets the unspoken message that she should reciprocate in kind. In order to deserve such well-behaving parents, she had better be very well-behaved herself. This pressure can be very constricting for a young child.

Sometimes toddlers' behavior is truly annoying and unacceptable, and it goes on and on in spite of the parent's best efforts to be firm but civil in stopping it. The parent's eventual anger (whether perfectly modulated or quite out of proportion) carries an important message for the child: *your inappropriate behavior has consequences that you will not like.*

Toddlerhood is the time to begin understanding this. Toddlers learn best through feeling—their own and the feeling of others. A parent's outburst can be actually helpful for toddlers because it teaches them that they do not need to control themselves all the time.

Making Up After a Fight

The important question is what to do after the parent has lost her temper. Here, language can be of enormous help because it enables parent and child to discuss together what happened "when mommy and daddy got so angry."

No matter how righteous a parent's anger, it is always frightening to the child. This fear can be made more manageable by explaining how mommy or daddy felt, asking the child how he felt, and reassuring him that he is loved even when the parent is angry at him. When children

NANCY P. ALEXANDER

can find meaning in difficult experiences, their sense of security is temporarily shaken but not permanently impaired. In fact, repairing lapses in partnership again and again gradually inoculates toddlers against hopelessness and despair when the usually loving parent suddenly turns into a frighteningly angry one. They learn that closeness is restored after the tempers calm down.

What about those times when the parent "loses it" because of personal reasons, and the toddler's behavior becomes a pretext for an angry outburst? Here again talking helps. Telling the child "I am sorry" can spare her undeserved shame, reassure her that she is not to blame, and shore up her self-esteem. Of course, this only happens when parents mean what they say. Talking becomes cheap when it turns into a formula to alleviate adult guilt. Children are very perceptive in sensing when their parents are really trying to do better, and when they are saying "I'm sorry" simply to put the episode behind them until the next blow up.

Repairing episodes of conflict with the parent helps the child to acquire inner controls. The long-term goal of making up is to help the child build an internal model of the secure base that the parents represent on the outside. When this is successful, the child acquires a profound sense of centeredness and self-respect that can help through difficult times.

At age 4, Josh is able to tell his father after he yelled at him: "Dad, I am a small boy and adults should not yell at small children. You should be able to stop yourself."

These words are a summary statement of the truths Josh learned since he was a toddler from many exchanges in which he felt heard and affectively met by his father even in the midst of the emotional turmoil between them.

The Emotional Value of Disappointment

Partnership often involves modifying our plans to accommodate our partner's. Just as often, it means accepting that we will disappoint our partner because we cannot do what he or she wants. This is as true of toddlers as of adults. Disappointment is a very early experience, and toddlers need to learn that they can feel it without falling apart forever.

Nevertheless, parents often feel guilty for disappointing their children. Guilt can be a powerful obstacle to forming a partnership if the parents consistently give in to the child's wishes at the expense of their own. This automatic yielding gives a message to the child that her wishes are the natural order of things, and she learns to experience frustration and disappointment as dangerous emotions that should be avoided at all costs.

Guilt can also lead parents to overnegotiate. They plead with their child to agree to their requests and to accept the situation with a pleasant demeanor. I remember a very loving and sensitive mother who wanted to go home with her toddler at the end of a wonderful birthday party. Sophie, naturally, did not want to go. The mother cajoled her child in the most persuasive terms: "Let's go, Sophie. I know you want to stay, but you are tired. All the children are gone. Tommy needs to go to bed. You need to go to bed. Please let's go." Sophie's answer: to run away and continue playing. When the mother finally picked her up to leave, Sophie threw herself on the floor and screamed. The mother again pleaded and cajoled: "You are too tired, Sophie. That is why you are crying. Please let's go." This lasted for the next 40 minutes, with escalating frustration for mother and child, not to mention the hostess.

Paradoxically, this mother's effort to get the toddler's permission to leave actually robbed the child of her right to dislike something and protest it. She was deprived of the freedom to express negative feelings and was coopted instead by the pressure to please. Nobody, not even a toddler, should need to renounce the right to negative feelings. To give up anger, sadness, and disappointment is to give up the right to a part of oneself.

Toddlers who don't learn gradually about disappointment lose their resilience through lack of practice in give-and-take with other people's needs. They can become self-centered, demanding, and difficult to like or to be with. Sophie's mother would have done her daughter and everybody else a favor by overriding her protests, picking her up and taking her home.

Encouraging a Partnership

How does one get toddlers to comply in healthy ways? Let us count the ways.

- Give them a likable alternative. This works most painlessly for all concerned ("We'll go home now and then we can watch 'Sesame Street'"). Of course, this is not always possible or effective.
- Use a tone that conveys your visceral conviction that your request is important and meaningful. Then the child will also find meaning in it because toddlers are strongly disposed to believe and want to please the parent ("You need to come in from the rain. Children get sick if they are out in the rain for too long").
- The toddler's natural sense of fairness is the parent's ally in many circumstances. Explaining that a particular behavior bothers other people helps the child to learn that other people have different needs ("Please stop banging the table with your spoon. It hurts my ears"; or, "I don't want you to call me 'stupid.' It hurts my feelings").
- In many situations, the parent needs to explain that she is the one in charge of deciding what to do. Many toddlers have been cured of uncontrollable tantrums by their parents' newly found confidence in saying, "I am the one who decides that." There is nothing more reassuring to toddlers in conflict than the parent's benevolent authority, even if their strong protests make this hard to believe.
- If all else fails, humor sometimes works. If a parent can make a game out of a toddler's outrageous request, for example saying in mock disbelief: "You really want to eat your dessert before dinner? I just can't believe it!" and go on playing with this theme, the toddler may join in the spirit of the game and learn in a playful way what is permitted and what is not.
- Taking action is sometimes the only sane thing to do. This is particularly the case with toddlers between 12 and 18 months, who are still not very verbal. With older toddlers, taking action is best done as a last resort, when nothing else works or when it is important to react fast for the child's safety. Picking a child up to take him somewhere sometimes works better than cajoling, pleading, or explaining because it teaches the child that the parent is doing his or her job in taking charge of raising him.

What are counterproductive ways of encouraging compliance? Inducing fear or guilt are the more obvious culprits. At a more subtle level, admonishments such as "You need to cooperate" or "You have to share" make the child feel confused and hopeless at the enormity of the task. How is one to comply with such all-encompassing, abstract commands?

(In the same vein, can one really obey the injunction to "be good"? Even the Ten Commandments are more simple and concrete.)

If we replace the oppressively big word "cooperate" with the simple statement "I need you to help me," we appeal directly to the child's innate wish to please. If we say that "it's time to let Johnny have a turn now," we address the toddler's sense of fair play. Toddler-sized words speak to the child's feelings. This helps toddlers to learn directly about the values of reciprocity, fairness, and empathy that are the bases of good human relationships.

Parents worry sometimes that telling a toddler about their own needs and wishes will make toddlers feel guilty or dampen the child's natural exuberance. This is unlikely to happen for very long. Ira overheard his mother saying that she was feeling much better after a bout of flu. He immediately perked up and asked, "That means I can bother you again?"

Children's own needs and wishes reassert themselves spontaneously if the parents do not stifle them. In fact, toddlers and parents are quite well balanced in their ability to get what they want: only about 50 percent of parental requests are initially complied with by toddlers in the second year of life.

Opposition, negativism and temper tantrums are challenging for both parent and child. Their virtues, however, should not be overlooked: they force us to learn the complex but rewarding art of reconciling competing goals and building a life-long partnership.

CHAPTER FOUR

The Question of Temperament

BABIES ARE UNIQUE INDIVIDUALS FROM THE TIME THEY ARE BORN. SOME are cuddly, others do not relax into the parent's arms; some cry lustily, others barely whimper; some seem to be in constant motion, others hardly stir; some seem unaffected by changes in routine, others collapse in tears when their feeding or sleeping schedule is altered.

Observations like these indicate that infants come into the world already equipped with very personal ways of responding to their own body processes and to what happens around them.[1,2] Sometimes these responses become a stable part of the baby's personality, but in other instances the behavior may change or vanish as the child develops. Only time will tell.

Where do these individual differences come from? How do they evolve? What determines whether they persist or disappear? Can we find ways of categorizing the different patterns of behavior, or are they totally random and unpredictable? These and many other questions have long puzzled those who try to understand human development.

The concept of temperament is a useful tool for trying to answer some of these questions. Temperament is defined as the "how" of behavior: in looking at children's temperament, we try to describe how intense, moody, adaptable, and predictable they tend to be. The focus is behavioral style, not ability (the content or "what" of behavior) or motivation (its reason or "why").[3]

In describing temperament, we often find ourselves using adjectives that involve nonverbal, kinetic experience: high strung, low keyed, bursting with energy, slow to warm up. These terms overlap with what Daniel Stern[4] calls "vitality affects"—qualities of feeling that accompany the basic or vital processes of life, such as hunger and satiation, falling asleep and waking up, breathing in and out, moving around, experiencing different emotions surge and fade away. In this sense, emotionality and activity level are the hallmarks of temperament.[5]

For a long time, temperament was seen as immutable, a personal gift or burden one was born with and could use and endure more or less wisely but never quite shake off. Mark Twain, writing in 1909, has Satan proclaim:

"Temperament is the law of God written in the heart of every creature by God's own hand, and *must* be obeyed, and will be obeyed, and will be obeyed in spite of all restricting or forbidding statutes, let them emanate whence they may." (*Letters from the Earth*, p. 38).

This notion of temperament as a form of predestination is currently out of favor. Current views of temperament minimize the notion of fate, and emphasize that the child's development is shaped by the interacting influences between genetics, constitution, and environment. Temperament alone is not destiny.

This view of development emerged from the realization that temperament is not a single, unchanging trait but a set of relatively stable tendencies a person has to react in particular ways. These propensities may be magnified, downplayed, or changed in quality in the course of development, depending on the nature of the child's encounters with the environment.[3]

Just what are these propensities? How exactly do young children differ from one another? Not surprisingly, different experts have different ideas about which tendencies are based on temperament and which tendencies are learned from the environment. The pioneers in the study of temperament—Alexander Thomas and Stella Chess—identified as many as nine dimensions of temperament as they followed 136 children from toddlerhood to adult life. These dimensions involved *activity level, regularity of biological rhythms, tendency to approach or withdraw* as the first response to new situations, *adaptability* to change, *intensity* of response, *sensitivity* to stimulation, *predominant mood* (positive or negative), *distractibility,* and *persistence* in pursuing a goal.[3,6,7,8] Children could be high, medium, or low in any of these categories, giving rise to many subtleties in each child's temperamental make-up.

A child who rates consistently high or low in any one of these categories is not predestined to react that way always. She may surprise everybody by behaving quite contrary to expectations in a particular situation, or she may change dramatically at a given age on one dimension or another. Many parents comment that their children were very active and intense as toddlers but became quiet and mild during their school years. Even more common is the complaint that their friendly, outgoing, perennially happy school-age children became unrecognizably withdrawn and irritable as adolescents. At different ages, children's experiences and the way they perceive themselves and their world may mobilize new coping mechanisms or may elicit unsuspected vulnerabilities. The temperamental dimensions outlined above are not rigid categories of functioning, but rather useful guidelines to recognize recurrent patterns of response in a child.

Temperament Types

Nine categories are a large number to keep track of, no matter how useful each one may be. To make things less cumbersome, Thomas and Chess looked for recurrent combinations of these traits in the children they studied. They found three constellations that were particularly common in their sample. The children showing these constellations of traits were called *easy, slow to warm up,* and *difficult.* A fourth category, the *active toddler,* was not identified by these authors but emerges from many observations of young children.[1,9,10] Not everybody agrees with these labels, but the temperamental types they refer to are certainly worth considering because they have been extensively researched and seem to show continuity from early childhood to early adulthood. The sections that follow describe every one of these types, providing specific examples of how the child's temperament influences the relationship with the parents and the styles of secure base behavior and partnership that may develop.

Easy Children

The children in this category are flexible above all. Their biological cycles are regular and predictable. They are consistently in a good mood, are receptive to new situations, adapt rapidly to changes, and are mildly or at most moderately intense in their emotional reactions.

Because of these features, flexible children are easy to integrate into the rhythms of the household. Parents can plan their activities around the child's mealtimes or naps because these occur at about the same time every day. The toddler can be taken shopping, to visit friends, or even to work (if feasible or necessary) because he can be counted on to be in a good mood, to show interest in the new situation, and to adapt quickly if at first things are not particularly to his liking. Parental spontaneity is possible: plans can be made or changed in the spur of the moment without fears of eliciting a minor catastrophe in the baby's rhythms. Whether pleased or disgusted, the child will show his feelings in a thoughtfully mellow tone.

These characteristics make flexible children a pleasure to care for. As a result, their parents tend to feel effective and skillful in their caregiving. This is not surprising, since they are rewarded with a positive response to almost everything they do.

Joey is usually in a good mood. He tends to wake up with a smile and ready to play. This attitude prevails during the day. He accepts changes of routine with equanimity. For him, things easily

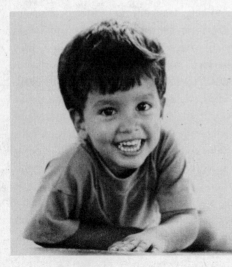

become a source of pleasure and interest. His responses are usually moderate in intensity, whether he is showing pleasure or pain. He greets his parents and other people he likes with a happy expression but without exuberance. New toys elicit laughter but not shrieks of pleasure. By the same token, he complains only quietly during medical exams. Even his reaction to vaccinations consists only of a moderate cry rather than intense wailing.

One possible problem with flexible children is that they are easy to take for granted. They tend to be so agreeable that one may push them beyond what in fairness they can be expected to tolerate. Even flexible children get sad and scared. Parents may need to remind themselves of this from time to time in order to remain attuned to the emotional needs of their flexible toddlers.

Children Slow to Warm Up

When faced with a new experience, children slow to warm up tend to withdraw at first and they take a long time to adapt. They are not particularly active and they tend to express their emotions rather mildly, escalating into an intense response only if pushed beyond their endurance into new situations. These children need some time to observe from the sidelines before they are ready to join in. Once they feel ready to participate, they can show just as much zest as their less tentative peers. Children slow to warm up are often considered shy or timid because of their reluctance to enter new situations readily.

Erin is low-keyed in new settings. She observes new objects and new people for a long time before engaging with them. She cries if pressured to approach more quickly than she is ready for. In physical activities, Erin has slow and measured movements. She prefers sedentary activities such as reading books and solving puzzles. She tires easily from active games although she enjoys them for short periods of time. She asks to be carried after walking just a short while in spite of her ability to walk, run, and jump very well for her age.

One possible risk facing children slow to warm is that people looking for psychological motives for their behavior may label them "anxious" or "insecure."

There is no evidence that slowness to warm up and insecurity go together. A child may be quite confident of her parents' physical and emotional availability, she may trust her own abilities to cope well with different situations, and she may still prefer to first observe from the sidelines and only later join in. Of course, insecurity may result if others criticize, ridicule, or try to change this tendency instead of accepting it as the child's personal and normal way of adjusting to new situations.

This raises the question of how the parents feel about their toddler's shyness. There is some evidence that shyness may be biologically based: in studies of adopted and biological infants, there is a higher correlation of shyness between infants and their biological mothers than between infants and their adopted mothers.

Parents with a shy toddler may respond to the child's slowness to warm up in a different way. Some parents empathize with the child and allow him to get into situations at his own pace. Other parents wish to protect the child by minimizing exposure to new and challenging situations. Still others try to help the child "outgrow" his shyness by encouraging him to join in before he is ready. There are a few parents who feel personally indicted by the child's behavior and respond with impatience or embarrassment, as though the child is shaming them.

These responses may reflect in part the parents' experience with their own temperament. Some shy parents feel mortified that their child shares this trait with them. Others understand instinctively what their child is feeling. Some outgoing parents feel slowed down and constricted by their child's reserve; others find their child's shyness refreshing because it relieves them of the expectation to be more socially available than they want to be.

Difficult Children

This label in itself is difficult to accept, but it carries a strong intuitive appeal when one is faced with a child who consistently challenges one's patience and best intentions. Fortunately, such children comprise only 4 percent of the population by Chess and Thomas' calculations, although every toddler (like every adult) can be exceedingly difficult for days or even months at a time depending on what he or she is going through. Efforts to find a less pejorative label have led to descriptions like "fussy," "feisty," and "inflexible." These children are often irregular in their biological functions, withdraw from new situations, have difficulty adapting to changes, are hard to please, get in a bad mood easily, and have intense emotional reactions. In short, they are difficult to predict and to modulate, and one cannot pursue one's plans without taking their reactions into account.

Jenine is often on the verge of a bad mood. Her parents feel as if they are "walking on eggs" because she gets upset so easily. She wakes up crying in the morning, and it takes her a long time to be ready to play. She dislikes novelty and her parents must hold her for a long time before she is ready to explore. Jenine has a hard time adapting to change. She cries when her baby sitter first arrives although she has a good time after a while. Similarly, she often screams on first climbing the slide at the neighborhood playground, although she also likes it very much and does not want to get off. Jenine responds to most situations intensely. When she is in a good mood, she greets the arrival of her favorite aunt with peals of laughter and a dizzying run towards her. When she is in a bad mood, she refuses to look at her for a long time. When she goes to her doctor whom she knows and likes, Jenine gets into a fist fight with him when he tries to examine her ear. When he offers her a toy after it is all over, she gives him a tight hug.

Not all difficult toddlers are exactly like Jenine. Difficult toddlers express their difficulties in their own personal ways. Some have frequent and prolonged tantrums. Others cry easily. Still others have problems with eating, sleeping, and elimination.

Parents often find it reassuring to learn that such trials and tribulations may result from their child's difficult temperament and not necessarily from some ingrained fault in their child-rearing methods.

All toddlers need their parents to provide a secure base that can become the building block for a rewarding partnership. Difficult toddlers need this process even more because their own moodiness and readiness to withdraw work against them in many situations. People often respond to the difficulties of toddlers with moodiness and withdrawal of their own. This is a pity. Sometimes the most difficult toddlers are also the most interesting to be with because their intense emotions and sensitivity help them to notice things other toddlers are not even aware of.

The prescription that most parents of difficult children find useful for managing everyday life has five major ingredients: not taking the child's behavior personally; a sense of humor; patient availability when one is with the child; clear guidelines for behavior; and a support system that allows the parent "time out" and breathing space from the child.

This recipe is not restricted to the rearing of difficult toddlers but is crucial to keep one's perspective at the most trying times. Through the book, parents of difficult toddlers should pay particular attention to the suggestions offered to help children through taxing situations such as separations and reunions, sleeping difficulties, discipline problems, sibling rivalry, toilet training, and so on. All toddlers deserve sensitive handling of these challenging situations, but difficult toddlers need it more than most.

Active Children

The impact of a high activity level on the child's behavior is particularly apparent in the toddler years, when the child's judgment about what is permissible and what is not is still very rudimentary. Active children tend to have a different, more expanded definition of the perimeter for secure-base behavior. Rather than staying within a radius of proximity considered safe by their parents, active toddlers may take off and move on without looking back.

Adam is a very active toddler. As a baby, he crawled very early and was always on the move. In his second year, he runs rather than walks, climbs on tables and cabinets, and loves high-energy games such as chases and playing ball. Adam does not hesitate to run into new situations and barely takes the time to look at a new object before grabbing it. He becomes restless and irritable when forced to be still, for example during long car rides or while being dressed.

Adam illustrates the fundamental temperamental feature of active children: a high activity level. When they also have a high propensity to approach novel stimuli, active toddlers can seem unstoppable because they not only crave movement for its own sake, but they are also irresistibly attracted to the many objects that surround them.

Active toddlers are not necessarily sociable. Some of them are so absorbed in physical pursuits that people do not hold a special interest for them. Even other children may serve primarily as partners in physical pursuits. Sedate social exchanges are not up to the active toddler's speed.

These toddlers and their parents often encounter many obstacles in their daily lives. People are frequently bothered by their high vitality level, and resent the constant motion these children engage in. Parents of active toddlers report that they often feel subtly or overtly criticized for not "setting limits," as if the child's need for physical activity were completely under the parent's control. "House proofing," a necessary method for keeping the peace in any home with a young child, becomes essential for safety with an active toddler. One problem is that many people resent having to childproof their house when an active toddler is visiting for a few hours, and the parents then feel additional pressure to keep their child within acceptable bounds. This situation can set up many conflicts between the child and the adults because constraints are so aversive to the active toddler that the child can become cranky and testy in response. Many a social visit ends with a feeling of failure as a result.

The Socialization of Temperament

Temperament is nobody's fault—not even its owner's. What one does with one's temperament, how one builds on it and tames it when necessary, is what education and character building are all about.

This is where parenting as an acquired art comes in. The way that parents and caregivers respond to a toddler's temperament will help to determine whether the vulnerabilities of the child become magnified and entrenched in his sense of himself, or whether, hopefully, these difficulties are framed by the more competent aspects of the child and do not become a dominant part of his personality.

The temperamental styles of children tend to be outside of their control in the early years. A toddler is not likely to wake up crying on purpose in order to spite the parent. She is also unlikely to hide behind her mother at a birthday party because she is trying to manipulate the situation to get people's attention. Yet toddlers are often unfairly blamed for behavior they cannot control.

When a child's behavior irritates or embarrasses us, we often respond by seeing murky motives behind it. In a way, we are trying to justify our negative reaction by looking for equally negative motives in the child. This is very human, but it is neither fair nor helpful to the parent–child relationship or to the child's emotional development. As mentioned earlier, temperament describes how the child responds, not why he is responding that way.

Keeping in mind that these tendencies are part of the child's innate makeup will help us to empathize with the child's experience and to find ways of responding to behavior we do not like in ways that preserve the child's self-esteem. For example, it will help to comfort rather than scold a toddler who wakes up crying, and to give time to a child who needs to stay near us at a party before being ready to move off on her own.

The Child's Temperament and Secure Base Behavior

The toddler's temperament influences the ebb and flow of secure base behavior. As described in chapter 2, secure base refers to the balance

between moving away from the mother in order to explore and coming back to her to restore the emotional connection or to seek comfort and reassurance.

Children's temperamental propensities tend to color the style of their secure base behavior. In general, toddlers who are active and love novelty leave their mother's side readily. Children who are slow to warm and withdraw from novelty tend to stay longer by the parent's side.

Toddlers with long attention spans and high persistence often stay away from the mother for long periods, because they like to spend much time manipulating and sorting out things. Conversely, these same children may also spend more time close to their mother once they decide to approach her, because they get quite engaged in whatever they are doing with her.

Highly adaptable children are likely to move away from the mother to explore a wide range of novel surroundings; less adaptable children need a long time to get comfortable with change and may explore only in familiar settings.

Even the child's mood quality and intensity of reaction may affect secure base behavior. Children with strong negative reactions to new stimuli are likely to stay close to their mother and may need encouragement and reassurance before they can move off and explore on their own. The examples below describe how the easygoing Joey, the slow-to-warm Erin, the difficult Jenine, and the active Adam organize their secure base behavior.

Joey is a very curious, precocious, exuberant 2½-year-old. He seems to be perpetually in a good mood. His episodes of distress are usually short-lived: his mother describes him as "the image of resilience." Joey can entertain himself for a long time with activities that range from pretend play like putting his turtle to sleep and building a block "house," to talking to himself, looking at his books, or using the climbing equipment just outside his room in the backyard. At these times, Joey's mother needs to keep an eye on him every once in a while to make sure he is all right. At other times, Joey shows no interest in playing by himself and wants to be near the mother for long periods of time, singing to her, asking to cook with her, or asking the mother to join him in play. If the mother cannot be available on demand, Joey becomes distressed and is not easily redirected. He then shows none of his exceptional ability to entertain himself when he takes the initiative to do so. However, he accepts speaking with his mother and singing together as substitutes for close physical contact. This child's secure base behavior shows a clear dichotomy between "times on his own" and "times with mother."

Erin is a quiet, mild-mannered 2¾-year-old. She is somewhat shy and tends to be watchful at first, but she easily becomes interested in novel surroundings. Her expressions of pleasure as well as distress tend to be low-keyed. She neither ventures too far from her mother nor clambers up or clings to her. Her movements away from her mother and back to her are subtle. She may move away a little bit at a time, and her approaches may also be gradual, as if they were a side effect of pursuing a rolling ball or becoming interested in a toy that happens to be near the mother. Erin's secure base behavior, like her overall personality, seems to have no dramatic swings: a well-modulated balance between attachment and exploration behaviors predominates.

Jenine is a bright 2½-year-old who has much difficulty managing her mood. When she is at home and in her mother's presence, she can delight in playing with her toys and chatter happily in an animated description of what she is doing. However, she easily becomes angry and despondent when things do not go exactly as she wants. Should her mother leave the room, for example, Jenine becomes alarmed, cries, asks where she is going, and often follows her while wailing. When Jenine and her parents visit friends' houses, Jenine stays close to her father and mother. An older child may persuade her to play for a little while, but Jenine soon becomes distressed and seeks her mother again.

In unfamiliar situations, Jenine refuses to move away from her mother and often screams in distress if her mother tries to get Jenine off her lap and interested in nearby toys.

Jenine's secure base behavior can be characterized as including short bouts of exploration away from her mother and prolonged periods of proximity and contact with her. Because the child has a low threshold of sensitivity to stimuli, she is easily alarmed even by routine events like her mother's comings and goings about the house and periodic visits to friends' houses. Her high intensity of response means that she responds with marked distress to these situations and needs prolonged contact with her mother in order to feel safe again.

Adam is a rambunctious 2-year-old, who seems always in motion. Even while he sleeps he thrashes about in all directions. He walked at 10 months, and locomotion is his favored mode of expression. He approaches novelty with glee, reaching out to dogs on the street, stopping to pick up little pieces of paper, plastic, or any object that he enounters as he moves about. He is seldom wary and rarely frightened by unfamiliar situations. When not held firmly by the hand, he races ahead without looking back, making little noises of excitement or delight as he marches on. Although quite affectionate when he chooses to be, Adam has little patience for extended cuddling and scrambles off his mother's lap after a few minutes. He occasionally approaches her in the course of his explorations to touch her knee or give her a toy, but he more often looks, smiles, or speaks to her from a distance, often showing her the toy he is involved with. He accepts his mother's overtures to play together with pleasure, but is equally contented to play on his own. His secure base behavior can be described in terms of sustained periods of exploration interspersed with brief but satisfying instances of proximity and contact with his mother.

All these are normal children with distinctive patterns of attachment and exploration. Each of them has a very personal style. Their different use of the parent as a secure base helps us to understand whether they are introverted or extroverted; needy or self-reliant; whether they feel protected or endangered and alone; whether the world is a source of joy or a reason for fear. More subtly, secure base behavior carries the stamp of the child's individuality in her sense of herself, her way of interacting with those closest to her, and how she negotiates familiar as well as unexpected situations.

Parental Style and Secure Base Behavior

Parents have unique styles of encouraging or dampening exploration and attachment in their toddlers. Two distinctive parental patterns consist of holding on and letting go. When things are unfolding well enough for parent and child, these two patterns complement each other in response to the child's developmental needs to go away and then come back to the parent. When the parents' own emotional needs distort their perception of the child, there is often a tendency to overemphasize one or the other pattern, holding on too tightly or letting go too readily.

Parents' and toddlers' patterns influence each other. An over-protective parent may increase a shy toddler's tendency to hold back by giving the message that the world is a dangerous place and that the child can be safe only by staying near. Alternatively, similar parental overprotectiveness may trigger a very different response of rebelliousness and even reckless testing of the limits in an active, feisty child.

The toddler's style may also influence the parent's patterns. A daring, adventuresome child may delight shy parents by acquainting them with new horizons, or may terrify a parent who is not so ready for such feats. A cautious toddler may trigger impatient urgings to explore in one parent, while another parent may find this behavior very compatible with his or her own style.

Temperament, Partnership, and Goodness of Fit

Not only children have temperaments; parents do too. When the temperaments of parent and child are compatible, parents find it easier to work with the harder edges of the child's behavior. This compatibility contributes to the pride and satisfaction that the parents derive from who their child is.

At the same time, parents do not have omnipotent control over their children's development. Erik Erikson[11] expressed this simple but often overlooked truth most eloquently when he wrote:

> We distort the situation if . . . we consider the parents as 'having' such and such a personality . . . and then . . . impinging it upon a poor little thing. For this weak and changing little being moves the whole family along. Babies control and bring up their families as much as they are controlled by them; in fact . . . the family brings up a baby by being brought up by him.

This brings us back to the question of partnership explored in the previous chapter. When the parent and child are well matched in their temperament styles, it is easier to establish a partnership because each of them feels comfortable with the other's pace and emotional tone. On the other hand, mismatches of temperament can interfere with finding mutually acceptable solutions when the parent and child have competing agendas and conflicting expectations.

Compatibility does not mean sameness. It means that the parent and child fit well with each other. "Goodness of fit" exists when the parents' expectations and demands from their child can be met by the child's motivations, capacities, and behavioral style.[3,6,7,8] A poor fit occurs when there is a mismatch between the parents' expectations and the child's ability to fulfill them.

Goodness of fit can be observed in the course of the moment-to-moment transactions that take place between parents and toddler. At the end of the day, a methodical observer may emerge with a score. For example, "good fit: 50 percent of all interactions; medium fit: 30 percent; poor fit: 20 percent." These particular scores would probably reflect a daily routine in which parents and child manage to be reasonably well attuned to each other's needs and wishes for a good portion of the day. We can imagine some of the sequences that contribute to the final tally:

At 5 a.m., when the parents are still badly in need of their sleep, Andy demands breakfast. Mother groans and buries herself under the blanket. Father musters his most authoritative voice to say it is still sleeping time. Andy (a persistent sort by temperament as well as emerging habit) insists that he is hungry. Father remembers that the child fell asleep before supper the previous

night; by this reckoning, he hasn't eaten for about 12 hours. Convinced that the child might indeed be hungry, father gets up, prepares a bottle, and tells the child firmly that he will need to drink it in his crib and let mommy and daddy continue to sleep. Andy complies grudgingly. He calls a few more times from his crib, but gives up when the father replies he needs to sleep now. Soon father and son are fast asleep. (Score: high goodness of fit between parent and child's mutual expectations and abilities).

It is 7:30 a.m., and parents and toddler are up. Mother needs to take Andy to a regular pediatric check-up by 9 a.m. She discovers that he is badly soiled and that only a bath will remedy the situation. Rushed, she overlooks the fact that this child is used to long leisurely play with her in the morning. She gives him a bath, which he (being a basically adaptable child with predominantly positive moods) accepts with pleasure. But he protests intensely when mother tries to make the bath short and businesslike. He is an active child who is well rested and naturally wants to splash, play with his duckie, and roll around the tub. Mother impatiently says there is no time for play today and abruptly takes him out. He screams. Mother realizes she is pushing him too hard, hugs him, and uses a corner of the towel in which he is wrapped to play "where is the baby?" This is all he needs to get back to a cooperative spirit. Grateful for his resiliency, mother begins telling him step by step what they will do during the day, distracting him with this story as she quickly dresses him. Andy likes the idea of a car ride, which mother highlights because she knows he will be receptive to it. The process of getting ready is completed without further disagreement. (Score: high goodness of fit. Both mother and child are able to experience conflict with each other through different expectations and plans, and to negotiate a way out of this conflict that satisfies both of them.)

It is 8:40 a.m. On the way to the doctor's, mother is feeling pleased that she managed things on schedule that morning, but she is also apprehensive about the pediatric check-up. She knows that her child has an excellent memory and that he will remember the medical exam and the shots he received in the previous visit as soon as they enter the medical building. At that time Andy cried and fought the doctor off for a long time. She decides not to say anything about going to the doctor in order not to spoil the child's good mood prematurely. Her forebodings are confirmed as soon as they park in the back of the building. Andy cries: "no doctor, no shot," and refuses to get out of the child seat. Mother is mortified. She is rather shy and hates public scenes that make her the center of attention. She is now keenly aware of people looking at them as she tries unsuccessfully to reason with her child. The mother decides that the child is too upset to go through the pediatric appointment and decides to cancel it. She tells him so, and he calms down immediately. She drives away and calls the doctor's office from a public telephone in order to reschedule. (Score: poor goodness of fit. In her embarrassment about the child's tantrum, the mother mistook her own difficulty in withstanding a public scene as Andy's inability to cope with the pediatric visit. Occasional stress, by itself, need not be damaging to children. They have the ability to experience and tolerate strong emotion provided they have access to a trusted and supportive adult and provided also that the situation is developmentally appropriate by cultural standards. Withdrawing children protectively from situations that they need to go through undermines their confidence in their own ability to cope with anxiety.)

It is 6:30 p.m., dinner time. The father, who is very concerned about good nutrition, heaps the child's plate with chicken, mashed potatoes, and vegetables. After eating his fill, Andy starts experimenting with the mashed potatoes while the parents finish their dinner. He kneads the potatoes between his fingers, and eventually, bored by the lack of attention, begins to alternatively smear it on his hair and drop it on the floor. The father tells him to stop and cleans him up with a napkin, but he wants Andy to remain in his high chair until the parents finish dinner. Andy becomes increasingly restless. The mother and father allow him to get off the high chair and play on the floor next to them. (Score: medium goodness of fit. It is hard for a toddler to be good company at the table when he is no longer hungry. After a bout of somewhat unrealistic expectations, the parents realize this and change their demands to a more age-appropriate approach.)

It is 8:10 p.m., and bedtime is nearing. Father and child are playing hide-and-seek. Father announces that after two more times, it will be time to go to bed. Andy protests, and father reassures him that he will still "find" Andy two more times. After this time is up, the father tells the toddler that now it is time to get into his pajamas and brush his teeth. As the child complies with the routine, he asks for more play. The father says, "We'll have more play tomorrow." The child is reassured by this promise, and the bedtime rituals of reading a book and singing a song with the lights out proceed smoothly. (Score: high goodness of fit. The father gives the child some time to adjust to the transition from play to bed, and is appropriately firm but sympathetic as the child expresses his understandable reluctance to give up the game.)

These examples were selected to emphasize that goodness of fit does not imply absence of conflict. Rather, it involves the ability to keep conflict within manageable emotional levels. This is possible when the parents can perceive accurately the child's capacities in a particular situation and when the child is receptive to reasonable parental wishes and demands.

Chronic Conflicts Between Parent and Child

There are times when the conflicts between a parent and a child are a predominant component of their relationship and are not simply a reflection of the regular ups and downs of daily life. In these cases, the parent feels chronically frustrated and irritated with the child. Moments of spontaneous pleasure between them are rare and short-lived. There seems to be a fundamental discrepancy between who the child is and who the parent wishes him to be.

The child's temperament may play an important part in this situation. He may be indeed a difficult child—one with unpredictable mood swings, intense reactions to mild frustrations, signals that are difficult to read. More often than not, however, it is not only the child's temperament but how the parent perceives it and responds to it that leads to a poor fit between parent and child. For example, one parent may see a crying child as manipulative and slap him to "really give him something to cry about." Another parent may interpret the crying as a sign of distress and try to find out the reasons for it.

A study by Susan Crockenberg illustrates this point.[12] She found that very fussy, irritable newborns tended to have an anxious relationship with their mothers at 12 months, but only when the mother consistently ignored their crying and had little social support herself. In other words, when their mothers feel supported in their daily lives and are responsive to the child's cries, even irritable babies can become secure in their attachment relationships.

Why do some parents respond appropriately while others get tangled in conflicts with their toddlers? It is easier to ask this question than to answer it, because the answer has many layers and individual variations. As Tolstoy observed, happy families resemble one another; unhappy families are unhappy in their own particular ways. A comprehensive answer needs to encompass the biological, psychological, and social levels of family life. A sketch of these levels is offered below.

1. *The temperamental make-up of the parent is at odds with the child's temperament.* For example, the parent may be active, extroverted, sociable, intense; the child may be slow, introverted, shy. When the parent cannot find pleasure in these differences, a mismatch may occur: what a parent considers fun, her toddler may find painfully overstimulating. Conversely, the activities that enthrall the toddler may be excruciatingly boring to the parent.

Mrs. Barker is an outgoing, energetic, athletic woman who takes pride in "working hard and playing hard." She talks loudly, laughs uproariously, and moves fast. Her child Ashley is the antithesis of her mother: retiring, low-keyed, easily scared. Mrs. Barker feels impatient trying to tone down her behavior to match her daughter's slower rhythms. Ashley, on the other hand, seems to quiver in her mother's presence, as if overstimulated by her.

Alternatively, the toddler may be active, sociable, intense, and the parent may be slow, quiet and shy. In such a pair, the child is constantly searching for more stimulation, and the parent feels always on the verge of exhaustion by the child's demands.

Mr. Preston is a bookish man who would stay home all day reading if he had the choice. His son Kevin, in contrast, can best be described as "hell on wheels": adventurous, unstoppable. Kevin tries to entice his father to play ball, climb playground structures, run after him. Mr. Preston tries to get Kevin to read quietly with him. The two seem always at odds with each other, because they cannot open themselves to the activities that give pleasure to the other.

These examples show the discomfort that can result from mismatches between parent and child. On the other hand, parents do not need to have the same temperament as their children for their relationship to go well.

Building a partnership often involves compromises. Mrs. Barker found a much-wanted area of compatibility with Ashley when she discovered that both loved the water and could go swimming together. This commonality made her more willing to go slow when her daughter needed her to. Mr. Preston and Kevin found a different solution. They "traded" times together by agreeing to go to the playground after reading a book together or vice versa. In other words, each of them was willing to do something for the sake of spending time with the other.

In a recent study, very active toddlers played more competently when their mothers did not intervene very much. Conversely, less active toddlers were able to play better when their mothers were highly stimulating.[13] These findings suggest that active children probably need their autonomy and feel cramped by an equally active parent when they are interested in playing alone. Less active children may feel supported by the parent's help. The match between parent and child at any given time affects what the child is able to achieve on his or her own.

2. *The parent's level of self-acceptance.* Some parents feel at ease with who they are and what they have become. Others feel divided inside themselves, guilty about their imperfections, dissatisfied with their achievements.

It is difficult to be an accepting and contented parent if one is displeased with oneself. We often project on our children our deepest longings and most secret fears, and when this happens we tend to see in them what we suppress in ourselves. The young child can become for the parents a mirror of their own most shame-producing attributes, a reflection of their hopelessness and their frustrations. More encouragingly, the child can give the parents new hope and stimulate them to find more fulfilling ways to live.

The symbolic role the child acquires in a parent's life can have pervasive effects on their relationship because the objective characteristics of the child may become virtues or defects depending on how the parent perceives them. For example, a child's assertiveness may be seen as aggressive by a parent who feels uneasy about this trait, whereas another parent may take great pleasure in the child's ability to speak up for herself.

Mr. and Mrs. DeCarlo have a child, Anthony, who is very clear in stating his likes and dislikes. Anthony does not give in when he wants something, and protests loudly when he does not get his way. Mr. DeCarlo, who thinks of himself as too stubborn and has problems yielding to other people, believes Anthony's "willfulness" should be curbed. His wife, who sees herself as overpowered by her husband, is delighted by her son's feistiness and thinks it would be damaging to set firmer limits. Each of these parents is perceiving Anthony from the perspective of their own psychological needs. The father consciously wants to spare the child the problems he himself has, but he also wants to control Anthony and bring him in line with his own wishes. The mother relishes Anthony's outspokenness because it compensates for her own feelings that her husband always has the last word.

3.   *The parent's subjective experience of the child.* Each child makes his own unique imprint in the parent's psyche. The parent may feel delighted, irritated, threatened, enraged or conflicted by the child's existence at a visceral level. This may have to do with many factors (for example, the circumstances of the child's conception; who the child resembles; the child's birth order; the child's temperament and emerging personality; the parent's sense of self). Ultimately, however, the parents' visceral reactions have much to do with how they recognize themselves in the child.

Parents sometimes believe that they are able to detect the very essence of their child. How this essence is perceived may be fateful in shaping who the child can become.

One mother who was sent for treatment by Family Court was convinced that her 14-month-old son would become a juvenile delinquent. This mother perceived her husband as controlling and insensitive. She had been physically abused by her father when she was a child and she feared her husband would eventually become physically abusive as well. Her toddler was enmeshed in the harshness of the mother's experience. He was, in fact, an active child with a sunny disposition. However, he had become the carrier of his mother's anger at her husband and at

her life in general, and she interpreted his mildest protests or expressions of displeasure as a portent of his future as a "good for nothing."

This mother had relatively unconflicted relationships with her other three children, all daughters. She could not entertain the notion that her perception of her son was a projection of her own anger at her abusive father and her controlling husband. Instead, she thought that her feelings for her child showed that she knew him better than anybody else. Her behavior towards him was shaped by this conviction. She spoke openly to him about his disobedient nature and treated him with a mixture of punitiveness and rejection. Only as she could get in touch with her own pain and anger at her abuse by her father was this mother able to become more aware of her son's need for her. She gradually began to perceive his protests and signs of displeasure as the normal responses of a toddler in need of firm but affectionate guidelines rather than as the signs of a delinquent in the making.

This example shows a distortion of the normal parental experience of attributing to the young child a variety of virtues and defects. These parental attributions often say more about the parent's wishes, fears and expectations than about the child's true nature. Attributions may be flexible or rigid and they may be more or less influenced by the child's actual characteristics. Most often the attributions are positive and benign, and largely attuned to the child's own emerging individuality ("she will be such a tomboy, you can see it from the glint in her eye"; "he sure will be a success with the ladies"). In these cases, the parent-child relationship unfolds on a basis of mutual trust and hopeful expectations. When the attributions are negative or malevolent and cannot yield to disconfirming evidence, the parent and child are headed for a relationship filled with conflict and mistrust.

4. *The quality of the parent's support system.* It is difficult to establish and maintain a good relationship with a child when one is stressed out and isolated. Under these circumstances, parents have few supports to help them feel secure. They are sometimes so absorbed in coping with difficult circumstances that there is little time and energy left for the child.

We usually think of support systems in human terms—a spouse, a parent, a sibling, a friend. This is understandable because human relationships are essential to a sense of personal well-being. However, support systems consist also of community networks that provide supplies and services: adequate housing, sufficient food, efficient transportation, safe streets, good schools, accessible medical care.

When these services are readily available, they are "psychologically silent": we do not notice the enormous contribution that they make to our personal well-being, to our ability to have harmonious human relationships, and to our capacity to be adequate parents. It is only when one or more of these supports are lacking that their importance can be appreciated because of the stress that the family experiences in their absence.

How is this related to temperament? As the examples below suggest, parental responsiveness to their child's individual needs can be severely tested when the parents struggle to secure basic needs and services for themselves and their children.

Mrs. Fisher needs to work full time and can only afford a mediocre day-care center with too few caregivers for too many children and a high staff turnover. This setting makes it impossible to accommodate her child's unusually strong, temperamentally based needs for predictability and consistency in his daily routine. As a result, since attending day care 2-year-old Dave has become prone to severe and prolonged temper tantrums. He is constantly anxious, sucks his thumb, and follows his mother around the house.

Mr. Morgan became unemployed when the high-tech firm he worked for went bankrupt. His unemployment benefits have run out and the family has no medical insurance. He and his wife worry about the present and fret about the future. Mrs. Morgan, who left her teaching job to raise their daughter, is trying unsuccessfully to find another position. The parents are so intent on the daily effort to make ends meet that they have less time and patience for their daughter Annie, 30 months old. Always a sensitive, easily frightened child, she has begun refusing to eat in order to save food. She also started biting her nails and has

regressed in her toilet training. She constantly asks her mother: Are you O.K.?"

Mrs. Compton and her family live in a deteriorating inner-city neighborhood. Their small apartment has deficient plumbing in the kitchen and bathroom and is often infested by cockroaches and mice. The manager of the building has promised repairs for six months but nothing has been done. "It's the same in every apartment," he says. Because of concerns about crime, the family is afraid to go out at night. The parents would like to move to better conditions but cannot afford it. There is frequent quarrelling as a result of frayed nerves and hopelessness. This situation is affecting little Ricky, an intense child who responds strongly to even minor stimulation and who would optimally need a calm, predictable environment to help him organize and modulate his behavior. At 30 months, he has frequent nightmares and cries easily at minor frustrations. His attention span is very short and in spite of good intelligence he is unable to persist at trying to solve an age-appropriate task. He often seems worried and distracted.

In these situations the strain on the parents, the child, and the parent–child relationship originates in a social failure to provide an adequate safety net for families in need. While all children suffer from exposure to inadequate conditions, some children are more temperamentally resilient and able to cope with fewer emotional costs, while other children are more vulnerable.

The examples above illustrate the concentric circles of influence on a child's well-being. The child's temperament and personality unfold within a family context which in turn exists within a larger social and political context. Each context has its own complexities, but no individual—no matter how strong, talented, or resourceful—exists on his own. Each one of us is helped or hindered in innumerable, often invisible ways by how our temperamental propensities are supported or undermined by the conditions in which we live.

The next two chapters will focus on two temperamental styles that are quite common among toddlers: shyness and its counterpart, bold activity. The chapters will describe the specific patterns of behavior that characterize these styles and the pleasures and special difficulties that they might bring.

While temperamental differences are very real, most toddlers are shy sometimes and boldly adventurous at other times. Because of this, parents may recognize familiar aspects of their child in both chapters, even if they do not usually think of their toddlers as either particularly active or particularly shy.

The Active Toddler: Racing Ahead

TODDLERS ARE BY NATURE TIRELESS EXPLORERS. EXACTLY WHAT THEY like to explore varies with the child and with the developmental stage. Some children resemble miniature scientists, bent on laboriously pulling apart every object they can get their hands on to see how it is made. Others experiment with language: they mix and match, make up words, engage in feats of linguistic construction. Still others build elaborate structures that seem to defy the imagination as well as physical gravity. Some do all of this and more, while others focus on different activities at different stages in their development.

Among these explorers, there are also toddlers who are mesmerized by movement and by the pursuit of a far-off goal. They careen through the world with their eyes set on whatever is just out of reach, with little regard for what stands in their way. They seem undaunted by obstacles, bumps, or falls.

Exploration from a Secure Base

In the balance between the exploration and attachment behaviors that define secure base behavior, very active, fearless toddlers show a clear preference for exploration. Parents learn to cherish the brief moments when the child is so tired that she needs to cuddle up for a while. This does not mean that these tiny adventurers have no feelings of love or wish for closeness. It is simply that at least for the time being, action and novelty exercise an irresistible pull. For them, secure relationships consist of the willingness to take risks away from the parent. It is as if the parents' love for the child fuels the child's love for the world.

This is not fanciful thinking: toddlers raised in sterile institutions show little energy or interest in taking off because they have no loving base to take off from.[1] Secure, actively exploring toddlers can risk leaving the parent's side because they rely on her ongoing availability. Rather than needing to stay close for protection, they take off fully expecting that the parent will be there should the need arise.

Movement and Language in Active Toddlers

Active children are not always overly active as babies, but they often walk early following a relatively brief crawling stage. Their first steps may be at 8 to 10 months (instead of the more usual 11 to 13 months), with autonomous walking following about a month later.

Some toddlers begin to walk months before they say their first words. Most infants use their first words by about 12 months, but there are very marked individual fluctuations in the timing of this achievement. Toddlers also differ in the rate of acquiring new words and in how quickly they move from single words to two-and three-word sentences.

There is also great variability in the importance that language has for different toddlers and in the pleasure that they derive from using it. Some 2-year-olds are very attuned to language; others are not. Toddlers who thrive on activity and experimenting with movement are often not interested in talking or listening until they get older and their motor skills become better integrated with their overall sense of themselves. Until this happens, they pay little attention to the "no's" and "stop's" of the adults. This makes language an ineffective tool for trying to restrain them.

Toddlers with a strong motivation for racing ahead and being on the move show a combination of at least three traits: a high activity level, high intensity of response, and a short attention span when it comes to sedentary activities. Such a child is unlikely to spend much time looking at books or trying to assemble puzzles. On the other hand, if she has access to a climbing structure she may practice going up and down and in every other possible direction until she (and her parents) collapse from fatigue.

Particularly in the 12 to 24 month period, movement is so central to the active toddler's sense of well-being that enforced immobility, cramped spaces, or simply being indoors for too long can set off irritability, restlessness, and finally temper tantrums. This the child's way of indicating that the urge to move and explore needs to find an avenue for discharge.

In the section that follows, a little boy called Adam will be described to illustrate some typical features of a well-developing, unusually active, and seemingly fearless toddler. The description also highlights some of the adaptations his parents had to make to cope with his high energy level and tireless urge to explore.

A Tireless Explorer: Adam

All toddlers carry a measure of bold initiative inside them, and in this sense Adam illustrates vividly what is a normal state of affairs at this stage. He just did it more often, more intensely, and for longer periods of time.

Adam's First Year

Adam began walking at 9 months. From then on it seemed as though he could never stop. His mother described herself as feeling like a seeing-eye dog, because she was always vigilant to Adam's whereabouts and ready to rescue him from danger. (She was a veterinarian, so the analogy came easily to her.) Some highlights of Adam's life between 9 and 30 months are provided below.

10 months. Adam is walking by himself and refuses to be carried anywhere. His parents observe that he is so enthralled by attractive distant objects that he fails to notice the obstacles in his way, such as steps or pieces of furniture. He trips over objects, falls down, bumps himself. He is often covered with bruises in spite of the family's concerted efforts to move faster than he. The house becomes thoroughly child-proofed, with gates everywhere. This proves somewhat helpful.

Diapering time is "a nightmare," in his mother's words. For Adam, a dirty diaper is a minor nuisance compared with the indignity of lying down and staying put while being changed. He kicks vigorously, protests, cries. His mother decides to switch from cloth diapers to disposable ones to minimize the hassle for both of them. Adam's mother is constantly exhausted, but there is some respite. He sleeps soundly at night and takes two naps, for a blessed total of about 14 hours of sleep a day.

Adam's mother feels as if her little boy grew overnight. She longs for the tender moments of quiet cuddling they had in earlier months, and her arms feel painfully empty at times. On the other hand, her own legs never stop now because she is always catching up with Adam. She says laughingly that their way of being together moved down from the torso to the feet.

12 months. Adam says his first word, "cat." This word choice may not be a coincidence and may be related to Adam's fascination with movement. The family cat is an important member of the household, the center of much conversation, and an agile presence that jumps easily from the floor to the kitchen counter, flees swiftly when pursued by Adam's eager hands, and moves gracefully and at will throughout the house. Maybe the cat represents Adam's fledgling version of an "ideal self," seemingly free to move everywhere and happily unconstrained by cumbersome realities like gravity, loss of balance, and parental efforts at holding him back.

The word "ousside" appears soon afterwards. When expected to stay indoors, Adam stands by the door, banging at it and repeating this magic word again and again. If he is not taken "ousside," he becomes increasingly agitated and distressed. Adam's mother finds herself spending a lot of time in the yard and following him as he insists on going further and walking up and down the block. She reports: "I got to know all my neighbors really well during that time."

Adam from 14 to 30 Months

14 months. Adam begins hitting his head when he cannot succeed at doing something he wants. How can we understand this behavior? Adam is a precocious child, and he has high expectations of himself. He wants to climb on his highchair all by himself, or to open the front door to go "ousside." When he cannot live up to his own standards, he refuses adult help and instead punishes himself quite deliberately. He stops what he is trying to do, looks for a good hard surface such as an uncarpeted portion of the floor, and bangs his head loudly and repeatedly.

This dramatic behavior looks worrisome and is very scary to watch but is actually common among toddlers with a high intensity of emotional response. This does not mean parents should ignore it. Doing nothing gives the child the message that punishing oneself is an appropriate reaction to feelings of failure and frustration.

Adam's mother responds to his head banging by placing him in his crib while telling him that she cannot let him hurt himself. At first she feels guilty, and worries that putting him in the crib is punishing Adam for punishing himself. However, Adam responds well to this maneuver. He bangs his head softly on the mattress, as if rehearsing a discharge of motor tension in a safe setting. His mother stays near, sometimes talking soothingly to him, sometimes letting him be on his own. Adam eventually calms down. This positive response convinces his mother that she instinctively found the right way to soothe her child.

The crib serves as a comforting container for Adam's unruly emotions. It is noteworthy that this very athletic child does not begin climbing out of his crib until 30 months, in spite of being physically able to do so much earlier. He clearly likes his crib and regards it as a safe place to be in.

Some children respond best to being held and cuddled while having a tantrum. Adam's mother found that this did not work well for him. When Adam was upset, he refused to be held—arching his back, squirming, and pushing away. At these times he did not experience being held as a loving act but as a physical restraint which was extremely unpleasant to him.

This is a common response at his age when the toddler is experiencing a conflict of ambivalence: he simultaneously wants to be comforted by the parent and to assert his own autonomy. This conflict may be expressed by turning against the mother or father and hitting them or pushing them away. The parents are serving here as the recipient of the child's inner conflict.

It is better not to leave toddlers alone when they are having a tantrum. They need their parents as a secure base that will not leave them in the lurch when they are feeling alone, angry, and scared by the intensity of their emotions. If the parents can respond calmly rather than with anger or emotional withdrawal, the child's ambivalence will resolve itself in the course of development as he becomes better able to negotiate being close versus being separate and autonomous.

15 months. Adam learns to kick a ball, and a beach ball becomes his favorite toy. His parents put a basketball hoop in the kitchen at his height level, and he delights in putting the ball through the hoop again and again. He loves watching sports on TV, although neither parent relishes this activity. He cries when they try to change the channel, saying, "fooball, fooball."

16 months. Adam and his mother take a five-hour plane ride to visit his grandparents. He is miserable unless he is going up and down the aisle. He climbs on the few empty seats and tries to talk on the flight attendants' telephone. Adam's mother does her best to catch up and keep up, but the frowns of the crew are hard to bear. She mumbles to herself: "I bet they've never been around a kid."

Before this visit, Adam's mother had looked forward to staying at her

parents' house and sharing Adam's care with two other adults. Images of going for a walk by herself or even reading a book in the middle of the day had floated dreamily through her mind. These fantasies fail to materialize. Her parents are clearly unable to match Adam's speed and energy level. Much as they enjoy him, they are clearly unsettled and exhausted after a two-hour stint as his sole caregivers.

18 months. Adam begins to cry bitterly when his mother leaves. She has to peel him off as he clings to her. This continues until he is 30 months. The distress on separation indicates that Adam is very conscious of his mother's role in making him feel secure. However, he accepts substitutes well, and develops a warm relationship with two baby-sitters who care for him while his mother works a few hours every day. He greets his mother warmly when she returns home.

19 months. Adam begins attending a toddler group for two hours a day, twice a week, with five other children. His mother stays with him during this time. The teacher is experienced, cheerful, energetic. All the signs seem to indicate that this will be a good experience for Adam and his mother, but events prove otherwise.

The first day of the group, Adam climbs to the highest rung of the climbing structure and falls down, luckily without hurting himself. The teacher proceeds to unscrew the two upper rungs, commenting that no toddler had ever tried to go beyond the first three levels. The mother is grateful for the teacher's flexibility.

The second day Adam upturns a heavy wooden bench and uses it as a climbing structure. The teacher removes the bench from the area, saying cheerfully: "Adam is teaching me about possible dangers I never knew about."

The third day Adam cries continuously because it is raining and the children can't play "ousside." He does not mingle with the other children. He climbs on the furniture and invents games based on movement that the other children find fascinating and try to imitate. Mostly, however, he is very unhappy about being there.

The fourth day, after watching Adam's preference for moving on his own rather than playing with the other children, the teacher says to the mother: "I think Adam is not ready for this." His mother is devastated. She thinks: "If only I were more creative and energetic and came up with novel ways of channeling his energy, he would fit better." Adam's father is philosophical. He consoles her by saying: "He is just fine. I was just like him. Actually, I still am."

20 months. Adam and his father go for an outing and come back radiant. They have spent the whole day riding buses and finding exciting things to do between bus and bus. On the bus rides, Adam gleefully climbs on the mostly empty seats and goes up and down the aisle in the back of the bus.

Adam's mother wishes such outings could happen more often. His father works very long hours and often comes home just before Adam goes to sleep. Everybody in the family regrets this situation. When singing a homemade version of "Old MacDonald Had a Farm," mother asks: "What does the daddy say?" Adam replies: "Bye bye." He is only too aware that much of his daily experience of daddy consists of seeing him leave.

It becomes clear that Adam has an internal motor map that allows him to navigate the world with an inner sense of competence. He is like his father in this regard; his mother has no sense of direction. When driving through the neighborhood where his best friend lives, he points in the right direction yelling "Tony, Tony."

22 months. Mother's best friend comments that she doesn't feel she has a relationship with Adam. "He never lets me do anything for him, and he doesn't like to do things like solve puzzles or read books with me," she laments. Adam's mother worries that maybe he is not sociable enough to be liked by other people.

Adam says his first two-word combination. Not surprisingly, it is: "No, myself."

23 months. Adam balances himself on a swing, refusing help by using his handy new utterance, "No, myself." But there is a new twist: his mother hears him muttering to himself: "Be careful," as he eases himself down.

Adam begins to use "be careful" whenever he embarks on a new feat. He also begins to ask for help: "Mommy help." This marks a transformation in his mother's perception of him. She begins to trust that he can take care of himself. She is right: his reality testing regarding danger has become more accurate. He has internalized his mother's protective role, and he can now use her help as well as his own coping devices to make himself feel secure.

24 months. On Adam's second birthday, his mother reflects: "It's a miracle we never had to end up in the Emergency Room." In spite of his bold behavior and his many falls, Adam has never been badly hurt. This is probably a combination of Adam's innate sense of his own capabilities and of his mother's and caregivers' readiness to spring into action.

As she thinks of herself during the past year, Adam's mother reflects: "I feel like a hypervigilant, overprotective mother." Is she accurate in her self-assessment? Truly overprotective mothers do not generally know this about themselves. They believe they are protecting their children from very real and immediate dangers, but in fact they tend to overestimate the risk of a situation. Adam's mother, on the contrary, was clearly responding to her child's need for protection before he could reliably take over this function by anticipating danger and protecting himself. She learned to accept and admire his boundless determination to explore as a personal trait that she needed to monitor but could not change. Because of his mother's availability, both physical and emotional, Adam was free to be himself without conflict or shame.

On the other hand, it is worth noting that Adam's father was less compelled than his mother to retrieve and rescue him. Adam did not get hurt more often in his father's care, although he did get banged up more. Adam's mother worried more about physical safety than his father, but this was all right. Individual differences between the parents can be very useful in giving children alternative but equally valid perspectives on how to negotiate the world.

30 months. Adam continues to be very active, but now his activities are modulated in a way that conveys new skills at self-control. During a trip to the beach, he makes a beeline for the water but stops right at the edge; he then runs all the way back to a line of trees but does not venture into the woods.

After an initial moment of panic as she watches him running between the water and the woods, Adam's mother realizes that he knows when to stop and gives up trying to run after him. She positions herself by the edge of the water where she can keep an eye on him as he covers this exciting new territory. She is ready to spring into action, but she has a new confidence that she will not need to.

Adam spends long periods of time building with blocks and solving puzzles. His attention span has been redirected to quieter pursuits now that movement has been mastered. This has a good effect on his ability to relate to adults, who prefer sitting with Adam rather than running after him.

Language has become a major avenue for partnership between Adam and other people. At the doctor's, he follows the nurse's instructions to the letter. At home, his parents can now tell him what to do and he does it without physical coaxing. He also reports to his parents what his day was like. Conversations become based on taking turns, and he listens while others talk. He puts feelings into words, describing himself and others quite accurately. He shows awareness of and empathy for his parents' and his little friends' experiences.

Adam is happy in his preschool. He has friendly relations with all ten children in his class. He fits in just fine.

He loves being naked. He discovers his penis and is enamored of it. He notices and comments when he has an erection: "Mommy, my penis is big. Touch it, right here." He is also interested in differences between boys and girls. He plays with a little girl: "This is my eye. Where is your eye? . . . This is my nose. Where is your nose? . . . This is my penis. Where is your penis?" These developments indicate that Adam's interest in the body is switching from an unwavering focus on movement to a growing fascination with how he is made, how he is similar to other boys and how he differs from little girls.

Adam's second year shows the trajectory covered by a little child with a boundless craving for movement as he or she learns to modulate a high activity level. The key to developmental progress is the child's ability to gradually integrate physical movement with cognitive and social milestones in development, such as the ability to interact with peers and adults, the use of language, and the evolution of fantasy play.

A *time-limited* period. Parents who do not share the child's level of activity (and very few do) may have a difficult time during this period. Mothers of very active toddlers often comment that they feel at times like social pariahs because of their children. Family friends fret over their belongings when the child comes over. There is a covert or overt social message that the parents should always do more to keep the child "under control." One mother commented: "People did not understand that for Danny a coffee table was not a coffee table; it was something made to climb on." She went on to explain that her own self-esteem suffered as a result because she was ashamed of her child's wild behavior. This mother believes that her child's early self-esteem might have suffered as well because he was constantly experiencing the disapproval of the adults. (She might well be right, but her son did not seem to carry this early hurt into his preschool years. He was a happy, talented, and much-liked child).

The good news is that the period of unbridled motor exploration is generally time-limited and begins to wane at about 30 months. By 3 years of age, children are generally much more in control of themselves, and life in the household becomes quieter and more pleasant.

The next two sections describe what happens when the child's high-activity level becomes a source of friction between parents and child. The last section offers some suggestions that may help to defuse conflict and build islands of quiet activity to promote partnership between parents and child.

Conflict in Motion: Melinda

When a toddler does not feel emotionally supported in her search for a satisfying balance between closeness and exploration, movement may become the carrier of conflict in the parent–child relationship.

This was the case with Melinda, the youngest of four children and the only girl. Melinda's parents had longed for a girl for many years, and they were overjoyed when she was born eight years after their youngest son. Mrs. Powell experienced a resurgence of youth and hope as she cuddled her little girl, dressed her in frilly outfits, and daydreamed about playing with her daughter the way she herself had played as a child. She had saved a beautiful doll house from those happy days, and she began collecting miniature furniture to outfit it in style by the time Melinda could play with it.

But Melinda's emerging personality did not fit in with Mrs. Powell's dreams. She was a smiley, sturdy little girl who loved her mother but was totally mesmerized by her boisterous and playful older brothers. As soon as she could walk she ran after them when they played outside, trying to catch a frisbee or kick a ball. The boys sometimes welcomed her and other times resented her intrusions. As a result, they alternated between including her and shoving her away. Melinda was giddily happy when her brothers played with her and screamed in rage when they did not.

Mrs. Powell went along with Melinda's interest in her brothers' games until she was 2 years old. The mother believed that a 2-year-old should start learning to play like a girl rather than a boy. Melinda's second birthday present was her mother's childhood doll house, fully equipped with doll-size furniture and dolls to match. Melinda played with it briefly, broke the leg of a doll, pulled out the stuffing of a tiny armchair, and then trotted off to see what her brothers were doing. She played "tag" with them, running wildly around the yard.

Mrs. Powell was hurt, but she could not allow herself to admit it. Instead, she became more firmly convinced that Melinda was now a little girl and must not be allowed to be so wild. The mother became curt and critical whenever Melinda was exuberantly active, which was often. When Melinda came close to her mother after falling down or getting hurt in the course of her play, Mrs. Powell said harshly: "That is what happens to you for being so wild." If Melinda was sweaty and covered with dirt after playing in the yard, Mrs. Powell snapped: "Don't come near me when you are dirty like that."

Melinda soon learned to associate physical excitement in active play with rejection by her mother. She also began to acquire a dim sense that little girls should not "run free." Instead of finding a receptive mother when she returned from her forays, she found emotional distance and disapproval.

Melinda continued to have happy moments with her mother, but only when she was quiet and controlled. By 28 months, she became aware that doll playing and tea parties made for moments of rewarding intimacy together. She began to purposely seek out her mother for this kind of play, bringing her a doll or saying: "Let's have tea, mommy." Mrs. Powell's heart seemed to melt at those times, and she stopped whatever she was doing to play with her daughter.

In spite of these times of closeness, some incidents suggest that Melinda's relationship with her mother had become emotionally constricted. When she got very excited, she often stopped herself abruptly and looked worriedly in her mother's direction. When she fell as a result of daring activities, she sometimes said to herself "bad girl" and did not seek out comfort from her mother. At these moments, it seemed as if Mrs. Powell's disapproving demeanor had become part of Melinda's sense of herself.

If everyone in this child's world had adopted her mother's attitude and frowned on her activity level, it is possible that Melinda might have internalized the adults' disapproval and begun to feel bad about herself for not living up to the ideal of a properly feminine little girl.

Fortunately, this conflict about activity did not become pervasive, because Melinda's father and brothers continued to play rough-and-tumble games with her and to enjoy her liveliness. At those times Melinda seemed to be truly happy, particularly if her mother was not present. If she got hurt during these activities, she readily went to her father or one of her brothers for a cuddle.

If Mrs. Powell had been less wounded by her daughter's failure to be the sedate little girl she wanted, she might have become more accepting of Melinda's boisterous behavior and more able to help the child learn that enjoying tea parties and climbing trees, far from being mutually exclusive, could be two integral parts of herself and her world.

What is the long-term outlook for Melinda? If the family continues functioning as it is now, it is possible that Melinda will learn to associate physical and emotional freedom with being a boy, and self-constraint in the physical and affective spheres with being a girl. As she grows up, this might contribute to unnecessary conflicts over being a woman.

On the other hand, a turn for the better could well occur. After all, mothers and fathers grow and learn from their mistakes. It is possible that Melinda's mother might become less uptight about what she sees as Melinda's "tomboyishness." There are signs that her family and friends were working to make this happen. Mrs. Powell was good naturedly ribbed by her family for what they called her "prissiness" towards Melinda. Her husband often spoke up in private, telling her she was being "too hard" on the child. A close friend made a helpful comment when the mother poured her heart out about her worries and wishes about Melinda: she pointed out that Mrs. Powell often felt lonesome at home among "all the boys" and was relying too much on Melinda to provide some female companionship which was beyond the capacities of a 2-year-old.

These reactions might help Mrs. Powell to become more aware of how her own needs are affecting her attitude towards her daughter. If she becomes more accepting, Melinda could in turn feel more secure about being good and lovable just as she is, tomboyishness and all.

Reckless Accident Proneness: Paul

Some children express their conflicts over the parents' lack of availability as a secure base in the form of an uncontrollable urge to explore recklessly that often ends up in accidental injuries. These reckless toddlers may wander away from the house, dart across the street, get lost in supermarkets and shopping malls, pull the contents of shelves on themselves, and in general constantly get into trouble. It is not the occurrence of a couple of incidents that define a reckless toddler; it is the frequency of fairly serious accidents or enough close calls to warrant ongoing concern for the child's welfare.[2]

Sometimes it is difficult to know when a toddler is reckless as a result of inner conflict and when he or she is simply still too young and too active to be able to anticipate danger. One clue that something might be wrong is that reckless children remain uncontrollable long after outgrowing toddlerhood. Unlike Adam, they do not become more aware of danger and more careful and attentive as they enter their third year.

Another sign of trouble is that, paradoxically, reckless toddlers tend to also show numerous symptoms of anxiety in a variety of areas. Although all toddlers show age-appropriate fears, reckless toddlers are often overwhelmed by them. They might be excessively afraid of the dark, of animals, of strangers, or of unusual noises. They might have frequent and intractable tantrums; be afraid of going to sleep or wake up screaming several times during the night; suffer from acute separation anxiety interspersed with episodes of darting away. Their apparent fearlessness in exploring seems to be counterbalanced by their excessive fear in other realms. Sometimes their anxiety emerges in the form of anger and aggression: hitting, biting, and kicking.

At 28 months, Paul showed all of the above behaviors, making him a very difficult child to live with. His parents and pediatrician were so worried that they undertook an extensive medical evaluation to determine whether he was hyperactive. When the results were negative, Mr. and Mrs. Donahue were actually a little disappointed. They wanted a concrete medical reason for Paul's behavior, something that could be cured by taking pills. They did not want to get into the amorphous realm of psychological difficulties. Nevertheless, they were concerned enough about Paul to agree readily when their pediatrician recommended a psychological evaluation.

The best place to observe a toddler's psychological functioning is at home, where he feels least restrained by the demands of an unfamiliar situation. In the course of a two-hour home visit, Paul was quite ready to show me what his parents were worried about. While they spoke about his uncontrollable behavior, he climbed precariously on a window sill and jumped down noisily, twisting his ankle; he pulled down a portrait of himself and his family by climbing on a piece of furniture; he got into a fight with the cat by pulling its tail and getting scratched; and he hit his mother when she tried to look at the scratch.

In spite of all this turmoil, Paul quieted down and looked at me with wide, sad eyes when I spoke with him. I told him that he was showing me that he and his parents were having a hard time together, and that I had come to help things feel better for them. These words had the effect of calming him down. He clearly understood what I was talking about.

In the sessions that followed, a curious pattern emerged. Mr. and Mrs. Donahue were so convinced their son was an aggressive, powerful, and uncontrollable "little demon" (as they called him) that they could not see the ways in which he was also a fearful little boy. They were frightened of him, and perceived his night terrors, difficulty in going to sleep, and fitful crying on separation as cunning efforts to keep them under his control. "He is just pretending," they would say. "He is afraid of nothing. He is just trying to fool us into doing what he wants." The Donahues had become so angry at their son that they had no empathy with his plight. Their own suffering blinded them to Paul's own desperate bids for help.

How had all this come about? Observations of Paul with his parents showed that Mrs. Donahue had little patience for any behavior that might be construed as dependent or needy. When Paul became alarmed by a fire truck and clung to her skirt, she laughed and told him he was being silly. When he cried as she left him in a toddler group, she said: "You have no right to cry. You are always running away from me. See if you like it when I do it to you." When he cut himself on a piece of glass he had broken, she told him: "It is your own fault for being so destructive."

Mr. Donahue, although less active than his wife in Paul's life, followed a similar pattern. He encouraged Paul to be "strong" and was critical of him when he was frightened or hurt. In addition, Mr. Donahue tended to spank Paul quite hard to keep him in line. Paul had begun to hit him back, which alternatively amused and enraged his father. When he was amused, Mr. Donahue laughed appreciatively at his son's feistiness and said "You are tough like your old man." This approval reinforced Paul's readiness to use aggression to fight back. But when his father was not in the mood for such feistiness, he became enraged and hit the child even harder to "show Paul who is the boss." At these times Paul collapsed in tears and was then sent to his room, where he screamed in protest for as long as 40 minutes at a time.

These exchanges with his parents gave Paul the message that he was on his own. He had no secure base to which he could turn when he felt fearful or needy. His father could not help Paul modulate his anger because Mr. Donahue could not control his own. His mother disliked any show of weakness and encouraged him to be independent, but she also scolded him for the often disastrous results of his efforts to "stand on his own."

Mr. and Mrs. Donahue misinterpreted Paul's high activity level as a sign of defiance that needed to be punished. They also mistook Paul's efforts at physical closeness or proximity as symptoms of dependence, and dependence was not acceptable to them. They rejected Paul's efforts to establish a secure base with them because they did not understand that this was age-appropriate behavior.

Thoughts and feelings that are unacceptable to the parents can easily become unacceptable to their child. From this perspective, we can understand Paul's recklessness and darting away as an effort to counteract his wish to come close, which he knew would be rebuffed by his parents. The more he fought off the desire to approach his parents for comfort and reassurance, the more scared Paul became of succumbing to this wish. The sleeping problems and the separation anxiety were efforts to engage his parents' help and to ensure he would not be left alone with his fears. This active child was using motion as a defense against anxiety, but the fears surfaced at night and when his parents were leaving—that is, in situations where he could not run away.

Children like Paul are asking: "How far do I need to go before mom will bring me back? How much danger is too much so that dad will protect me? How scared do I need to be for mom and dad to help me feel safe?"

Mr. and Mrs. Donahue had to struggle long and hard before they could understand the urgent reality of Paul's fears, and before they could respond to his recklessness as a cry for help. In the process of learning to know their child, they had to remember their own fears and longings as little children who were punished too harshly and expected to do too much too soon.

The repetition of a painful past in a painful present is often at work when parents are at a loss to protect their child. The Donahues were helped in infant-parent psychotherapy to reexperience their own early, unheeded wishes to feel protected and secure. This helped them understand their child's fears better, and then they could begin responding to Paul's call for help. For example, they held their son when he clung to them and said: "You are O.K. I will take care of you" instead of pushing him away. They retrieved him when he darted off in unfamiliar places and told him: "I get scared when you run away. I don't want you to get hurt." They helped him when he asked for help. As the child began to heal from his anxieties through these loving ministrations, the parents found that through experiencing empathy with their child they were also beginning to heal themselves of the wounds left by their own harsh childhoods.

Some General Reflections: Temperament and Partnership

The cases of Adam, Melinda, and Paul show how the child's temperamental style and the parents' acceptance of it can have a powerful influence on the kind of partnership they are able to develop. When parents accept the child's style and adapt to it, their partnership promotes successful development. When the parents are rejecting or critical of the child's style, conflict and alienation may result.

Adam's mother did not have the same temperamental style as her son and often longed for a less active child. However, she managed to remain emotionally available and attuned to his whereabouts by reminding herself that he was not an extension of herself but a little individual with very strong predispositions of his own—that he was, in fact, more like his father than like her.

Melinda's mother, in contrast, could not accept her daughter's active style; she was too disappointed by the child's inability to fulfill her dream of quiet mother–daughter intimacy.

Paul's parents went one step further in their inability to be receptive to their child. They became punitive in response to his difficult behavior and rejected him when he came close; these were the only responses they had learned from their own parents as they were growing up.

Adam, Melinda, and Paul showed distinctive adaptations to their parents' treatment of them. In response to his mother's acceptance, Adam explored in a manner that was self-assured and free of conflict, and was progressively able to internalize his mother's protection to modulate himself. Melinda, aware of her mother's disapproval, learned to inhibit her exuberance in order to please her, but indulged in the pleasure of bold activity with her father and brothers. Paul internalized his parents' harshness and punished them as well as himself through his aggression and proneness to accidents. We see through these three children how one developmentally dominant behavior—an exceptionally high activity level—may lead to three very different early personality configurations as a result of differences in parental response.

The other side of this process is the extent to which children educate receptive parents to become accustomed to their style. Adam's mother, after much daydreaming about how peaceful life would be with a less active child, had the chance to baby-sit for just such a toddler. She spent the day with a quiet, docile, companionable little boy. Much to her surprise, she found herself bored and restless and had to suppress the impulse to push the child to become more active.

Living with an Active Toddler

How can one try to cope productively with an exasperatingly energetic child? The first step is to remember that active toddlers are just as eager to please their parents and to form a partnership with them as are more sedate children. They are simply unable to stop themselves even when they want to because the urge to explore is so strong. The parent's strategy needs to involve an effort to instill gradual self-control around specific unacceptable behaviors.

One way of doing this is to address the situation at hand rather than the child's essence. It is not helpful to a toddler to be told that he is being a nuisance because he would not know what to do to change and because such a global statement would only make him feel bad about himself. It is better to tell the child the specific behaviors that he needs to stop, including a simple explanation so that the child can start to learn about the connection between his behavior and its effects. For example:

- "I am very angry because you ran away"; "I got so scared that you would get hurt—I love you very much and I don't want anything to happen to you."
- "I don't like it when you don't do what I tell you"; "You need to stop when I tell you to stop."
- "You need to be in your room until you are ready to be with people again."

If words are not enough, take firm action to stop the child and then tell her why you did it. Young toddlers in particular learn better from the parent's protective actions than from their words alone.

Intense children often need an intense parental response to match their inner experience. A mild "Don't do that" is not likely to persuade such a

child that the parent means it. If a parent says "I am angry" with the conviction of his emotions, the child will hear it as a genuine statement that must be taken seriously. No threats will be needed to encourage compliance, because the parent's approval is incentive enough.[3]

There are also other ways of helping very active children remain true to their nature while minimizing parental burnout and family conflicts. The suggestions below may help.

- Set up areas inside and outside the house where vigorous play is possible and permitted. This helps the child to discharge energy, and increases the likelihood of quiet moments following high-energy play.[4]
- Make the best of quiet moments. Enjoy the brief moments of cuddling to the fullest. When the child rests, try to take a rest as well.
- Active children crave novelty. Try to come up with new ideas that will keep you and your child from getting bored. While you cook, give him scraps of vegetables and ask him to make a salad, or mix some flour and water to make "bread." Hide toys that he has tired of and make them reappear some weeks later. Schedule outings and arrange times together with other parents and their children. Try to get to know your neighbors so that they can become part of a neighborhood network of social support.
- Keep an eye out for subtle cues of wariness or fear, and be receptive to calls for help. Sometimes it is easy to typecast children as "fearless" and assume that they are self-sufficient all the time. This is not true. Even the most intrepid of toddlers gets needy and scared.
- Try to share the care of your child. Children between 8 and 13 can be great baby-sitters at this age if you stay around. As a rule, they are too young to leave alone with an unruly toddler, but they can match your child's energy level and help to bring some organization and good judgment to physical feats. Responsible adolescents are generally able to care for toddlers on their own. They can provide the parent with a welcome relief from the ever-vigilant stance that active toddlers demand.
- Relax your standards for as many things as you can get away with: meals, household, entertainment, even your work standards if you can afford to. You can catch up later, when your toddler is no longer an obstacle to other pursuits.
- Pick your battles with your child carefully, and do not be afraid

to give in if the issue at stake is a relatively trivial one. As one very wise mother put it: "His capacity to passionately insist on wanting something outlasted my capacity to say no." After all, negotiating and giving in are part and parcel of building a partnership. In the middle of a struggle, learn to ask yourself: What is the point here? If your answer is that you are doing something important, hold on to your position. If, on the other hand, you are trying to be "consistent" or to save face, do yourself a favor and find a graceful way to give in.

Occasional yielding will not spoil your child, unless it becomes such a habit that you no longer have the will to enforce basic rules about safety, regard for others, or care of property. On the contrary, your flexibility can help teach your child the value of persistence and give her confidence in her ability to make her point well. It will also save you precious energy that you need for the here and now and for more important battles in the long run.

Remember that your child is your best partner in working out conflicts over keeping close and moving away. Games of hide-and-seek, mutual chasing, and "tag" enact these conflicts about secure-base behavior in the language children understand best: the language of play. The emergence of fantasy play also contributes to the gradual mastery of these conflicts. Henry Parens describes a little girl, Cindy, who at 14 months showed inexplicably increased irritability and testiness towards her mother. She started moving away from her only to stop abruptly, go closer to the mother and have a tantrum. After a week of repeating this sequence again and again, Cindy found a symbolic way of trying to master her dilemma. She sat close to the mother and engaged in a game of throwing her doll off the sofa and then lovingly retrieving it. Six weeks after playing this game again and again, Cindy was able to move away from her mother for increasingly broader perimeters.[5] She had found a way of coming to grips with an inner impasse about her use of her mother as a secure base, and she moved on to a new integration of daring and intimacy.

CHAPTER SIX

The Shy Toddler:
Taking One's Time

BUOYANT AND IRREPRESSIBLE AS TODDLERS CAN BE, THEY ARE ALSO CApable of a mood of quiet reserve. This state of mind is most likely to occur when the child encounters an unfamiliar situation. At these times, activity level subsides, the facial expression becomes sober or worried, and there is a strong tendency to stay close to or even hide behind the parent. The toddler may stare fixedly at what is happening, avert the eyes, or hide the face in the parent's body. The child's whole demeanor seems to be saying: "I need some time to process this and to feel safe with what is happening."

While all toddlers react in this way at one time or another, for some children it is a typical response that may last for 20 minutes or longer. Jerome Kagan, who has been studying this set of behaviors for more than a decade, calls it "inhibition to the unfamiliar" and believes that about 20 percent of Caucasian American children exhibit an extreme form of this response.[1] There are no estimates of its incidence in other national or ethnic groups.

The Profile of Early Shyness

Children slow to warm up have three major temperamental traits: they are inordinately shy with strangers, cautious towards novel obejcts, and timid in unfamiliar situations. However, they do not differ from other children once they are well acquainted and comfortable with their companions and with their surroundings.[1a]

In their secure base behavior, shy toddlers tend more than other children to stay near their parents rather than to explore when they are faced with an unfamiliar setting. Parents learn to prepare themselves for a warm-up period that may involve holding the child or at least letting the child hold on to them or stay very close. Once a shy toddler adjusts to the new situation, pleasure in exploring may be quite intense. However, shy toddlers are more likely than other children to keep an eye out for unexpected changes and go to the parent if any occur.

There is considerable evidence that slowness to engage with novel

situations is a stable temperamental feature with a reliable physiological profile. Kagan compared the toddlers he calls "inhibited to novelty" with a group of very outgoing age-mates and found that the timid children had higher levels of arousal of the sympathetic nervous system. For example, they tended to show large increases in heart rate and pupil dilation in response to mildly stressful stimulation, suggesting that they were more reactive to situations likely to elicit wariness or fear.[2]

Do shy children continue to be shy as adults? Kagan and his colleagues were interested in studying the long-term stability of this pattern of behavior. In one early longitudinal study, 3-year-olds who were extremely shy were more likely to become introverted adults than very outgoing peers.[3] A more recent study shows that shyness can be found even earlier in development. Extremely shy 2-year-olds continued to show this behavioral profile and its distinctive physiological pattern when they were 8 years old.[4]

The tendency to withdraw from novelty becomes a reliable feature of the child's personality only in the second year of life, but some responses during infancy may predict that the child is likely to show the pattern later on. For example, 4-month-old babies who responded to unfamiliar stimuli by crying and motor activity continued to be more distressed by novelty at 14 and 21 months than toddlers who had not cried or become physically active when they were babies. Here again, the evidence suggests a physiological basis for the behavioral response.[5]

In spite of this evidence, shyness is not completely stable as a personality trait. About half of extremely timid 2-year-olds do not appear to be shy in later childhood. It is possible that this decline in initial shyness is a result of social pressure, since mainstream American culture values friendliness. As a result, retiring youngsters might be coaxed by parents, teachers, relatives, and peers to overcome their initial reserve in new situations. This possibility is supported by findings that children who used to be shy but no longer behave that way continue to show a higher level of sympathetic arousal. Behavior seems easier to change than physiology.[6]

A Typical Slow-to-Warm Toddler: Erin

Erin fits well the profile of a toddler who in new situations takes her time, watches carefully, and ventures out only after a warm-up period. Erin's mother reports that she developed a standard strategy to mediate between her daughter and strangers eager to make her acquaintance at social gatherings. She told the stranger: "She'll be shy for one hour and then she'll be your friend."

Erin's First Year

Erin was 2 months old when her mother got a first glimpse of her daughter's sensitivity to overstimulation. This happened when mother and child attended a mothers' group of about eight women and their babies. Erin cried nonstop and could not be consoled. This was in stark contrast with her behavior at home, where she seldom cried and was easily comforted. Ever since the group meeting, Erin's parents could predict how their daughter would behave. In familiar surroundings she was placid and composed; in unfamiliar and busy places she was restless and unhappy.

Even in her earliest weeks Erin liked to observe her surroundings. The family had a sunny and colorful home with bright walls and interesting ornaments. When Erin was only 3 weeks old she could spend long periods scanning the room and looking at different objects with eyes wide open and a transfixed expression. Erin's mother, who stayed home for the first six months, wondered at these times whether she should try to entertain her daughter more actively. However, Erin herself seemed very content with these private times.

Her interest in looking included people as well. At 6 months Erin was a very sociable baby, who showed only fleeting wariness on meeting strangers. During outings she fixated her big eyes on those around her and people would fall in love with her as she smiled and cooed in delight while looking straight into their eyes.

Erin's first year was peaceful and uneventful. There were only two areas of sustained difficulty, both of which involved transitions. One was the transition between being awake and falling asleep. Erin cried very hard and seemed to fight off sleep even when she was very tired. The other area of intense distress was being undressed, given a bath, and dressed again. She seemed to hate having her skin exposed to too much stimulation.

Erin's parents found good ways of helping her during these difficult periods. The transition to sleep was made easier by movement and sound. The parents put her in a stroller and pushed her all over the house. When this did not work, they rocked her while making wide sweeping movements with their arms. Erin loved sound (her parents were musicians and music often flowed through the house), and the monotonous sound of the vacuum cleaner had a soothing effect when nothing else seemed to work.

Erin said her first word at 9 months, and language became a major tool for relationships soon afterwards. She also began to crawl at 9 months. In fact, she said her first word and began to crawl on the same weekend. Her first steps did not occur until she was 13 months, and this event formally ushered the beginning of toddlerhood.

Erin from 13 to 36 Months

13 months. Erin takes her first steps. She seems tentative but delighted with herself. She practices valiantly, falling down and getting up again and again. Her mood as she does this is sober and intent rather than giddy. She seems to be working hard at mastering and controlling this new and unpredictable skill.

Rather suddenly, Erin becomes quite shy. This is when her mother begins to caution people that she will take quite some time to open up to them. Erin's mother remembers her pain when the child changed from outgoing sociability to reserve. She remembers thinking "People won't even have a chance to find out how wonderful she is."

14 months. Erin becomes clingy and grumpy. Whereas earlier she liked to spend time alone and was in a good mood most of the time, she has now become irritable and difficult to please. She cries when her mother leaves the room, and insists on following her everywhere. Her mother finds this change very frustrating, and wonders why her child seems so insecure.

Erin has a very good relationship with her baby-sitter, a warm and responsive young woman who has cared for her since her mother went back to work when Erin was 6 months old. This relationship helps her during her separations, but Erin remains demanding and easily frustrated when her mother is around. There are times when her mother remembers thinking: "She has become a pest."

15 months. Erin and her parents go to the birthday party of a little friend, a strictly timed two-hour affair. For the first half hour, Erin stays very close to her mother, intermittently hiding her face on her mother's skirt. The second half hour is spent playing with some toys at the mother's feet. Erin then agrees to go with her father to watch the other six children as they run around in the adjacent family room. The birthday boy hands her a party favor, and this seems to finally break the ice. Erin follows her little friend as he goes on to climb on an indoor slide, and she laughs happily as she slides down. She gets very unhappy when it is time to go home.

Erin remains difficult to please at home. She continues to have happy interactions with her mother and father, but she gets easily frustrated. Contrary to her general good mood during her first year, she now cries easily and needs frequent reassurance. This behavior comes and goes, with two or three weeks of good cheer interspersed with periods of intense clinginess. This pattern lasts until her second birthday.

16 months. Father and Erin go to a small grocery store where the friendly owner exuberantly praises her beautiful eyes and hair, coming close to her and lightly touching her cheek. Erin bursts into tears. Her father explains to the grocer: "She is becoming self-conscious." Erin is using short sentences well and is beginning to talk about feelings. Once, half asleep, she puts her arms around her mother's neck and murmurs: "I like my mommy."

17 months. Erin and her father go to a new playground, and Erin refuses to try the new structures for the first half hour or so. Her father walks around the whole perimeter of the playground with her, talking lightly about the scene. He points out a dog peeing against the slide, and they both laugh merrily. They sift sand between their fingers and look for little bugs in the surrounding grass. Then they sit and watch quietly as the other children go up and down the structures. Erin suddenly says: "Me too." She then plays actively and happily for a long time.

18 months. Erin's mother takes her to a toddler's gym where about ten toddlers play on different structures and have a brief "circle time" with songs and a little dance. Erin watches the children intently with a "tight little face," in her mother's words. She does not try anything new. Her mother berates herself for raising such a timid child. "What have I done," she thinks to herself, worrying that she has been hopelessly over-protective and that she is completely to blame for making her child insecure in new situations. When all the other children are putting their socks on to go home, Erin has a sudden upsurge of activity. She runs wildly from structure to structure, trying on everything. She does not want to leave.

(The issue of mothers berating themselves for developmentally or temperamentally normal behavior cannot be underestimated. Mothers are prone to torture themselves with self-blame when their children are having a hard time. Knowing this might help a little when one catches oneself doing it.)

Erin's parents take her to the gym every week because they believe (with good reason) that it makes sense to expose her to a setting where she needs to make some efforts to overcome her discomfort with novelty. For a whole year, Erin goes through a similar sequence: a long warm-up period followed by a surge of activity when no one is looking, and then reluctance to leave.

20 months. Erin develops a fear of masks and of the full moon. She cries, averts her eyes, and refuses to look at them. She tries to run away from the moon and insists that the masks should be hidden somewhere. She cannot articulate what frightens her about these objects, but toddlers do develop seemingly inexplicable fears on the basis of their fantasies about how the world operates. The difference between reality and make-believe is very tenuous at this age, and it is possible that Erin thinks in some half-conscious way that these objects are real but disembodied angry faces that can do her harm. This fear persists for about four months.

There are other examples of Erin's difficulty in distinguishing fantasy from reality. She bursts into tears and cries "no, no, no, I don't want to go to sleep" when her mother plays a game with her dolls in which the mommy doll tells the baby to go to bed. Another time Erin tries to "scoop" the babies and animals off the pages of her books. These and similar behaviors are very common at this age.

22 months. Erin goes to a party attended by about ten adults and six other children. She behaves very similarly to the way she does in the gym. She stays very close to her parents, watching the other children with wide eyes. She starts playing with them after about one hour of careful scrutiny. When it is time to leave, she complains: "But I did not get to play very much."

Erin's parents develop a strategy to help her leave a social gathering. They tell her in advance that they will leave in ten minutes and then keep apprising her of the time: "We'll leave in five minutes; we'll leave in one more minute; now it's time to go." Although Erin still protests departures, the advance notice gives her time to prepare herself for this unwelcome event.

Erin plays happily with individual children that she knows well when the gathering occurs in her own home or in the home of close family friends. She has early and intense friendships, and plays with her friends for long periods of time. She also loves playing quietly with her mother. With her father, she dares to do things she does not try with anybody else: he swings her so high in the swing that her mother can hardly watch, but Erin loves it and asks for more. These examples suggest that Erin needs a secure interpersonal base before she can risk exploring new horizons. Close, one-to-one relationships are her most comfortable and enjoyable forms of social exchange.

24 months. Erin seems to undergo a transformation. She seems more relaxed, confident and independent. She is less demanding at home and easier to please. Her fear of masks and of the full moon disappears. She begins to ask "why." Her curiosity about how the world works seems insatiable. She wants to know why it rains, why the cat licks herself, why pancakes get burned, why mommy needs to go to work, why so-and-so got angry. She listens with rapt attention to her parents' explanations.

Erin seems freer to be exuberant than in earlier months. A friend's mother comments that "Erin really let go of herself" as she brings her back home from an outing with her little friend. Still, there is a quality of self-restraint to Erin's moods. She can laugh merrily but does not get hyperexcited; she does not have intense tantrums; she does not say "no" very often. The extremes of emotion seem alien to her.

On the other hand, Erin loves to entice her little friends to do exciting things: "jump higher"; "run faster." It seems as though she gets vicarious pleasure from the excitement of others, and wants to expand her own experience by watching how others feel.

26 months. Erin's pleasure in strong one-to-one relationships becomes more apparent. When she meets her friend Stephanie after not seeing her for a week, the two children run towards each other with open arms and hug each other tightly.

Erin internalizes her parents' formula of counting time to help her with transitions. Waiting for her friend Ansel to stop going down the slide so he can play dolls with her, she says: "Two more times, Ansel. Now one more time. Now you come play babies with me."

28 months. Erin begins to spontaneously initiate social contact with other children in unfamiliar situations. At a restaurant, her booster seat is back-to-back with another booster seat at the next table. She leans back, smiles at her little neighbor, and says in a very friendly voice: "Hello."

Being thrust into a large situation is another story. Erin still takes her time before she joins in. These warm-up periods are a stable part of her response to new situations. She does not require coaxing or being won over. As her mother puts it, "She comes around on her own if you don't bug her."

30 months. Erin finds a creative way of saying good-bye to her mother, something she does not like to do. She invents a separation ritual: she runs all over the house to find a special small object (a leaf, a shell, a marble, a small toy) that she ceremoniously deposits in her mother's hand. This object may represent a precious part of Erin's own self, which she wants to put in her mother's safekeeping while they are apart.

32 months. Erin becomes more assertive in her efforts to be alone with someone special. If her father comes home while she is playing with her mom, she greets him briefly, and if he lingers around them she says: "Mom and I are playing." After her father returns from a trip, she hugs him tightly, then says to her mother: "Would you go away, mommy?"

33 months. Erin begins preschool for 4 hours, 5 mornings a week. She spends the entire first morning with her mother. Nevertheless, the experience is difficult for her. After coming back home she has one of the few tantrums of her life, and emerges from it sweaty, short of breath, and exhausted.

Erin establishes a very close relationship with a friend at school, Jonathan. They announce plans to get married and they spend many hours playing dress up and other forms of pretend play. When Erin arrives at school before Jonathan, she sometimes plays by herself while waiting for Jonathan. The friendship with Jonathan continues to be a central feature of Erin's life 12 months later, a testimony to children's ability to form very close, enduring relationships even at this early age.

Erin seems incapable of defending her toys and watches passively when another child takes them away. Her mother blames herself for this trait, thinking that she has encouraged Erin to be "too nice." She begins to encourage her child to be more assertive, and Erin learns to say a forceful and effective "no!" by the time she is 36 months. This is a good example of how shy children can learn more self-assertive behaviors when they perceive that it is socially approved.

The sleeping problems that Erin evidenced as a baby still persist, but in a different form. Erin has no difficulty going to sleep, but she experiences night terrors two to three hours after falling asleep. At these times, she seems to go through the temper tantrums that she does not indulge in during the day.

After a fight with a friend during which she was very self-controlled, Erin relives the scene at night. She sits up on her bed while still asleep, yelling: "I don't want that. Give it back to me. Don't do that." She gesticulates with great intensity as she talks. Her mother gently tells her that things are fine and talks her back into a calm sleep. Erin is clearly dreaming, and the intensity of the dream spills over into motor discharge. Even at this early age, the dream is fulfilling one of the functions it has through the life span: to enable the dreamer to grapple with unresolved tasks left over from waking life.

36 months. Erin becomes freer in expressing difficult emotions. She now initiates talking about her mother's departures. She asks her mother: "When are you coming home?" If she dislikes the answer, she replies: "That is too long." After her mother returns, Erin tells her: "I didn't want you to go."

Erin seems very aware of feelings and relishes talking about them with her mother. They develop a game: "Tell me a time when you were happy; a time when you were sad; a time when you were afraid; a time when you were mad." Erin has no problem remembering times when she was happy, sad, or afraid. When it comes to anger, however, she says thoughtfully: "I can't remember a time when I was mad." Anger is not a familiar part of her sense of herself. It tends to go underground and emerges when she is not fully conscious, particularly during sleep. Not all shy toddlers are uncomfortable with anger. However, many shy toddlers try to avoid intense excitement of any kind because it does not fit well with their innate reserve. The feeling is there, but the child is too self-conscious to express it freely.

Erin's parents (themselves quite comfortable with a full range of emotions—including anger—but not overwhelmed by them) make concerted efforts to encourage their child to become more aware of her anger as a first step towards helping her to feel safe with it. They begin to oppose her more actively when this is appropriate, and they become less worried about making her angry. They assert their own preferences rather than yielding to her as they did before out of a wish to keep her happy. This is a very good move. It enables Erin to get more practice with the experience of being angry, with the result that anger becomes less frightening for her.

Erin becomes very interested in pregnancy and in babies. After her baby-sitter gets pregnant, she announces: "I am having a baby in my tummy." She then asks: "When will my baby be born?" When her mother tells her that her baby is not in her tummy yet and that it will be born when she grows up, Erin asks with much distress: "But where is it now?"

Erin becomes interested in collecting things that she finds during her walks. She treasures pebbles, leaves, shells, pieces of colored paper, and she gives them away as a special gesture to people she particularly likes. She continues asking why, but now goes to great lengths to come up with her own explanations. When she can't explain something, she says thoughtfully: "It must be magic."

A Well-Developing Shy Toddler

How can we understand Erin's initial holding back in new situations, given her zest in exploring and her pleasure in people once she is comfortable with them? What function does her slowness to warm up serve for her?

We can speculate that this behavior has a physiological origin for Erin, as it did for the children studied by Kagan and his colleagues. Nevertheless, temperamental traits acquire a psychological meaning both for the individual and for her companions. What psychological meaning did Erin's reserve have for her?

We cannot know for sure, but there might be a parallel between Erin's difficulty with the transition from being awake to falling asleep and her difficulty with the transition of going from familiar to unfamiliar situations.

Both types of transition involve moving from a comfortable and safe state of being to a different, more demanding state. Falling asleep calls for letting go of one's human connections and venturing alone into a mysterious realm. Going to the gym, to a party, or to preschool involves leaving one's familiar activities in order to engage with other people and other tasks.

From the time she was a baby, it was clear that Erin liked individual people and objects very much and was capable of intense involvements on a one-to-one basis. Individual relationships were her preferred way of relating to the world. Perhaps, in this context, Erin's slowness to warm up was a way of coping when the social situation was so large and complex that she could not be alone with someone special. Holding back and surveying the scene bought her time until she could identify a particular person or object with whom she could be most comfortable (such as Jonathan in the preschool setting).

Conversely, it is possible that Erin preferred very focused one-to-one involvements because these individual relationships offered a way of coping with the bombardment of stimulation from large situations. In any event, it is quite apparent from her developmental course that Erin's reserve has not impeded her cognitive, social, or emotional progress in any way. On the contrary, it is quite possible that her initial holding back served for her as a helpful mechanism to fend off overstimulation.

Erin illustrates the typical behavior of a well-developing shy toddler. Her preference for close individual friendships rather than group situations, familiarity rather than novelty, and mild rather than intense stimulation is characteristic of healthy, well-adjusted shy children of this age.

There are, of course, individual differences even in those common elements. Some shy children find some new situations so compelling that they forget their reserve and rush forward. One 18-month-old became so thrilled by his first visit to the zoo that he moved from cage to cage as in a daze, calling out to the animals and trying to climb over the fences separating him from them.

Other shy children like specific kinds of intense stimulation. Cindy loved being thrown up in the air by her uncle, but not by anybody else. Albert devoured every spicy food, including chili peppers, and seemed to have a sixth sense for detecting it and going for it. Estela adored reggae music and danced like a swirling dervish when it was played, crying "more, more!" when it came to a stop. Maria took quickly to any new situation if there were crayons available that she could draw with.

These examples show that shy children should not be stereotyped. They are not only shy: they are also curious, energetic, loving, and growing and changing. Their pleasure in exploring can help them surmount their reserve in a new setting. For parents, the important thing is to become familiar with their child's specific range of responses and to continue introducing novelty in gradual, nonstressful ways in order to cultivate the child's flexibility of response. The final section of this chapter offers suggestions on how to go about doing that.

A Fearful Toddler: Tobias

Sometimes a toddler's natural shyness can become transformed into a pervasive fear of new situations and unfamiliar people. When this occurs, the child refuses to go to new places or cries when meeting new people. Sometimes the child develops multiple apparently senseless fears that can become quite crippling of his ability to explore and learn about the world.

Tobias was a little boy in this situation. His parents asked for a consultation when he was 32 months old because they felt that life in their household was becoming increasingly tense and unhappy due to their child's excessive fears. In the course of a few home visits and playroom sessions, the following picture emerged.

Tobias was a lightly built, pale child with a thoughtful expression. He moved carefully, spoke softly, and liked to spend long periods of time playing by himself. He used wooden blocks to build elaborate structures that he adorned with whatever he had at hand—books, nesting cups, feathers, cans of food from the kitchen—so that when he was finished, his buildings looked like elaborate masterpieces from many architectural periods. He also liked to look at books, talking to himself as he pointed to the pictures. He was unusually adept at puzzles, and family friends knew that the puzzles they gave him as gifts had to be at least two years above his age level. His manual dexterity was extraordinary, and he loved toys that he could take apart and put together again. His favorite toy was a red plastic car that he could assemble and disassemble with a plastic wrench and a plastic screwdriver. His father predicted he would be fixing real cars by the time he was 12.

Tobias developed uneventfully until he was 26 months. He was slow to warm to unfamiliar situations, he did not seem particularly interested in people, and he was very cautious in trying new physical feats. On the other hand, he was affectionate with his parents, had a couple of good friends he played happily with, and seemed to be always busy and content tinkering with something or other around the house. His mother commented: "He has a personality all of his own."

The biggest challenge in Tobias' life was his brother Andrew, 15 months younger than him. Andrew was hell on wheels. Where Tobias was light and slender, Andrew was strong and sturdy. Where Tobias was slow and gentle, Andrew filled the room with loud chatter and fast-paced movement. Where Tobias liked to spend time alone, Andrew craved company. A red-headed, freckled-faced boy with an impish grin and twinkly eyes, Andrew attracted delighted attention and praise wherever he went, while Tobias stayed behind watching quietly from the sidelines.

Andrew would not leave Tobias alone. This is understandable from an adult's perspective, but for Tobias his brother's intrusions were an endless irritation. Andrew was particularly entranced by the constructions Tobias put his heart and soul in, and he wasted no time in bringing them down. Tobias said "no" and tried to defend his masterpieces, but his mild manner and soft voice were no match for Andrew's self-assured rambunctiousness. To make matters worse, Andrew could get away with it. Their mother thought of Tobias as a mature little boy who could control himself, and she told him not to get angry at Andrew and to simply rebuild his structure once again. Tobias obeyed dutifully with a resigned, hopeless expression on his face. At these times, he looked much too old for his age.

By the time he was 30 months, Tobias started displaying multiple fears.

ROBERT MAUST

He refused to go to his play group, which he had attended for six months and had always enjoyed, and he cried for a long time after his mother left. He developed an intense fear of going to sleep and was convinced that there was a monster lurking in his closet. He became literally afraid of shadows and clung to his mother whenever he saw his own shadow or that of another person or object. He refused to try new foods. Each of these fears, by itself, is a frequent enough occurrence in the toddler years. It was their number and intensity that signalled something more serious in this little boy's life.

Every day seemed to bring in a new fear. If he was at the corner grocery store, he became afraid of the noisy, old-fashioned cash register. In the park, he was terrified that the dog trotting along next to its owner would bite him. One day he panicked when he saw a man with a totally bald head. Another day he clung to his father when he saw a man dressed as a clown in a toy store. His parents said: "You name it, he is scared of it."

Life became unpredictable as a result of Tobias's fears. The parents never knew whether an outing would proceed smoothly, whether it would become an endless exercise in reassurance, or whether it would have to be cut short because Tobias insisted on going home.

Andrew sailed through the family turmoil. He seemed oblivious to his brother's distress and went on gleefully kicking down towers and snatching toys. Andrew had a free reign because of his parents' attitude that he was "too little to know any better." This parental attitude had very negative consequences for both children: It encouraged Tobias to become a victim and it allowed Andrew to behave more and more like a bully.

Tobias's predicament can be understood as a heroic effort to suppress his anger at his brother in order to live up to his mother's expectations that he be "a good little boy."

This effort asked for a degree of self-control that was beyond even his considerable ability in this area. The only way that Tobias could be the precociously selfless child his mother wanted him to be was to cut off any conscious awareness of his aggressive impulses. In doing this, he had to suppress the normal ebullience and impetus for self-assertion of this age, because he was afraid that in the process of being assertive he would lose control of his impulses and end up clobbering his brother and losing his mother's love.

Children cannot maintain a total suppression of angry feelings without paying a price. The feelings want out and will find a way of expressing themselves. Tobias could not think of himself as angry without immediately becoming terrified of his own badness. He dealt with the situation by projecting his anger on unfamiliar people and objects. In his eyes, he managed to be good, but anybody he did not know and love was bad and out to get him. He developed a litany when he was out with his parents: "Is that man bad? Is that dog bad? Is that truck bad?" He was really asking: "Am I bad?"

At first, Tobias's parents did not like my explanation that their older son was angry at his brother but could not express his anger for fear of displeasing them. Anger was an emotion that made them feel uncomfortable. Indeed, these young parents were unusually formal and correct with each other and with their children, as if good manners counted above all else even in family relations. To think of Tobias as struggling to contain angry feelings came too close to their own experience of trying hard to be "good" at the expense of their emotional spontaneity.

With much support, these well-meaning, thoughtful parents began to accept the idea that no 2-year-old could be as self-controlled as they hoped Tobias would be. Watching from behind a one-way mirror, they saw Tobias's initial tentativeness and eventual glee as he threw blocks around the playroom and as he made two dolls hit each other until they fell to the floor in exhaustion. The parents were moved by Tobias's blissful expression of agreement when I told him that "sometimes it feels so good to be angry."

In joint sessions with Tobias and Andrew, the parents had an opportunity to practice new ways of responding to their children. They started to respect Tobias's right to play by himself and to stop Andrew from messing with him. It was a sight to behold the surprised expressions of Andrew and Tobias when their parents restrained Andrew and took the side of Tobias. The parents themselves were surprised and greatly encouraged that they had the power to tell Andrew what to do. Andrew, in fact, obeyed them when they meant what they said. This relieved the parents because they had been feeling as helpless as Tobias in the face of Andrew's seemingly unstoppable power. It probably came as a big relief for Andrew, too, that he no longer was the most powerful figure in the household at the tender age of 20 months.

A few months after the end of a four-month intervention the mother called to report on how things were going. Tobias was 39 months at the time; Andrew had just turned 2 years. Mrs. Novak had taken Tobias to the playground the previous day and they had spent a delightful two hours together, in keeping with the parents' effort to build in more time alone with each of the children. After swinging on the swing for a long time, Tobias said: "Mommy, once there was a little boy who was scared of everything. That little boy died, but another little boy was born who is not afraid." Tobias was talking about himself.

Shyness, Suppressed Anger, and Fear

Tobias illustrates a very common occurrence with mild-mannered, shy toddlers who want to be good but worry that their natural feelings of anger and frustration mean that they are bad. They become afraid of their anger, but in their effort to suppress it they become preoccupied with badness and with danger and end up being afraid of the world at large.

This does not mean that toddlers' fears are always an indication that they are suppressing anger. Some fears are the result of age-appropriate fantasies and misunderstandings about how the world works. Others fears originate from being exposed to frightening experiences. Still other fears do stem from suppressed anger, and these fears are often the most difficult ones for parents to understand.

Tobias happened to focus his anger on his brother, although he was also indirectly angry at his parents for not defending him and for allowing Andrew to run wild. Other children become directly angry at their parents and worry about those feelings because they fear losing the parent's love.

Lenny adores being alone with his mother and resents his father when he comes home. At 22 months, he hits his father when his mother and father kiss. At 30 months, he becomes more articulate. He says to his mother: "Love me, not daddy." By 36 months, he is even more explicit: "I'll marry you when I'm big, but daddy can live with us." Lenny loves his father but is also afraid of him. He startles when his father comes into the room, and when he does something wrong, he pleads with his mother: "Don't tell daddy." The father is a gentle, loving man and there are no objective reasons for Lenny's fear. It is likely that Lenny is afraid that his father will be angry at him for wanting to be the only one in his mother's love.

Sonya, 26 months, became very frightened of animals after a one-week separation from her parents during which she stayed with her beloved grandparents. When the parents returned, Sonya turned away from them and buried her face in her grandmother's lap. After about ten minutes, she allowed her parents to hold her and kiss her but seemed constricted and reserved. Over the next few days, she was unusually well behaved and compliant with her parents' requests, but the fear of animals emerged, and at about the same time she refused going to sleep

at night. Sonya's anger at her parents for leaving had to be suppressed for fear that they would leave her again. She became an excessively good little girl, but the cost of this effort was expressed in her fear that she would be attacked by animals when she went to bed and was away from her parents. The fears dissipated when the parents helped Sonya to express her anger at them through words and play and reassured her that they would always come back no matter how angry she got at them.

These examples show that the fear of their own anger is a common response in young children, particularly when this anger is felt towards the most important love figures in their lives. Shy children may not express their anger easily, but they can feel it just as keenly as other children, and they may suffer silently from their difficulty in showing it. Because of this it is particularly important for parents of shy children to be aware that their children may be showing anger under the guise of excessive fears.

When Shyness Turns to Aggression: Nadia

Timidity is not ordinarily associated with aggression in people's minds. One thinks of shy children as slow to anger as well as slow to warm up. However, shyness can take an aggressive turn under some circumstances, such as enduring physical or emotional abuse, witnessing violent exchanges between parents, or being overwhelmed by stimulation, including parental demands that the child cannot meet.

Shy children can also become aggressive when they have not learned to tolerate moderate levels of frustration because they have been overprotected. When parents take their child's vulnerabilities too seriously, they allow themselves to be cowed by them. This can create an expectation in the child that she is entitled to instant gratification because she is too fragile to withstand anything else. When frustration finally occurs (as it inevitably must), aggression becomes the only coping mechanism available to the child to fend off the feared damage to herself.

When shy children become aggressive, they may do so for the same reasons that other children do. For example, they may be trying to control and master a frightening situation by taking action that makes them feel less helpless. They might also imitate aggressive adults they are exposed to. What is most characteristic of shy aggressive children is the use of aggression to ward off overstimulation. Because children slow to warm up are often highly sensitive to stimuli, they may feel forced to strike out to protect themselves when withdrawal does not work.

At 2½, Nadia often scratched and bit her friends. She flew into a rage in response to seemingly minimal frustration. At these times she hit, bit, or scratched the offender and then looked greatly relieved. Unfortunately the relief lasted only briefly because other adults rushed in to admonish Nadia and protect the victim. When scolded, Nadia cried in anger and shame for a long time.

Nadia did not attack the adults she knew, but she did spit at adult strangers when they tried to make friends with her faster than she could tolerate. She was also quite aggressive with baby-sitters, and her parents found that potential baby-sitters were always "busy" when asked to spend an evening with Nadia. This pattern of behaviors developed gradually and it was the culmination of a slow process that began when Nadia was a baby. The process took different forms at different times.

During her first months, Nadia was a very alert infant who formed an unusually early and close relationship with her parents. They reported that she refused to be held by anybody other than them from the time she was 6 weeks old. Nadia cried intensely in new situations, turned beet red, and often ended up vomiting from gastric distress. Her parents seldom went out during the first 6 months of Nadia's life because they felt unable either to take her along or leave her with somebody else.

As the first year progressed, Nadia began to cry less but she still took a long time to adapt to unfamiliar situations. She clung to her mother with an anxious expression, scrutinized strangers with an intense and unwavering gaze, and burst into tears if someone she did not know tried to make friends with her too quickly. Her mother commented: "All the books say that stranger anxiety develops at 8 months, but Nadia was born with it."

Nadia's parents were very attuned to their child's moods and did their best to keep her happy. They believed that Nadia was a psychologically fragile child and tried hard not to hurt her in any way. Conversation around Nadia was mostly child-centered. If the parents were immersed in a conversation and Nadia made some social signal, they immediately interrupted what they were doing to attend to her. Reflecting back on the first year, the father reflected: "We thought she needed always to come first in order to feel secure."

While Nadia did feel secure in many ways, she had few opportunities to learn to experience ordinary frustration as an unpleasant experience that was well within her capacity to endure. As a result, she often panicked and turned to her mother to make everything right when she encountered something she did not like. In a paradoxical way, her mother's sensitivity and responsiveness tended to reinforce Nadia's feeling that she was unable to cope with unpleasant feelings on her own.

This situation came to a head when Nadia entered her second year and began to be interested in peer play. Two-year-old peers are fun as playmates but cannot be counted on as sensitive caregivers. They do not set aside their own plans out of deference to a friend's needs and wishes. Playing with friends became Nadia's first consistent encounter with people who refused to do what she wanted. She did not like it, but she could not withdraw (which she preferred to do in unfamiliar situations) because she was too emotionally invested in what was going on. The only response to frustration available to her was to hit back because she had not learned to tolerate discomfort or to negotiate a way out of it.

A similar mechanism was at work with overly forward strangers and unwary baby-sitters. Neither situation allowed Nadia a gracious retreat from frustration. The stranger who persisted in his attentions had to be faced; the unwanted baby-sitter had to be endured. Angry at these impositions and unable to escape, Nadia resorted to physical attack as a form of psychological self-defense.

Nadia learned to modulate her anger when her parents realized that they had been overly protective of her as a result of their intense empathy with her distress in unfamiliar situations. They started training themselves not to become emotionally undone by Nadia's protests, and they began to encourage her to solve small problems on her own instead of rushing to help her at the first sign of frustration. They made themselves wait a little longer before responding to a request or a demand, and they helped Nadia to wait by saying: "Just a minute, Nadia. I need to finish this first." This approach helped Nadia to understand that other people's plans and wishes, not only her own, needed to be taken into account.

Nadia's aggression declined as she learned to wait, to tolerate frustration, and to pay attention to the needs of others. She also learned to recognize when she was about to lose control of herself and strike out. At these times her favorite phrase became "You are bothering me." People recognized this statement as an early warning signal, and for the most part respected it. Everybody was happier as a result.

Helping Shy Children to Enjoy
Who They Are

As a temperamental trait, slowness to warm up is characterized by high sensitivity to stimulation, gradual adaptation to change, and a tendency to withdraw under stress. Within this general framework, a variety of individual differences is possible, as the personalities of Erin, Tobias, and Nadia illustrate. Depending on the pressures and supports they encounter and on their own talents and vulnerabilities, different shy children will resort to different coping mechanisms to adjust to the inevitable challenges of meeting new people and facing novel situations.

Erin's ability to form very close, deep relationships with her parents, baby-sitter, teacher, and a small number of peers shows that shyness need not entail emotional distance from others. Shy children may be more selective but are not less loving than their outgoing peers. Similarly, Erin's glee in trying daring new feats with her father shows that timidity does not preclude boldness if the child feels secure. Erin's ability to take physical risks in her father's protective but encouraging presence highlight the particular importance for shy children of relying on an adult as a secure base from which to explore.

Shy children's sensitivity to stimulation means that their parents and caregivers need to strike a careful balance between two extremes of caregiving in serving as a secure base. They have to find a way of protecting the child from overwhelming stimulation without becoming overprotective as a result.

It is only too easy to overlook a child's special need to be buffered from overstimulation. This is particularly the case if, like Tobias, the child is trying hard to be "good" and does not protest in the face of stress. In these circumstances the child may suffer quietly and become increasingly fearful and withdrawn in the effort to put up with a situation that is overtaxing his coping skills. When a child shows excessive withdrawal or too many fears, the parents will do well to look for specific sources of stress in the child's life that they have not been aware of.

On the other hand, it is also easy to become overly protective in trying to minimize a child's distress. When parents become anxious, they cannot encourage their child to tackle a taxing situation that is age-appropriate and within the child's ability. This can be a setback because slow-to-warm children become discouraged with themselves when they watch their peers enjoying a situation that is daunting to them, such as playing in a swimming

pool or getting on a swing. If they become routinely hopeless under stress, shy children can lose their resilience and become overly reliant on adults as a source of comfort. They can also become demanding and angry when their distress is not immediately relieved by a sympathetic adult. Adults can help by reminding children that they usually enjoy themselves after they get used to the new situation.

Perhaps the most useful formula in helping a slow-to-warm toddler tackle new situations is "step-by-step and one step at a time." This approach involves gradual but steady encouragement to explore. The following sequence of steps can enable a shy toddler to surmount the initial hesitation to enter a novel setting.

- Do not send the child over to the new situation. Go with him and draw him in. Take time together to simply observe what is going on. Make little comments about what is happening, focusing preferably on aspects that are already familiar and safe. For example, if a group of new children is playing with some toys, you might want to point to a toy your child already knows and likes: "Look at their beach ball. It is just like yours but orange. Remember how we played with it yesterday? We had to run all over the place just like they are doing, because it bounced so much!"

• Stay near until the child's mood has changed reliably from caution to enjoyment. Then step back.

• Remain "on call" for a while but do not hover in anticipation
that the child will need you.

• If the child calls you, modulate your response to match the
intensity of his need as you see it. If he seems truly anxious, do
not hesitate to approach. More often, a wave from a distance or
some reassuring words may be sufficient to let him know you are
available if needed. Try a minimalist approach: start out with the
least active response, and see if it works.

• Children are often the best helpers in enticing a shy child into
a novel situation. You might facilitate this by starting a conversation
with a child who seems like a compatible partner for yours. The
rest may follow on its own.

Ronald Lally and his colleagues suggest that the sequence outlined
above may be summarized in the following series of moves by the parent
or caregiver: "being with, talking to, stepping back, remaining available,
moving on."[7] The rhythm of these steps needs to be coordinated with the
child's own rhythm, but the adult's confidence will enable the child to
"move on" when the time is right.

CHAPTER SEVEN

Early Anxieties

HUMAN BEINGS HAVE A DEEPLY INGRAINED CAPACITY TO ANTICIPATE DANGER. We respond with anxiety when we believe that something dangerous is about to occur. Anxiety is not only a reaction to objective threats but may be experienced also when unfamiliar or unexpected events take place. Because of this, anxiety has a strong subjective component. The perception of danger is enough to provoke anxiety, whether the danger is real or not.

While unpleasant to experience, anxiety has an important role in survival because it serves as a signal of impending danger that gives us time to protect ourselves. The events that trigger anxiety are not dangerous in themselves. They get their emotional force from the fact that they often precede danger or are associated with it.[1] For example, waking up to find ourselves alone in our darkened house is not dangerous in itself but can make us anxious if we imagine unseen dangers lurking in the dark. If we turned on the light and saw actual danger, we would move quickly from feeling anxiety to downright fear. Our anxiety is relieved when we find that nothing unusual is happening.

Anxiety is increased by helplessness and lack of knowledge, which makes babies and toddlers particularly prone to it. Very young children face an unfamiliar world that operates in unknown ways. They are small and vulnerable and rely on others to feel safe. Young children also do things that can have unpredictable and even frightening consequences, including making their parents angry at them. For all these reasons, the opportunities to experience anxiety are ever-present in infancy and the toddler years.

This chapter describes the origins of anxiety in the first year of life and how the early anxieties change in the course of toddlerhood. The great adventures of the second and third years described in chapter 2—discovering the world and discovering the body—have a dark side. With new knowledge comes the fear of harm by being abandoned, unloved, or physically damaged. This chapter describes how toddlers experience normal and excessive anxiety and the range of coping mechanisms available to them. The next chapter provides specific guidelines to help parents help their toddlers with the more common anxiety-arousing situations of this age.

The Early Origins of Anxiety

Anxiety in toddlerhood should be understood in the context of early development because the child's basic feelings of security or fearfulness are established in the first year of life. This section describes the origins and manifestations of anxiety in infancy as a backdrop for understanding the toddler's anxieties.

It is likely that emotions are felt by the fetus even before birth. Early investigators reported facial expressions of disgust, sadness, happiness, and fear,[2] and these pioneering observations were confirmed with the invention of the ultrasonogram, which allows for close monitoring of the facial expressions of the fetus on video screens.[3]

Embryos also seem capable of acting on their sensations. For example, they withdraw from noxious stimulation such as a light touch as early as 7.5 weeks gestational age, using a global response that begins with the bending back of the head and then spreads progressively to the hands, trunk, and shoulder.[2] This withdrawal response suggests that the fetus may be capable of feeling a rudimentary form of anxiety because the same form of physical avoidance is a common expression of anxiety after birth.[4,5] During gestation, the capacity to withdraw from unpleasant stimulation occurs at an earlier age than the capacity to approach using, for example, the prenatal rooting reflex.[6] This may indicate that the motivation for self-protection develops earlier and may be more basic to survival than the motivation to explore.

The fetus, of course, does not need to seek proximity to a source of nurturance and protection. It is already embedded in a secure base—the mother's womb. The healthy newborn's response to departing from this safe haven is a lusty cry that represents both protest and a call for human contact and assistance. This cry may signal the first experience of anxiety after birth.

Once born, the baby cannot take care of herself. She needs the care of a loving adult, who in most cultures and circumstances is primarily the mother during the first years of life.

This is no accident. In the course of pregnancy, mother and fetus gradually form an intimate connection with each other.[6] By the time babies are born, they are well equipped to recognize and form a primary relationship with their mothers. For example, newborns recognize and prefer the mother's voice. This was demonstrated in an ingenious experiment in which babies learned to suck for longer or shorter periods of time, as needed, when the reward for sucking was hearing their mother rather than a stranger read from a Dr. Seuss book.[7] Newborns also discriminate and prefer the mother's face within hours after birth.[3] Similarly, they recognize and prefer their mother's smell: They consistently turn their heads towards their mother's nursing pad rather than the pad of a different mother.[8]

Newborns start to make use of these social skills right away, because being born involves a major developmental challenge. They need to regulate their cycles of hunger and sleep in a way that complements their mother's expectations and fits more or less smoothly with the family values and daily routine.[9,10] Recognizing and preferring the mother's face, voice, and smell help the baby to engage with the mother as a partner in the joint venture of regulating the rhythms of the body.

This process is accomplished in fits and starts, through trial and error. The baby's earliest anxieties are based on distressing bodily sensations: hunger, the urge to suck, gastric upset, elimination strains, fatigue, and the need for physical contact in the form of touch, holding, and cuddling.

Most of the mother's care during the first two or three months of life is geared to helping the baby find relief from these sources of distress. As shown in the chapter on temperament, babies differ in their levels of irritability as well as in their readiness to be soothed. However, each baby can learn to manage anxiety if the caregiver can find the specific interventions that are most helpful for her child.

Because babies cannot take care of their own needs but have to rely on somebody else, the pleasures and anxieties of the body acquire very quickly a social character. Mother and baby can look, coo, smile, talk, and cuddle with each other while feeding, diapering, bathing, getting dressed, and falling asleep. Conversely, caretaking can be short, abrupt, impatient, or simply matter-of-fact and business-like.

The feelings that go with these early experiences teach the baby a great deal about what to expect from relationships. A young baby who cries when hungry and is fed lovingly learns that there is a connection between his cry for help and a successful outcome in the form of an appropriate maternal resonse. When this experience is repeated again and again, the baby learns that pangs of hunger or pain will not last forever. He is giving a signal and help is on the way. Such a baby learns to wait with hope in the face of internal stress. The mother's sensitive response helps to keep his anxiety within manageable limits. The mother, in fact, protects the baby from experiencing excessive anxiety before he can protect himself.

When a baby cries and cries and nothing happens, a very different internal experience begins to unfold. He finds that his signals of need are not effective in securing help, and he cannot learn a causal connection between needing and receiving. As bodily discomfort mounts, so does anxiety that this state of affairs will go on forever. Despair replaces hope, and the baby has only two avenues of response open to her: disintegrating into frantic, angry wailing, or withdrawing into lethargic sleep. Rather than protecting against anxiety, the parent actually becomes the cause of it.

Lack of synchrony between the baby's signals and the parent's response can occur in many areas of interaction. The baby may smile beseechingly and be ignored by the parent; cling to the parent and be put summarily to bed; come close and be pushed away; call for help and not be heard.

When these emotional rebuffs become the norm rather than the exception, they shape the baby's sense of herself and her emotional relationships. Babies who get little help when they are distressed tend to be dispirited, angry, and to cry often. They lag behind in experimenting with verbal communication and other social signals because they lose faith in their competence to bring about good experiences for themselves.[11]

Such babies become chronically anxious about their mother's physical and emotional availability; they cannot have a confident expectation that the mother will respond to them when they are in need. Gradually, this anxiety about the mother gets internalized to become an integral part of their sense of themselves and how they see the world. Conversely, babies whose signals receive consistent and appropriate responses internalize a feeling that they are worthy and deserving of good care. In trusting others, they learn to trust themselves.[5]

The intricate patterns of reciprocity between mother and baby prompted the noted British pediatrician and psychoanalyst D. W. Winnicott to quip that "there is no such thing as a baby."[12] He meant that a baby's individuality unfolds in a particular mothering context, so that his very essence is profoundly affected by the kind of care he receives.

At the same time, mothers may well feel that there is no such thing as a mother, because each responds to the unique characteristics and specific demands of her child. Although there is a basic core of mothering attitudes and practices that each woman brings to the caregiving situation, the same mother may respond differently to her different babies, depending on how comfortable she feels with herself, with being a mother, and with each particular baby at different times in her life. Of course, the same is true of fathers as well.

How Unique Is a Mother?

A mother is special to her baby because of the intimate bodily and emotional experiences that they share from pregnancy onwards. But this does not mean that only the mother and nobody but the mother can help babies to become secure in their human relations.

Children can thrive in different kinds of child-rearing settings provided that they have satisfying relationships with a small number of consistent caregivers who are responsive to their needs. Adoptive parents, fathers, grandparents, and other adults can raise a child equally well. The mother is used in these pages as the reference point because she is so often in reality the primary caregiver: the baby's emotional reference point. Speaking about "mother" is simply a way of giving credit where credit is most often due in raising the very young child.

At the same time, fathers have become increasingly more involved in child care in the last decade. Kyle Pruett studied a group of families where the father was the primary caregiver while the mother worked. He found that the nurturing capacities of the men were more than up to the task of raising their children. The children thrived in their fathers' care.[13]

In fact, babies establish distinct relationships with different people from a very early age. At 4 weeks, they already respond in predictably unique ways to their mother and their father, and these two patterns in turn differ from the much more diffuse responses shown in relation to a stranger.[14] By 12 months, infants can have a secure relaitonship with one parent but an anxious relationship with the other.[15] These different patterns are strongly influenced by each parent's sensitivity and responsiveness to the child in the preceding months. In this sense, the first twelve months serve as a laboratory in which the baby learns what she can expect from important people in her life.

How much an anxious relationship with a parent or caregiver affects the child's emotional development depends on the centrality of that person in the child's life. In a group of middle class children raised primarily by their mothers, toddlers who were anxious with their mothers between 12 and 18 months showed more insecurity at age 6 than those who had a secure relationship with the mother in the first 18 months. In contrast, early anxiety in relation to the father did not predict later insecurity in this group.[16] For these children, the mother was the more central caregiver and their relationship with her clearly influenced their emotional development.

Insecure attachments are particularly forceful indicators of a major normal anxiety of infancy: the fear of losing the mother, or separation anxiety. Between 6 and 10 months, babies protest the mother's departure energetically and are much less willing than they were earlier to accept substitutes with good grace. In the course of multiple interactions occurring in many contexts and moods, the baby has become fiercely, uncompromisingly attached to the primary caregiver. She has become the center of his emotional life.

The quality of this bond has many individual variations. It may be secure or anxious; exuberant or affectively muted; passionate or tranquil; conflictful or harmonious; simple of multifaceted; ambivalent or wholehearted. It may be all of these things or different things at different times. Most of all, it just is, and the threat of its not being unleashes intense agonies in the baby's heart and mind.

Once it emerges, anxiety over separation and loss becomes a steady human companion. One cannot have an intimate, intense emotional relationship and be spared anxiety about the stability and the permanence of that relationship. Some adults (as well as some babies) are more prone to it and experience it more intensely than others, but fear of losing the loved one is the ever-present, although often hidden, darker side of love.

The Anxieties of Toddlerhood

The 12-month-old baby enters her second year of life with a rich and well-established emotional world. She has a hierarchy of relationships—with mother, father, grandparents, siblings, caregivers, even the family cat or dog—that have special meaning and are not interchangeable. Some of these relationships are more central to her sense of well-being than others, and she resists and protests separation from them. However, she also uses other familiar and trusted people as substitutes until the preferred attachment figure returns. The more secure a 12-month-old baby is in her primary attachment relationship, the better equipped she is to negotiate the special challenges of the second year.

As we saw earlier in the book, the developmental course of separation anxiety is such that it becomes most acute at about 18 months. It seems paradoxical that separation anxiety increases just as the toddler experiences the urge to leave the mother's side, but this is as it should be. The momentum away from the mother calls for a psychological counterweight of equal magnitude in order to keep the toddler within reach at least sometimes. Separation anxiety provides that counterweight.

Like everything else, separation anxiety becomes more complicated in

the second year. In the first year of life, the mother's sensitive response was enough to relieve the baby's distress. Now the toddler fights within himself about wanting versus not wanting the mother's help. He wants to be the one to decide, but most often he cannot decide on his own.

The target of that internal struggle is often enough the mother herself, but the issue the toddler is trying to resolve is really an internal one. He is simultaneously saying, "I still need you" and protesting, "But I can do it myself!" The inner subtexts indicate the self-doubt underneath the assertiveness: "Can I really do it myself?" and "Will you be there to help, even if I send you away?"

Mixed messages are common in the toddler years because the salient emotional issues are usually compounded ones. (No wonder tactfulness is traditionally considered a female virtue. A mother needs plenty of it to help her child without being blamed for undermining his autonomy.)

Fear of Losing the Parent's Love

As the growing toddler acquires a greater awareness of what constitutes right and wrong behavior, another source of anxiety comes to the fore: fear of disapproval and anxiety over losing the parent's love.

Mario and his mother have a big fight. She yells at him to go to his room. He refuses. She grabs him by the arm, takes him to his room, and shuts the door. He screams. She sits outside the closed door, shaking with anger, helplessness, and guilt. After the tempers calm down, they talk quietly about what happened. The mother tells Mario she is sorry she lost her temper with him. Mario asks: "When you are angry with me, do you still love me?" His mother says yes, and asks: "Do you love me when you are angry with me?" Mario is silent for a minute and then says: "Oh, I don't know." He adds: "Later I do."

Mario is struggling with the problem of remaining aware of one's love in the midst of one's anger. Toddlers' increasing self-awareness leads them to scrutinize their feelings quite closely, and to ask many questions about what feelings occur when, and how different feelings fit with each other. They are trying to make sense of ambivalence in themselves and in others.

Toddlers' anxiety over losing the parent's love is fueled by their experience that they no longer love the parent when they are angry at her.

Because of their cognitive limitations, young children find it difficult to understand that others may feel differently than they do in a given situation. As a result, a young child cannot believe they the parents still love him even if he is not feeling any love for them at a particular time. This perception may actually be quite accurate, since even the most caring of parents will find it hard to feel love in the middle of a fight. The parents' anger is so graphic and real that it can make the child believe that the dreaded loss of love (that ultimate catastrophe) has finally occurred and will last forever. This is why it is so important to make up after a fight. The parent's reassurance is of immense importance to the toddler's emotional wellbeing.

Body Anxieties

Not all of the anxieties of the second and third years are based on separation and loss. The body, that old troublemaker, continues to elicit fears. The early anxieties over digestion, hunger, and sucking needs are presumably well enough mastered by now, but as new challenges emerge so do new uncertainties.

Bowel movements and urination can produce much anxiety in toddlers because they cause uncomfortable body sensations that the child cannot control. Particularly when the child is prone to digestive cramps, diarrhea, or constipation, bowel movements can become associated with a feeling of being threatened from the inside.

More commonly, however, it is the pressure of toilet training that generates anxiety in toddlers. When children become toilet trained because they are motivated to grow up, this anxiety does not occur. When they are asked by the parents to control their body functions before they are ready, toilet training creates anxiety about who is in charge of the child's body and a feeling of shame for not living up to the parents' standards. Chapter 8 provides specific guidelines for deciding when to start and how to proceed in toilet training the child.

Gender differences are another source of body anxiety. By about 15 months, children become very attentive to differences between boys and girls. They cannot yet ask clear questions or put their worries into words, but it is clear from their behavior that they are aware of body differences, and they can become anxious about having or not having what the other sex has. In a longitudinal study of 70 boys and girls in a nursery school, Roiphe and Galenson observed that from 15 months onwards children watched their own and each other's genitals closely and some of them expressed distress at the differences.[17]

Nursery school teachers are very aware of this phenomenon. One of them reports on a boy, Timothy, who at 15 months watched with absorbed attention as the teacher changed a little girl's diapers. When his turn came to have his diaper changed, Timothy ran away and hid under a crib screaming "No! No!" He had never done that before. It is possible that Timothy, not understanding the source of gender differences, feared that his diaper change would make him look like the little girl he watched. The teacher guessed this fear and said: "Timothy, I won't hurt you when I change your diaper. You are a boy and you will stay a boy. Lindsay is a girl and she does not have a penis." The explanation worked. Timothy allowed his diaper to be changed.

Fear of the Unknown

Throughout the life cycle the age-specific sources of anxiety have to do with those life tasks we understand only imperfectly and have many fantasies about. For junior toddlers, this may center on movement and toilet training; for senior toddlers and for 3- and 4-year-olds, on the differences between boys and girls and how babies are made; for young adults, on the secrets of love; for very old people, on the mysteries of death and the world beyond.

We tend to be afraid of what we do not know, and toddlers are no exception. To compound matters, they often reach faulty conclusions because their reasoning is still based on their wishes and fears rather than on objective information. In addition, toddlers overhear many things they cannot understand. Adults do not routinely edit their conversations so that toddlers can understand them, and often they do not even know that the child is listening. Yet the toddler can be full of anguish over his very personal understanding of what he overheard.

During the Persian Gulf war, Philip, 27 months old, refuses to play in the yard or to go to the playground. He develops intense fears of going outside, and clings to his parents whenever they do go out. The source of his fears becomes clear when his older brother overturns a stone to look at the worms under it, and Philip begins to scream. After patient questioning by his father, Philip sobs: "There is a bad man in a rock, and he kills people, and I don't know in what rock." This was his best interpretation of the anxious family discussions about Saddam Hussein of Iraq.

Anxieties about the parents' love, how the body works, and how the world is made are manageable if the toddler is largely confident that his mother or father will listen and intervene on his behalf. At any age, fears become magnified if one is alone with them. Philip could trust his parents with his information about "the bad man in a rock" because they made clear to him that they were concerned about his fears. Their patient, persistent questions and attentive listening were clear signs to him that they wanted to help. (Tell me what makes you scared. Did something happen to you outside? Do the worms scare you?) If his refusal to go out had been dismissed as irrational or ridiculous, Philip would have suffered silently and unnecessarily for a much longer time.

What Is Optimal Anxiety?

In the most desirable conditions, the child learns to manage anxiety by being exposed to just the right amounts of it, not much more and not much less. This optimal amount of anxiety varies with the child's age and temperament. It may also vary with cultural values. However, even within a particular culture, knowledgeable adults differ in their views of how much anxiety, frustration, or stress are "just right" for an individual child. There is no mathematical formula for calculating exact amounts of optimal anxiety. This is why child rearing is an art and not a science, and why parents need to stay in touch with their personal convictions in deciding how much anxiety their child can tolerate.

Nevertheless, we can entertain some different possibilities to guide our thinking on this topic. Let's go back to the example of a newborn crying with hunger. If the mother responds right away, the baby eats with gusto and falls asleep peacefully. If the delay is long enough so that the crying escalates sharply, the baby will not be immediately soothed when food is offered. He will continue to cry with the nipple in his mouth and may even choke on the flowing milk. If we look at this picture in units of time, we find that when a mother responds to her baby's cry within 90 seconds, the baby calms down in only 5 seconds. If she waits 3 minutes, the baby takes about 50 seconds to be soothed.[18] In other words, doubling the response time leads to a tenfold increase in the length of a baby's crying. Once the baby's distress gets out of control, it is much more difficult to help him reorganize emotionally and reengage with the world.

It is not difficult to infer what optimal anxiety means in this context. A hungry newborn does not have the internal resources to wait for food without collapsing in distress. As she grows older, however, she will have more experiences in regulating her inner cues and will have a reassuring inner expectation that her hunger signals will be reliably attended to by the parent. She will be able to tolerate hunger with the parent's verbal reassurances and will distract herself with various activities, including watching the parent prepare his food. She will have learned to wait with trust.

Learning to cope with the anxieties of toddlerhood follows a similar course. Toddlers throw tantrums and protest loudly when they don't like what is happening. If they recover from a tantrum and go back to being their regular self, the experience that led to the tantrum was most likely a manageable one. Such an experience is actually valuable because it helps the toddler learn about frustration and anxiety as unpleasant states that can be tolerated as part and parcel of life. If the parents remain available and supportive, toddlers learn to manage situations of disappointment and distress without emotional damage. Tantrums decrease and eventually disappear.

By the time they are preschoolers, children can control their behavior better and they begin to speak about what they want and how they feel about not having it. They do not feel as overwhelmed by disappointment and no longer assume that they have an inherent right to have all things their way.

Play and the Mastery of Anxiety

Anxiety can be a very useful emotion if it is managed well. The child's impulse to master age-appropriate anxiety is a powerful incentive to learning. Mastery is possible when the child's capacities are tested but not overwhelmed by the challenge. If, on the other hand, the parents are overly lenient and try to spare the child the necessary developmental frustrations, she will grow unsure of her coping skills and may become anxious in the face of even minor trials and tribulations.

How does the toddler learn from anxiety? Anxiety serves as a signal that something dangerous is about to occur but has not yet happened. This gives the child an opportunity to search for ways of coping with the danger. The search, and the eventual solutions found by the child, spur the transformation of anxiety into the pleasure of discovery. This process of transforming anxiety into mastery is a basic component in the development of creativity.

The parents of Cecilie, 15 months old, go out for the evening. She cries although she very much likes her baby-sitter. As the evening wears on, she is alternatively cheerful and cranky, enjoying games with the baby-sitter and calling tearfully for her mommy. She then hits upon a game: she crawls under her crib, closes her eyes tightly, waits a moment and then, unable to control herself, cries out "Me here!" as she waits for the baby-sitter to "find" her. She plays this game countless times, and laughs glee-

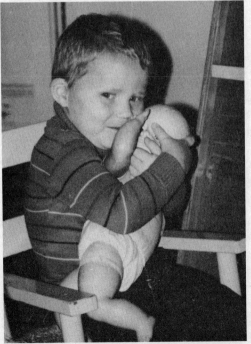

NANCY P. ALEXANDER

fully when she is retrieved. This improvised game of hide-and-seek helps her to practice and strengthen her fledgling knowledge that mommy always comes back, just as Cecilie herself can be hidden from view and then be seen again.

Rafi, 20 months old, has just discovered that girls do not have penises. After an unusually long period without hearing from him, his mother finds him sitting in his room, naked from the waist down. He is absorbed in covering and uncovering his penis with a plastic cup. He is checking that it is always there, even when it can't be seen. His anxiety about body integrity has led him to devise a scientific experiment which he repeats systematically in order to be sure that the results generalize from one trial to the next.

Michael's mother has become sick with the flu and is out of commission for a few days. Michael, 24 months, is allowed into her room but cannot come close to her for fear of contagion. He sits watching her quietly for a long time. He then takes a doll which he checks from top to bottom, trying to find "what is wrong with her." He cradles the doll tenderly in his arms. He then turns to his father and announces cheerfully: "All better now."

Play is a major avenue for learning to manage anxiety. It gives the child a safe space where she can experiment at will, suspending the rules and constraints of physical and social reality. In play, the child becomes master rather than subject. She is the one who decides instead of being the one who must abide by the grown-up's decisions or the one who must endure whatever life brings—from a mother's illness to a troubling discovery. Play allows the child to transcend passivity and to become the active doer of what happens around her.

Erik Erikson proposed the theory that play is the childhood version of a lifelong human propensity: setting up model situations to experiment with different ways of controlling reality.[19] While playing, the child relives past events and in this process alleviates lingering anxiety and fear over what happened by "playing it out," just as adults find emotional relief from "talking it out."

Jessica, 25 months old, had her tonsils taken out. Although the operation went smoothly from a medical point of view, it involved many stresses for this little girl, including being wheeled away from her parents for the procedure and then being in pain for several days. After returning home, she becomes uncharacteristically clingy to her mother. She also flies into rages at the drop of a hat. During this period she is so anxious that her bouts of play are short-lived. Her parents help her by going over what happened again and again as she listens intently, asks occasional questions, and volunteers her own details. Over the next four months, as her anxiety over separation and body damage is assuaged, Jessica does not want to hear about the operation any more but she begins to play it out. She becomes the surgeon operating on her doll and gets quite angry with her doll as she "operates" on her, reflecting her perception of the procedure as an aggressive intrusion on her body. While Jessica's parents do not enjoy watching her play in this way, they realize that she needs to find her own way of expressing and working through the anger and helplessness she felt during her difficult ordeal.

Play helps in coming to grips with the past and also, just as importantly, to giving the right shape to the future: a "happy ending" to a troubling situation.

Maria's parents have a loud argument in front of the child. Maria, 32 months, watches silently for a while, but she then yells at them: "Don't fight! It's not nice!" Later, she reenacts the argument using her two favorite stuffed animals. She speaks for each of them, mimicking her parents' voices and angry tone. Then she brings them together in a hug, saying: "We won't fight anymore."

Humor is also a powerful tool in managing anxiety, and toddlers delight in their growing capacity to make use of it. They even begin to experiment with practical jokes that play on their own vulnerabilities as well as on their parents' rules and fears.

Iden, 28 months, climbs on the kitchen table, an activity his parents have forbidden again and again. He stands very close to the edge, pretends to fall down, and then yells: "Save me! Save me!" with a twinkle in his eye. (His parents were less amused than he by his wit.)

Children get used to many situations that originally provoked their anxiety because they learn that the event is not associated with a frightening, dangerous outcome. They find out that having a haircut does not hurt and that their hair grows back. They discover that most unfamiliar situations turn out to be rather benevolent and even fun. Most importantly, they discover that people and things do not disappear when they are out of sight, that mom and dad always come back, and that they can have a good time with other people while the parents are away.

Parents can help toddlers to play out their anxiety about a particular situation by giving them the space to do so but not setting the script for them. The essence of play is spontaneity, and toddlers know how to do it better than grown-ups do. Parents can give permission and can follow the child's lead but they need to be careful not to interfere with the child's own pace by injecting their own agenda about what the child should be solving through play.

Excessive Anxiety

Anxiety has its uses but also its abuses. It stops being effective as a teaching mechanism when it overpowers the toddler's resources for coping with it. Experimentation, play, and humor are no longer available and the child cannot learn from the experience.

When the toddler is exposed to excessive amounts of anxiety on a routine basis, he must resort to extreme psychological measures in order to keep functioning while minimizing inner collapse. These measures are defenses against unbearable psychological pain. Although useful in containing anxiety, these responses involve a high psychological cost, because they constrict the child's capacities to appraise reality, to feel, and to learn.

What situations give rise to excessive anxiety? The answer to this question can vary from child to child. Toddlers with different temperaments experience different situations differently, and some children may become excessively anxious in settings where their peers respond with excited glee. The different responses of toddlers to their first encounter with a swimming pool is a good example of this. Some toddlers are terrified and withdraw in a panic. Others cannot get enough of splashing about.

In spite of individual differences, there are situations that elicit intense anxiety in all toddlers.

• Frequent and long separations from the preferred parent in the absence of a trusted substitute is perhaps the most common source of excessive, unmanageable anxiety for toddlers.

• Threats of abandonment are terrifying because they make children doubt the parent's basic love and commitment to protect them. "I will leave you here if you don't come along"; "I'll call the police to come and get you"; "I don't love you anymore"; "I don't like you anymore." These are common but very damaging threats used by parents to control their toddlers.

• Global critical comments create anxiety because they make the child believe he or she is intrinsically bad. "You are bad"; "Dummy"; "You are so stubborn"; "You never listen" are common examples.

• Blaming the child for how the parent feels makes the child believe she is dangerous and can hurt the parent by simply being who she is. "You will kill me"; "You will give me a heart attack"; "You exhaust me."

• Recurrent or harsh physical punishment or threats of physical punishment frighten a child and make him watchful in efforts to anticipate when it will happen. Routine physical punishment such as spanking also teaches a toddler that might makes right and that it is fine to hit when one is stronger and can get away with it.

• Unpredictable changes in caregivers make toddlers anxious because they cannot rely on a stable substitute relationship when the parents are away.

• Ridiculing or dismissing toddlers' fears makes them feel alone with their very real anxieties about how the world works or what will happen to them.

• Favoring one sibling at the expense of the others by consistently coming to that child's defense. Children internalize the message that their needs do not rank as high as the favored sibling's needs, and this may set the stage for a lifelong "Cinderella" complex.

• Parental overconcern about the child's physical safety, so that they hover around the child and constantly caution the toddler to be careful even when there is no imminent danger: "You'll fall"; "You'll bump your head"; "You'll get hurt." This excessive worry about anticipating danger can get transmitted to the child, who may come to see the world as a dangerous place. Such toddlers become conflicted about the discrepancy between their own impulse to explore and the parental message that exploration is bound to hurt.

• Parents' overconcern about fostering their child's intelligence. When parents become too conscientious about enhancing their child's cognitive skills, they tend to see every aspect of everyday life as an opportunity to teach and to test the child's knowledge. In this frame of mind, it is easy to forget that the most effective early learning occurs in spontaneous, pleasurable exchanges that are responsive to the child's interests. Overly structured efforts at teaching the toddler can create early anxiety about performance, because the child associates learning with parental approval and not with the intrinsic pleasure of mastering age-appropriate skills.

• Excessive parental attention to the child's inner life and mental health. Some parents are so concerned about being sensitive and responsive to their child's emotions that they become oversolicitous in trying to understand what the child is thinking and feeling. They ask many questions and they explain at length to the child what he or she is feeling and why. They also try to minimize frustration in all circumstances, worry a great deal when their child is sad or angry at them, and go to great lengths to get the child's agreement when they need to do something their toddler will not like. Young children raised under such close scrutiny can become overly anxious about having negative feelings. The child knows that the parents become upset when she is sad, mad, or upset, and she assumes that this is because there is something inherently wrong with these feelings. Children who are expected to be happy all the time to make their parents feel good are robbed of their right to feel a variety of genuine emotions. The effort to please their parents through a happy, pleasing, cooperative demeanor that cannot possibly be maintained can become a lifelong source of anxiety that begins in the toddler years.

This list of anxiety-producing situations is long enough to make parents anxious about doing anything right. The good news is that it is all a matter of balance. At one point or another all parents do things that create anxiety in their children. In general, this does not matter very much. Our children love us enough to forgive our mistakes and keep on growing. Manageable amounts of anxiety go into building coping resources, and parents and toddlers are the better for it. It is only when one errs too much and too often in any one direction that there is reason for concern, and toddlers tell us eloquently when the anxiety they are feeling is too much to bear.

Coping with Excessive Anxiety

Every child struggling with excessive anxiety develops emotional strategies for fending it off. Many of these defenses can be understood in terms of the biologically based "flight or fight" response to acute danger.[20] In other words, children engage in behaviors that result in withdrawal from the aversive situations or respond with anger and aggression directed against it. Sometimes the same toddler may show different patterns under different circumstances: withdraw from the parent, for example, and fight the child-care provider or a peer. Other children may show either withdrawal or anger towards the same person at different times.

All normal toddlers show some or all of these behaviors at some time or another as a response to stress. A more serious problem exists only when the pattern is so intense and pervasive that it interferes for weeks at a time with the child's overall pleasure in emotional relationships and with exploration and play.

Avoidance. Physical withdrawal (or "flight") from the parent is a common defense against intolerable anxiety. If often occurs when toddlers are reunited with the parent after a prolonged separation that has stressed their coping resources.[1] The child may fail to greet the parent, avert his gaze, turn away, walk away or sit with his back to the parent. In more serious situations (for example, after a separation of a week or longer) the child may seem not to recognize the parent, a reaction that can last from a few minutes to a few hours.

In very severe reactions, the toddler may eventually recognize the parent

but respond to him or her in an impersonal and distant manner, showing more interest in the toys brought by the parent than in interacting with him or her. This extreme form of avoidance has been labeled "detachment."[1]

Avoidance can be understood as the child's effort to get control of his anger about the parent's behavior. In the case of prolonged separation and subsequent reunion, the child is caught between his anger at having been left and his excitement and relief at the parent's return. Avoidance may provide a temporary space for the child to sort out these intense contradictory feelings. After a stressful separation, the child is too emotionally vulnerable to risk an overt and immediate expression of anger that, in his fantasy, may drive the parent away yet again.

Many toddlers become excessively clingy and aggressive with the parent after their initial avoidance. It seems that they can allow themselves to express their full range of feelings only after being somewhat reassured that the parent is truly back and will not leave them again.

Fighting. Aggression is the most straightforward manifestation of the "fight" response to perceived danger. Toddlers who use it as a defense against excessive chronic anxiety are given the painful but all too common labels of "little monsters," "holy terrors," or "devils." These children perceive routine exchanges as potential attacks on them and have learned that the best defense is a good offense. They fight when they are given a bath, being dressed, or put to bed; they hit, kick, or bite the parent for no apparent reason; they throw monumental tantrums that go on endlessly and from which they emerge shaky, exhausted, and wet with perspiration.

Self-punishment is another form of aggression. It occurs when the child is angry at the parent but afraid of showing it for fear of punishment. Aggression is then turned against the self in the form of accident proneness, recklessness, and even self-inflicted injury. The child bites or hits himself. An unexplained puzzle in self-punishment is why the pain from the injury does not serve to inhibit this behavior.[20] It is possible that the child does not feel the pain because his emotions are too strongly aroused. Another possible explanation is that the toddler actually seeks out pain because he feels he deserves it.

Transformation of affect. Some toddlers transform their anxiety into behaviors that superficially look like giddy excitement or intense amusement. They run around the room while shrieking wildly, or break into silly giggles that cannot be stopped, or escalate a game until they become almost manic. Eventually they cannot withstand this overstimulation and suddenly burst into tears.

What gives these behaviors away as a manifestation of anxiety is that they are inappropriate under the circumstances. For example, Daniel runs around laughing wildly when his father threatens him with a belt. Joshua winces and then laughs when his mother angrily throws a ball at him and hits him in the genitals. Teresa looks at her mother with a phony smile while throwing toys in her direction in a provocative way. These three children have all been exposed to high levels of aggression and excessive punitiveness in their home, and they have learned to hide their anxiety behind a mask of false gaiety.

Inhibition. Some toddlers express anxiety through a generalized inhibition of exploration. They are reluctant to approach, touch, and manipulate objects and they withdraw from interaction with unfamiliar people.

These children do not show the broad range of emotion, from exuberant glee to despair, so characteristic of this age. Their mood tends to be sober or at best neutral. Some inhibited children cling to their parents and refuse to leave their side even after being familiar with their surroundings. Others tend to keep their distance from one or both parents as well, although they may look at them with a mixture of vigilance and fear.

Toddlers can respond with inhibition when they are afraid of what will happen to them if they are spontaneous and carefree.

A little girl, Aleta, used this response to an extraordinary degree. She never showed anger, upset or frustration. She displayed little curiosity or initiative in exploration, and remained immobile for long periods of time on her mother's lap.

For this little girl, inhibition of movement and of emotion was the safest stance. Her mother was very depressed and sat sullenly for long periods of time, unable to stir herself. These periods of stupor were often interrupted by sharp yelling at Aleta if the child dared to initiate an activity that the mother disapproved of. On one occasion, for example, Aleta moved from her mother's lap to pick up a rubber band from the floor. Her mother yelled "No" and slapped the child's hand quite hard. Aleta dropped the rubber band and leaned back against her mother.

Sometimes inhibition becomes so extreme that the child seems literally frozen, incapable of feeling or exploring.[20] This "freezing" can come to a sudden end with the toddler collapsing in tears and crying inconsolably while thrashing about. This occurred in the case of Aleta when the therapist gave her a toy. Aleta moved her fingers imperceptibly but did not extend her hand. When the therapist touched her hand with the toy in an effort to encourage her to take it, Aleta burst into tears and fell sobbing on the floor. This motor collapse is the other side of freezing. The child can no longer contain her inner despair, and her effort at self-control disintegrates in a total emotional collapse.

Inhibition should not be confused with shyness or slowness to warm up. Toddlers who are shy or slow to warm up are fully capable of a full range of emotions, including playfulness and spontaneous joy, when they feel comfortable in their surroundings. They also are just as likely as other children to develop secure emotional relationships with their parents and caregivers. Inhibited children, on the other hand, seem to have a vigilant stance, as if they are always ready to flee from danger.

Precocious competence in self-care. This defense is manifested through an emotional reversal in the roles of mother and child, so that the toddler routinely engages in protective behaviors usually performed by the parents and is unusually solicitous of the parents' (particularly the mother's) welfare.

Anxiously precocious toddlers take it upon themselves to keep track of the mother's whereabouts at all costs, even at the expense of playing. They are exquisitely aware of the mother's moods and they may dry her tears or offer her a cookie when they see that she is sad. They may ask the mother whether she has the keys of the car when they leave the house. In almost uncanny ways, they take on the role of protector in relation to their mother, whom they perceive as vulnerable and needing their help.

Of course, there are many toddlers who are very advanced in their ability to take care of themselves and who are aware of the parents' moods without being overly anxious. In precocious competence, there is a striking discrepancy between the child's apparent maturity and other behaviors that do not fit this pattern, such as excessive thumb sucking, pulling of her own hair, tics, or compulsive masturbation. The other side of excessive self-reliance can also be seen in night waking, eating disturbances, and a pervasive soberness of affect, as if the toddler were trying to behave like a miniature adult.

Social values stressing independence and self-reliance are so pervasive in our culture that it is easy to praise precocious children for being resilient and well-adapted, while overlooking the anxiety that sometimes underlies the positive coping strategies. The most worrisome aspect of precocious competence is that the child is trying to compensate for a profound insecurity regarding the parents' availability. The outward show of competence hides painful inner doubts about her own worth and lovability. For this reason, precocious competence can become the foundation for a "false self," where an impressive appearance is used to conceal a fundamental fear that one is not good enough.

Can Toddlers' Excessive Anxiety Be Relieved?

The defenses against anxiety described above can be alleviated if we understand their meaning for the child. Children can let go of these behaviors when they are no longer needed as a protective device. As parents become aware of the reasons for their child's excessive anxiety, they can take steps to alleviate it and to decrease the need for premature defenses that constrict the child's emotional spontaneity.

Sometimes professional consultation is needed in order to discover the factors at work and to develop more harmonious relationships between the toddler and her family. Infant mental health specialists are psychologists, psychiatrists, social workers, pediatricians, and other professionals who are especially trained in the emotional needs of infants, toddlers, and their families. Their services can be of great help when the child and the family are at a loss to resolve an emotional impasse through their own resources.[21]

There is, in fact, research evidence that early intervention with problems of anxiety can be effective in resolving the problem. In a study designed to investigate the effectiveness of our clinical approach, my colleagues and I found that toddlers who were anxious before treatment were functioning just as well after treatment as toddlers who had been secure in their relationship to the mother all along.[22] In particular, these toddlers received high scores in a measure of partnership that assessed their ability to resolve conflict with their mothers in a mutually agreeable way. Anxious toddlers in a comparison group not receiving treatment showed no improvement. The positive result of treatment came about from our working with the parents to understand the causes of their child's anxiety and to find ways of modifying their approach to child rearing to make it more responsive to the specific needs of their child.

Encouraging Emotional Security

Perhaps the most succinct formula for encouraging emotional security in toddlers is sensitivity plus clear and firm guidelines.

Maternal sensitivity to the baby's signals in the first year of life is strongly associated with emotional security in the infant–mother attachment at 12 months of age.[5] This security becomes a part of the child's sense of self and of the world. As a result, securely attached infants usually grow to cope with the developmental tasks of later years with greater ease and competence than anxiously attached babies. For example, securely attached 12-month-olds become toddlers who are more cooperative with the mother and more persistent and enthusiastic in trying to master a difficult task.[23] As 3-and 4-year-olds, they have more harmonious relationships with other children and get along better in the nursery school environment as assessed by their teachers.[24] As 5-year-olds, they are more flexible in finding solutions to problems. By age 6, they are less emotionally constricted and have fewer behavioral problems than their more anxious age-mates.[25,26]

Sensitivity remains an important component of the parent–child relationship across the developmental span. In fact, sensitivity is present in all fulfilling intimate relationships.

At the same time, some of the components of parental sensitivity change with age. The infant's signals become more varied and subtle in the course of development, and the parental responses need to become more discriminating in response to the changes in the child. It would be unimaginable to say "no" to a crying 6-month-old; sometimes saying "no" to a crying 2-year-old is the only reasonable response. In forcing us to develop more creative forms of response, children raise their parents as much as we raise them.

As the child grows older and the parent is confronted with an increasing variety of wishes and demands, the natural desire to be sensitive to the child needs to be balanced by the question: sensitivity to what?

In the second year, it was relatively easier to have a clear-cut answer to this question, since 1-year-olds want straightforward things and do not put up too much of a fuss when they are diverted from risky enterprises such as eating dirt, climbing on the stereo, or putting their fingers in those perennial electrical outlets.

The third year, ushering in as it does a definite sense of personal will, poses new challenges to the sensitive parent. Facing an adamant 2-year-old insisting on her rights (either verbally or through that most persuasive of devices, the temper tantrum), any empathic soul is bound to have inner doubts about the wisdom of persisting in denying the child's wishes. One wonders: Is this a contest of wills? A power struggle? Am I being as stubborn and defiant as my child? Am I damaging her psychologically by imposing things on her against her will? Should I negotiate a compromise? Should I be firm no matter what? Will I make her anxious by opposing her wishes?

In struggling with these questions, it is useful to know that childhood frustrations do not create anxiety if the parents hold a deep conviction that what they do has a personal or cultural meaning that justifies the child's distress. For example, a mother who knows that her working outside the home is important—either for her personal satisfaction or for the family's financial stability—will be able to pass on to her child an understanding that mommy's work is important and not only a cause for frustration. On the other hand, a mother who feels that what she does outside the home is trivial or selfish will be more likely to be overly apologetic when the child protests her departure. Her toddler in turn will not learn to respect the importance of the mother's outside activities. Toddlers learn meaning from their parents, and they can learn to tolerate distress much better if they have a sense that it is for a worthy cause.

CHAPTER EIGHT

Issues to Negotiate

WE SAW IN THE PREVIOUS CHAPTER THAT THE BASIC ANXIETIES OF TOD-
dlerhood revolve around the fear of losing the parent or the parent's love
and around the puzzles of how the body is made and how it works. This
chapter will focus on some specific manifestations of these basic anxieties.

Every one of the daily events involved in growing and developing can
serve as a stage for playing out the toddler's fears. Separation anxiety,
sleeping difficulties, refusal to be toilet trained, sibling rivalry, and discipline problems are common manifestations of anxiety about losing the
parent or losing control over one's body. The developmental background
of these struggles offers an approach that includes the toddler as a junior
partner in a shared effort to find satisfactory solutions.

Separation Anxiety

Zoë, at 18 months, attends preschool for the first time. For the first 20 minutes she clings to her mother, but she gradually lets go. She crawls inside a toy cabinet, closes the doors, and then opens them boisterously, running to her mother and holding her tight. She repeats this game again and again.

As we saw in previous chapters, young children manage their innermost fears through action. They play hide-and-seek to reassure themselves that things do not disappear when they are out of sight and that mom will come back when she goes away. They entice the parents to chase them in order to make sure the parents want them back. They move away to explore but keep tabs on the parent to make sure she does not leave them behind.

Sometimes children's actions are not enough to keep the parent as close at hand as they want. Circumstances may make it necessary for a mother to say goodbye and leave her child with grandmother, in day care, or with a baby sitter, sometimes for a few hours and sometimes every day for most of the day.

When the separation is emotionally manageable for the child, he may respond with some distress but be comforted by the substitute caregiver. Even while missing the mother, the child is able to take pleasure in peers, toys, and other caring adults.

In more difficult situations, the child panics and clings desperately to the parent, rejecting efforts to distract her or console her while the parent is gone. In even more extreme circumstances, the fear of separation becomes so dominating that the child constantly monitors the parent's whereabouts, refusing to let him or her close the door of the bathroom or be out of sight for even a few minutes. The child loses her zest for playing and social interaction when the parent is gone. Separation anxiety occurs when ordinary, expectable distress becomes so acute and all-encompassing that it interferes with the child's overall mood and daily routine.

The Emotional Cost of Major Separations

Everyday separations are a common occurrence in the toddler years and children learn to cope with them even while expressing legitimate protest.

However, lengthy separations are a major emotional risk factor in the first three years of life, and remain a source, of possible stress throughout childhood.

The emotional cost of separations for the toddler depends on many different factors. A separation is most difficult in the following conditions:

- It is prolonged (overnight or longer).
- It occurs abruptly, so that the child is not prepared for it.
- The child is left in unfamiliar surroundings and with unfamiliar caretakers.

Each of these three factors is very stressful in itself, but when they occur simultaneously the child is exposed to a potentially traumatic break with everything he holds familiar and dear. Under these conditions, even well-functioning toddlers deteriorate rapidly in their capacity to trust, and they become both angry and distressed. These emotional reactions are often played down by unknowing adults as transitory and reversible, but it is well documented that some toddlers become more prone to long-term depression and anxiety as a result.[1]

Temperamental differences play an important role in the toddler's ability to adjust to separations. A two-hour separation may represent a mild stress for one child but a major source of anxiety for a more sensitive, less adaptable toddler. Similarly, children differ in their ability to be comforted by somebody they do not know well. Individual differences in response to separations are vast, and parents need to learn their toddler's personal style in order to anticipate when a separation will be overly taxing.

Sometimes separation anxiety is the result not of actual separation experiences but of the child's fantasies about not being loved enough, which make them afraid of being abandoned. Here again, some children are more prone to these fantasies than others. In general, toddlers tend to interpret their parents' hectic life style, busy work schedule, short temper, or frayed nerves as indications that the parent is angry with the child and does not want to be with him.

It is sometimes difficult for an adult to keep in mind just how exquisitely attuned the average toddler is to a beloved parent's moods and whereabouts and how quickly the child can become prey to frightening fantasies.

Marc was the last child to be picked up at day care that day. Later that night, as he was being put to bed, he said to his mother:

"I thought you forgot me at school for the whole night." Only then his mother realized that it had become dark earlier than usual that evening because of the daylight savings time change. Marc had no way of knowing that she had picked him up only a few minutes later than usual. For him, it was dark and all the other mothers had picked up their children and gone home. Darkness and aloneness triggered the fear of abandonment, which he relived and was able to talk about as the bedtime separation was about to occur.

Alleviating Separation Anxiety

Dealing with separation helps to prevent separation anxiety for both the parent and the child. Parents need to prepare themselves and the child and build a mutual confidence that the experience will be manageable and the reunion joyous. This applies whether the separation involves staying with a baby-sitter for a few hours, going to full-time day care, or when parents are on a trip for a few days.

Although the specifics vary from one situation to another, the basic parameters for helping a child with a separation remain similar across situations:

- Try to avoid overnight separations until the child is older.
- Think about the separation before it takes place in order to get in touch with your own feelings and work them through.
- Make sure that your child is familiar and comfortable with the substitute caregiver and with the place where she will be staying.
- Help the substitute caregiver become familiar with your child's personal style, likes and dislikes, specific worries and fears, and daily routine.
- Leave the child with tangible reminders of your love: an audiotape where you speak to her, sing to her, and tell a favorite story; photographs where you are together; a beloved toy that can serve as a transitional object. These measures are particularly useful for younger toddlers because they are concrete reminders of the parents' presence and do not depend on the child's memory and verbal ability.
- For a major separation such as the beginning of a child-care

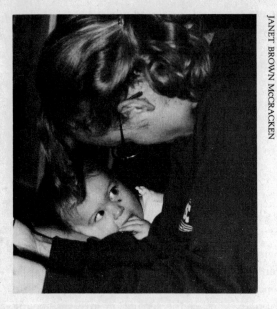

JANET BROWN McCRACKEN

arrangement, tell your toddler what will be happening at least a few days before it actually takes place. Choose language that is simple and straightforward, and use a positive tone of voice. Give your child room to ask questions and express misgivings. Tell him what he will be doing while you are apart. Reassure him that you will be thinking of him and teach him that he can think about you during the separation. These preparations work particularly well with older, more verbal toddlers, but younger toddlers can understand simpler explanations and a reassuring, loving tone of voice.

• Stress what you will do when you are together again. "And I will come back, and we will hug each other, and I will make your favorite pancakes for dinner, and we will play horsey." Concrete examples carry more emotional force than general statements.

• Encourage the substitute caregiver to speak to the child about you during the separation, to tell him that it is all right to miss you when he is distressed and calls for you, and to reassure him that you'll come back.

Paying attention to what happens after the reunion is as helpful to the child as a careful preparation for going away. The separation experience lingers on long after parents and child are together again. Some useful pointers are provided below.

• After the reunion, be prepared to encounter signs of ambivalence in your child. Some toddlers greet their parents joyfully, but others avoid looking at them, are quite lukewarm and aloof, or show overt anger. These are expectable behaviors and show that the child is making an effort to control his feelings of abandonment by keeping some emotional distance from the returning parent. Do not take offense or withdraw from the child. Often this initial ambivalence on reunion is followed by anxious clinging and a refusal to let the parent out of sight.

• Tell the child how happy you are to be back together, and find opportunities for talking about the time you were apart and telling the child that you missed her.

• Be prepared to recognize your child's fear of another separation in behaviors such as night wakings, relapses in toilet training, sudden tantrums, and a low threshold of frustration. Anxiety takes many unexpected forms, and children have different ways of expressing their fears. A little boy whose father was away on a long trip hit his mother quite hard with a toy hammer. After yelling at him, she thought of the father's absence and said: "I think you are angry at me because your daddy went away." He yelled: "You did it!" In his mind, his all-powerful mother was responsible for his father's absence, and his longing was naturally translated into anger at her for her imagined trespass.

• Engage your child in games that help master separation issues, such as peek-a-boo and hide-and-go-seek. Give her room to reenact the separation experience in playing with dolls or other toys. Children can express in play feelings that are kept carefully under wraps elsewhere. A very well-behaved little girl who seldom made trouble scolded her doll: "You bad girl! I will leave you all alone!" She was expressing her fear that the same thing would happen to her if she misbehaved.

Above and beyond paying attention to feelings before and after a separation, never threaten your child with leaving or loss of love in an effort to control her behavior. Children believe their parents assertions that "I will send you away," "I won't love you any more," "I'll go away," and are terrified with good reason. Fear is a very poor way of disciplining a child, and it can cause severe lifelong anxiety.

Being apart is always experienced by the child, at some level, as the equivalent of being left. There is an unspoken belief, "If you loved me most of all, if I was the most important thing in your life, you would never leave me." The only way to reconcile the child with this unmovable conviction is to provide abundant proof, through emotional availability and responsiveness, that he does not need to be the only important thing in your life in order to be loved well enough and deeply enough.

The Experience of Toilet Training

In the course of the second year, toddlers learn to recognize more subtle sensations in the anal and urethral areas. They also learn to contract and relax the muscles responsible for holding on and letting go of feces and urine. This increased capacity to notice and control sensations signals that the toddler is getting ready to be toilet trained.

Other factors are also influential in the child's readiness. The most important of these factors are the child's constitutional regularity or irregularity of the digestion-elimination cycle, the parents' tolerance of the child's individual pace, and the level of partnership that parents and toddler have already established in negotiating earlier developmental issues. Depending on all these variables, toilet training can be an uneventful process or a battleground between parent and child.

For all their earthiness, BMs have a profound symbolic meaning. No other body function represents so succinctly the polarities of experience of the human psyche. A BM is a precious treasure because it is part and parcel of one's body and its mysteries, and it is simultaneously something dirty, smelly, and yucchy; it is both something to cherish and something to discard.

Rafi, at age 2, looked skeptically at the potty his mother was offering him for the first time. He sat on it for a few seconds with his clothes on. He then got up, placed a chocolate gold coin inside the potty, smiled lovingly, and said: "There, mommy." The coin, with its dark sweet inside and its golden allure, was a perfect symbol of what Rafi's BMs meant to him.

If both these meanings of feces can be respected, toilet training can proceed with integrity. This means that the child's bodily production can be welcomed with pleasure but with no need for exaggerated accolades, and it can be disposed of matter-of-factly, without marked expressions of revulsion or disgust.[2]

Above all, feces need to retain their character as something that belongs to the child and it is in the child's power to produce or to withhold. In this sense, toilet training is the epitome of partnership through give-and-take, withholding, and letting go.

The Child's Readiness

The timing of toilet training has been a topic of much debate among parents and child psychologists alike. The current consensus is that it is best to wait until the child is ready to understand what is expected of her. She can then be a willing partner in the process.[3] This may vary from child to child, but it is unlikely to appear before 15 to 18 months of age, and it may not occur until about 24 to 30 months or even later.

Toward the middle of the second year, children become increasingly aware of the relationship between cause and effect and they are deeply concerned with the question of standards. They worry about the consequences of their actions and become disturbed if things are not up to par, if clothes are dirty or toys are broken. Children may scold their parents for leaving crumbs on the table or forgetting shoes in the hall; they get upset at themselves when they get dirty or make a mess. They are quickly internalizing the norms of social behavior that are being implicitly or explicitly taught to them.

The beginning of toilet training is best timed to coincide with a child's emerging interest in standards, which makes them feel invested in living up to them. The wish to emulate what the parents and older siblings do in the toilet can then occur naturally and calls for minimal parental encouragement.

Many toddlers initiate the process themselves by calling the parents' attention to the fact that they are making pee or poo-poo or by becoming upset for being wet or dirty. Even then, some children are rather lackadaisical in their approach and do not see the point of making themselves uphold standards all the time. Going in the potty is something they do when they feel like it; at other times, going in the diaper works very well for them. These toddlers go back and forth between periods of being clean and dry and periods when they relapse because they are absorbed in other pursuits. Other toddlers are so ready and regular that they become fully trained in a few weeks.

Starting toilet training before the child shows clear readiness is not advisable. Precisely because they are interested in standards, children in the second year of life become very upset when they cannot keep up with external demands. Jerome Kagan has shown that 2-year-olds from diverse cultural backgrounds cry or protest when an adult expects them to perform a task that is too difficult for them. The same-age children respond with spontaneous joy when they meet a self-imposed standard, such as building a six-block tower or completing a challenging puzzle.[5]

If we extrapolate these findings to the question of toilet training, we can conclude that beginning this process prematurely can lead to frustration and negativism in the child.

When parents feel pressured by circumstances to start relatively early anyway, it is best to involve the child in a partnership by helping her to signal when she is urinating or having a bowel movement. This is easily done: if the mother comments casually on the event ("Mary is making a poo-poo"), the child will soon enough begin to notice it herself because

her action brings about that most important of occurrences—the mother's interest and attention. When the child herself tells the mother that the noteworthy event of urinating or making a BM is taking place, she is also signalling an increased readiness to progress to the next step: going to the potty.

Potties are better than grown-up toilets for beginning training and for a long time afterwards. A potty is made for the size of a toddler's bottom, sparing him the fear of falling into the toilet. It enables the child to keep her feet firmly on the ground in order to push, something that few modern toilets seem designed to do. Finally, a potty does not come equipped with rushing water, which frightens some children with the unspeakable fantasy that they too, like their poo-poos, will be flushed away.

When the child's readiness is not an issue, most conflicts in toilet training can be traced to a combination of the child's irregular cycles (including perhaps a physiologically based tendency toward constipation, loose stools, or a mixture of both) and the parent's misperception that toilet training is a process controlled by the adult. Each of these two factors represents a threat to the formation of a partnership around toilet training.

Physiological Irregularities

The child's physiology can confront him with bouts of abdominal or rectal pain when he is constipated and his feces cannot be eliminated smoothly. The child may withhold to avoid the pain, making the constipation worse. Alternatively, recurrent diarrhea or loose stools make it difficult for toddlers to hold feces back, and they may stop trying and give up. Both with constipation and with diarrhea, the child's confidence that he can take charge of his bowels is undermined.

The child's pediatrician is the best person to consult when parents suspect that their child's digestive process is not working well. A special diet and stool softeners may be prescribed if necessary. Suppositories, enemas, and other intrusive measures are coercive and psychologically damaging and should be avoided.[3]

Many healthy children have irregular physiological rhythms and need to eliminate at unpredictable times. This is a constitutional characteristic, and adults should not coax the child to use the potty at the same time every day because it is convenient for them although not natural for the child. A portable potty is very useful for children with unpredictable elimination patterns because it is reliably available when needed.

Can Parents Control Toilet Training?

The secret belief that it is up to the adult to control toilet training can creep up in unexpected ways even among parents who consciously believe otherwise. Parents can feel embarrassed if their child is the only one in his play group who shows no interest in even starting the process. Other parents long for respite from smelly laundry or from sizable disposable diaper bills. Still others feel pressure from friends and family to stop "pampering" the child and to help him grow up. Sometimes very thoughtful adults worry about their own motives in not toilet training the child (wanting him to stay a baby forever? being afraid of not knowing how to do it?).

There is always room for examining one's behavior, but it is likely that if the child has shown no interest in cleanliness, tidiness, standards, toilets or BMs, he is not ready to start.

On the other hand, if the child seems ready, it behooves the parent to follow, without asking tentatively for the child's permission but with quiet confidence that this is the right time. The child himself can let us know if we have read his cues accurately.

> **Max, aged 2, had no interest in toilet training in spite of his mother's entreaties. Eager to start anyway, she bought some doll furniture which included a toy toilet and encouraged him, none too subtly, to play with it. Max complied by sticking the mother doll into the toy toilet—head first.**

Toileting has striking rhythmic similarities with secure-base behavior. Both are based on an alternation of holding on and letting go, giving and withholding, opening up and closing down. In both processes, the child's comfort with the mother is reflected and ultimately internalized in her confidence with her body and with herself.

Nighttime Difficulties

Sleeping problems are one of the most common difficulties of the toddler years. They are so common, in fact, that several studies have focused on how to define sleep disturbances and what factors contribute to them.[5,6,7]

Sleep disturbances involve difficulty falling asleep, waking up repeatedly during the night, night terrors, or a combination of all three. In many cases, toddlers with sleep disturbances have a history of early biological vulnerability. For example, they were born prematurely, had other conditions requiring specialized neonatal care, or suffered from colic for longer than three months. These children often have a history of not sleeping well from birth. On the other hand, other toddlers begin having problems going to sleep in their second year. This may be because daytime anxieties emerge most vividly during the night, when the child is alone and the lights are out. It may also be simply because the child has never acquired a predictable sleeping pattern.

Sleeping Irregularities

Many children get the sleep they need in spite of the awakenings, but their parents do not. The mismatch between the sleep needs of the toddler and those of the parents sets up an explosive situation in which the parents are exhausted, frustrated, and helpless. They become inconsistent and angry with the child, and the toddler becomes scared, angry, and defiant in response.

In these circumstances, it might be useful to recognize that toddlers have little control over awakenings. One solution is not to admonish them to "go to sleep"—something they often cannot do—but rather to help them realize what they can and cannot do while they are awake.

Toddlers should be encouraged to sooth themselves when they wake up at night. Depending on her age, a toddler can hug her pillow or teddy bear, sing softly to herself, or talk to herself about the things she will do when it is time to get up. A musical mobile with a soothing lullaby works well for many very young toddlers. Regardless of the specific alternatives offered, the child needs to understand that she may not get out of bed or go to mommy's and daddy's room because they need their sleep. These solutions are within the capabilities of even very young toddlers when the parents have the resolve to carry them through.

Mismatches Between Parents and Child

A mismatch between the parents' and the toddler's needs for sleep may occur if the child is a very early riser and the parents are not. Toddlers can learn to accept this discrepancy in stride and entertain themselves if the parents convey to them a lighthearted, guiltless sense that this is the way things are going to be.

One mother helped her 11-month-old, Mike, to accept her need for early morning sleep by putting some very enticing toys next to her bed at night. When Mike woke up at 6 A.M., she picked him up, nuzzled and talked to him, brought him to her bedroom, set him next to her bed, and told him that mommy was going to sleep some more and he could play with the toys. Every once in a while Mike would talk to his mother or pull up to the side of the bed. Each time, the mother gave him a reassuring grunt and a pat on the head, and the child went back to play. This is an early demonstration of secure-base behavior under unusual conditions!

Another mother came up with a different version of this basic solution for her 2-year-old. She set up a child-size table and chair in front of the TV set. Every night she put a piece of banana and some other safe pieces of finger food on the table, and set the TV to the channel carrying a good children's program. She taught her child, Logan, to wake up, come to the parental bedroom, and have a prebreakfast snack while watching the children's program. Logan is now 9 years old and has become an unusually self-reliant youngster, in part because of his mother's supportive confidence in his ability to collaborate in taking care of himself.

When Night Wakings Become a Problem

Sleeping irregularities have a constitutional basis. Sleeping problems result when the night wakings become charged with strong emotional meaning for the parent and the child. In this situation, the anxiety surrounding the wakings often interferes with finding a solution.

The most common anxiety associated with night wakings in toddler-hood is the fear of separation. This fear exists both in the parent and the child. Nighttime brings about a basic disruption of the secure-base patterns so readily available during the day. Instead of easy daytime access, there is now darkness, bedroom walls, and crib sidings serving as obstacles between parent and child.

Night, darkness, and physical distance are archetypal triggers of fears and anxiety. This is why many cultures less invested than ours in personal and marital privacy enable mother and child to sleep together through infancy and the toddler years. Even in technological cultures, the young child's nighttime cry elicits in the parent an ancient fear that the child's well-being and perhaps his very survival are at stake. The immediate impulse is to go to the child and provide reassurance and protection. This impulse is at odds with the parents' more rational knowledge that the child is healthy, the household is safe, and sleep can be resumed.

Some studies have found that night wakings in toddlers are associated with the mother's own fears of separation and with maternal depression. Many mothers whose toddlers have sleeping difficulties report that they were not well cared for as children. They want to spare their own toddlers the anxieties that they felt while growing up, and they respond to night wakings by bringing the child into their bed or going to the child's bed. Of course, every parent does this sometimes. When it becomes the norm, this response causes problems because it interferes with the marital relationship and it gives the child the message that her anxieties cannot be managed without the parents' ongoing presence.

Klaus Minde and his colleagues report on a successful program that was designed to help toddlers soothe themselves back to sleep when they wake up during the night.[7] This program, characterized by remarkable common sense, helps parents overcome their own anxieties about not "rescuing" the child from the anxiety of night wakings. The program involves the following steps:

1. A review with the parents of what the sleeping problems consist of—difficulty settling down to sleep, repeated night waking, or both. The daytime routine is also reviewed.
2. If the toddler does not have a predictable daily routine, the parents are helped to understand that toddlers experience a sense of comforting self-control from being able to anticipate what will happen next. Parents are encouraged to develop a routine where meals, baths, naps, and other daily events take place at about the same time and in the same place.
3. Once daytime routines are established, the parents are encouraged to focus on bedtime routines that do not include a feeding

but involve quiet activities such as reading, singing bedtime songs, or praying.

4.   The sleeping problem is tackled next. Two main techniques are recommended. One is "checking." The parent checks on the crying child at regular intervals that are tolerable for the parent (five or ten minutes), patting the child or using words of encouragement but expecting the child to stay in bed. This "checking" continues until the child falls asleep. If the parent is too overwrought by the child's crying, an alternative "shaping" technique is recommended. This consists of moving gradually from one step to the next. If the child were sleeping in the parent's bed, the next step would be for the parent to go into the child's bed the first night, sit on the bed on the second night, on a chair the third night, and so on.

This method was found to improve the sleep of 85 percent of the 28 toddlers with whom it was tried. Interestingly, Minde and his colleagues recommend that fathers carry out this project whenever possible because they tend to be less conflicted about sticking to it. On the other hand, the interventions tend to fail when the father is unwilling to cooperate in restructuring the parents' response to their child's sleeping problem. A major benefit of the program is that solving the sleeping problem tends to give parents and child the skills to negotiate more effectively other areas of struggle as well.

Enlisting the Child in the Solution

The plan developed by Minde and his colleagues to deal with sleeping problems can be enriched by letting the child know about it in advance and helping her come up with alternatives to crying and calling for the parents. This can work particularly well with older, more verbal toddlers.

Such a joint venture between parent and child in finding a solution to the sleeping problem teaches the child that her agenda—feeling safe and protected—can be achieved without violating the parents' agenda—to remain asleep.

One possible way of phrasing this approach is saying to the toddler:

"Danny, you know how you wake up at night and call for mommy?" (Wait for an answer.)

"Yes, and mommy is so sleepy that I get grumpy and yell at you to go back to sleep?" (Wait for an answer, which may only be a serious face or a meaningful look.)

"You know, mommy doesn't like to be grumpy at you. But I'm so sleepy at night and when I'm sleepy I get grumpy and that's why I yell." (Wait for a response, which does not need to be verbal.)

"It's hard for mommies and daddies to wake up in the middle of the night. I've been thinking, what can you do to feel better when you wake up at night?" (Go over different possibilities with the child.)

"Let's try that tonight. When you wake up, say to yourself: Mommy is sleeping. I am going to hug my teddy bear and talk to him (or whatever alternative you agreed on). Tonight, before you go to bed, I will remind you. That way mommy can get her sleep and you can help yourself by talking to bear and we will not be grumpy with each other."

It is worthwhile to have this conversation during the day, when both parent and child are rested and not in the middle of the conflict they are trying to resolve. In this way, both parent and child can mull over the plan during the rest of the day, and be readier to implement it when the time comes.

For some parents and toddlers, talking will be sufficient for meaningful exchange. For others, it might help to have this conversation in the context of play. The adult may set up a bedroom scene where the baby wakes up and calls for the parents, and the actual nightly scene may then be enacted. As the child becomes involved in the play, the parents may wait for a natural pause and then say: "That is what happens to us at night, isn't it?" This can become a good starting point for a dialogue and for a play enactment of the possible solutions.

Here again, attitude is more important than words. The child needs to realize that the parents are not requesting that she go to sleep; they are helping the child to grow into doing what is expected of her.

Night Terrors

Sometimes the child wakes up in the middle of the night screaming in a panic. This deserves prompt parental attention. If she can speak, the child may talk breathlessly and between sobs about "the bad man," "the monster," "the witch," or any of a variety of other scary creatures that are staples of the child's imagination. This is a sign that dreams have made their appearance and have acquired the character of nightmares.

One way to reassure the child is to tell her during the day about the nature of dreams as pictures inside her head that are "make believe" and can do her no harm. Most children go through a temporary phase of having nightmares, particularly at times of unusual stress such as starting preschool, a change of caregivers, a difficult visit to the doctor, a scary encounter with a dog or other animal, or an overly stimulating story or movie. If the nightmares persist, it is usually a sign that the child is struggling with an unexpressed worry or fear or with more pressure to perform than he can comfortably manage. Exploring what these fears might be usually opens the doors to finding a solution.

There is evidence that some cases of night terror have a biological component and can be hereditary.[8] During an episode, the children's behavior follows a predictable pattern that includes thrashing about, excessively rapid breathing, very fast heart rate, perspiration, and sounds of distress that may escalate to inconsolable crying. The child may respond to the parent's effort to restrain her with intense fear, confusion, disorientation, and efforts to escape. Some children scream for periods ranging from less than a minute to 20 minutes or so. The child seems oblivious to the parent's ministrations and often has no memory of the event the next day. When this pattern is so frequent and intense that it disrupts family life, it is a good idea to discuss the possibility of a sleep disorder evaluation with the child's pediatrician.

The Importance of Rituals

Toddlers have many reasons to have trouble with sleep: fear of relinquishing control by letting sleep take over; resistance to giving up the fun of being awake with the rest of the family; anxiety over being all alone in one's solitary room and solitary bed; or fantasies about what happens in the darkness of the house.

The importance of bedtime rituals in helping with these fears cannot be overemphasized. Rituals provide a container for uncertainty, bind anxiety, and provide reassuring bonds of human connection.

Structuring the activities before bedtime can help the child develop a feeling of belonging that will carry off into sleep. Uninterrupted family dinners (without intruding phone calls or other distractions), a time for quiet play, and then the ceremonies of getting into pajamas, brushing teeth, going over the events of the day, anticipating what will happen tomorrow, reading a story, singing a lullaby, saying a prayer—these activities can be woven into a family ritual that becomes associated with feelings of safety and protection which the child can hold on to when the lights go off.

If the bedtime ritual is done with quiet assurance, there will be no need to stay with the child until she falls asleep. A reassuring comment from the living room that "I am here and everything is fine" will be sufficient to convey the message that any anxiety she may feel being alone in her bed is manageable and that the parent is right in expecting her to handle it on her own. Toddlers grow stronger from going successfully through this experience.

Sibling Rivalry

Having a New Sibling

The birth of a baby brother or sister is a profound shock to a toddler. This does not mean that it is psychologically damaging. On the contrary, it can bring about many important learning experiences and the opportunity for a lifelong emotional connection with the sibling. But the experience is deeply upsetting because the child feels displaced and uprooted from his or her familiar role in the household constellation. He is no longer the·one and only child in the parents' lives if there were no other siblings, or the baby of the family when he was the youngest one.

Depending on their age, temperamental style and developmental level, toddlers express their distress in different ways.

> Susanna, 15 months, tries to push the baby out of her mother's lap and asks for the mother's breast even though she has been weaned for months. She bites the baby whenever she has a chance. She becomes "hell on wheels," careening through the house even though she has learned to walk only recently. During the day she is aggressive and overactive, but at night she regresses to being a little baby herself, waking up often and asking for the mother's breast or its alternative, a bottle. She clings to her pacifier and is very distressed when it is out of sight.

Benjamin, also 15 months, responds very differently. He becomes withdrawn and subdued, and his face has a sad, worried expression. He bursts into tears at the slightest frustration. He seems to have lost all his smiles, and his movements lack zest and vitality. He becomes very rejecting of his mother but clings to his father.

Nancy, 24 months, hugs her baby brother so hard he turns red. When the mother rescues him, Nancy wails. She wants to hold him constantly, but always finds a way of making him cry.

Rebecca, 28 months, is seen walking around with a silk bow and a hammer. Her father asks what she is doing. "A bow for her head," says Rebecca, pointing to her 3-month-old sister's totally bald little head.

Peter, 30 months, looks at his week-old brother and says: "OK, now he can go back." On other occasions he asks: "Can we put him in the oven? Can we eat him? He'll be tasty!"

The same Peter, now 3½, looks on as his brother tries to blow his first birthday candle. He says: "He is very cute, isn't he? We won't kill him, will we?"

Janice, 4 years old, has a 5-month-old brother. She confides to a little girl friend: "Wait till you have one. You will get so mad when your mommy feeds him." She turns her back to the guests who are admiring the new baby, and looks at them reproachfully when they try to admire her as well.

These vignettes show the evolution of very young children's expression of anger and ambivalence about having a sibling. Susanna and Benjamin, at 15 months, express their feelings simply and directly using their own temperamental styles—Susanna strikes out, Benjamin withdraws. The older children's responses are more complex. They are struggling to contain and control their aggressive impulses and to integrate them with feelings of love. Rebecca, who loves to wear ribbons on her abundant hair, ostensibly wants to share this pleasure with her bald sister and finds no better way of doing it than hammering one on. Peter struggles at first with opposite wishes to send his brother back and making him a part of himself by eating him; by the time he is 3½, the side of him that loves his brother is gaining over the side that wants to kill him. By the ripe age of 4, a child like Janice can reflect on her feelings of anger as an internal state that will not be expressed through destructive action.

The toddler's fear of losing the parent's love receives a powerful impetus with the birth of a new baby. The spectacle of one's very own mother lovingly holding and ministering to another child must be convincing proof to a toddler that this fear came true. As if this were not enough, the father is also absorbed in the new arrival and every guest pays attention to the baby first. The fear of being replaced by someone better—an anxiety that haunts many adults—has one of its early origins in this experience.

A new baby brings many concrete changes in the toddler's moment-to-moment experience. He now needs to wait more often and longer than ever before for things he wants or needs. He spends more time alone. He is scolded or corrected more frequently as parents try to teach him what he can and cannot do with the baby. Some favorite activities—going swimming, going to the playground, playing a favorite game—often have to be curtailed or postponed because of the baby's needs. Things cannot be done spontaneously any more because the baby's schedule needs to be taken into account, and the time it takes to prepare the baby's bag can seem interminable.

These are important losses for a toddler. The example below shows how keenly a toddler feels them.

Sammy, 28 months old, has begun burying his face in his hands and sighing deeply after the birth of the new baby. His father asks: "Why are you doing that?" Sammy replies: "I am sad." His father asks why. Sammy looks at him sadly and says: "I want my mommy back."

These feelings exist even when the parents are patient and sensitive in helping their toddler through the stormy feelings of this period. Competitiveness toward a new baby may give rise to the toddler's first sustained experiences of jealousy, envy, shame, and guilt.

Even without a new sibling, toddlers feel sometimes younger and sometimes older than they really are. As Linda put it, "I am a baby and a big girl both." Having to tolerate a baby day after day can greatly intensify the toddler's wishes to be a baby all over again. Toddlers show this by wanting a bottle, losing the gains they made in toilet training, or using baby talk. On the other hand, they also experience pride and a feeling of superiority when they realize they can do many things that the baby can't.

Parents do well to play along with the toddler's momentary wishes to be a baby. Letting him have a bottle or a pacifier, carrying him to his room, holding him snugly, and talking baby talk—these brief relapses into the modes of a earlier age can reassure the toddler that his baby side is still getting attention when needed. With this knowledge in place, the child can continue to get pleasure from his increased competence.

The toddler's abilities to do things better than the baby can be a good antidote for feelings of jealousy. When parents comment admiringly on a toddler's skill at doing something, or point out that the baby cannot yet do that marvelous feat, the toddler gets the comforting sense that she is still special and appreciated.

Perhaps most important of all is the message that a mother or father's lap is big enough to accommodate both the toddler and the baby. When a toddler is pushed off the mother's lap because the baby needs to feed, this experience can feel to him like a stab in the heart. The father's habit of asking about the baby first when he returns from work can make the toddler feel hopeless about anybody ever again caring for him most of all. At the risk of losing some spontaneity, the parents will do their toddler a great service by making themselves think of how he might be feeling when he watches them with the baby. During the difficult initial period of adjustment, including the toddler and even giving him priority whenever possible will help him tolerate the baby and, more, open the way for love toward the new sibling to develop.

When the Toddler Is the Baby
of the Family

Sarah, 4 years old, is playing dress up in her room. A box with a treasured collection of hair ornaments is on the floor next to her. Her sister Robyn, 15 months, comes in, goes straight to the box, and puts one of Sarah's ribbons in her mouth, covering it with saliva. Sarah screams and hits Robyn. Robyn wails.

Mario, 6 years old, is playing ball with a friend. Ronnie, 24 months, wants to join in. "Me too! Me too!" he cries.

Ayana, 3½ years old, has been waiting for her mother to read her a story. When she and her mother settle down comfortably and are about to start, Omar, 18 months, whimpers that he is hungry. The reading comes to an end even before it starts.

Rachel, age 4, and Armon, age 2½, struggle furiously over who will sit next to daddy to watch television.

These very ordinary scenes illustrate the power of toddlers to disrupt the life of an older sibling. They are little and most of the time they do not know any better. In addition, they often cry in response to frustration and then they appear so sad and helpless that it is almost impossible not to take their side.

Perhaps the most common mistake parents make in dealing with sibling relations is to favor the younger child too much. This is often done because younger children seem so vulnerable and needy. Another common mistake is to punish either or both children without learning first what happened.

Parents can allow themselves some benign neglect when it comes to sibling relations. Letting children work out their disagreements provides a valuable experience to children of all ages. Negotiations are not always smooth and the stronger child may win more often than is fair by strict standards of justice. The problem is that parental intervention does not guarantee fairness; it only brings into the conflict an even stronger participant whose word is final regardless of the facts. One can end up with a situation where the parent is inflicting on the older sibling the same kind of arbitrary power that the older sibling is trying to inflict on the younger one. The parent's action to stop the stronger sibling's power can give the message: Do as I say, not as I do.

Children need to work out their own relationships. Parents can certainly help or hinder this development. One of the parents' roles is to ensure that each child has enough parental attention and care so that there is no need to compete with the sibling for a little place in the sun. The case of Tobias and Andy described in chapter 6 shows some of the emotional repercussions that may result from excessive or one-sided parental intervention. The more favored child can become a self-righteous bully, ever confident that the parent will come to her defense. The less-favored child will either become a secret bully, trying to get away with murder when the parent is not there, or will suppress feelings of anger and resentment in ways that interfere with emotional spontaneity and freedom of expression.

Of course, there are times when parents must intervene. In the first vignette, where Sarah hit Robyn, their father did the right thing when he told Sarah in a stern voice that she could be angry and scold Robyn but she could not hit her. He then told Robyn that she needed to let Sarah play by herself, and removed her from Sarah's room. This intervention was concise, to the point, and addressed both children at their own developmental level. Each of them learned something from it.

Parental intervention is best reserved for times when the squabble threatens to escalate into a major conflagration where uncontrolled screaming or physical fighting may result. By intervening in a calm, measured, and succinct manner, the parent is modeling important values in conflict resolution. The children learn that they can control their more negative emotions and look for a solution that is fair and equitable for all the

aggrieved parts. At first, the parent needs to take on the role of moderator. Gradually, the children will internalize this role and learn to exercise it themselves.

Marital Squabbles

Toddlers get anxious when their parents argue in front of them. Does this mean that husbands and wives should have their arguments when they are alone? Should parents try to spare their children the distress of seeing them fight?

Sometimes children are the best judges of what is good for them, and I asked a 5-year-old girl about her opinion. As luck would have it, her parents had just gone through a testy day with each other, so the topic was fresh in Lydia's mind. She took the question very seriously, thought for a minute, and then said with total conviction: "It's better when they fight in front of me. Then I don't get so scared because we can talk about it."

Lydia's answer shows her faith in the power of talking about worries. She equates talking with reassurance. Even when tempers get out of hand, she derives relief from being told afterwards what the argument was about and, once it is over, that her parents have made up.

Do toddlers, who are quite a bit younger, respond in the same way as Lydia? While not able to articulate it, they would probably basically agree with her. Toddlers are very perceptive about cold silences, sarcastic tones, and unspoken tensions. They feel something is wrong but they don't know what it is. Sometimes toddlers themselves get cranky and overly demanding when their parents are angry with each other but trying not to show it. The child acts out the tension she senses but does not understand.

When marital disagreements do not get out of hand, watching parents argue with each other and then make up is quite instructive for toddlers, because they learn about the cycle of anger and reconciliation as the two most important adults in their lives go through the process. This experience puts in perspective their own episodes of getting angry with the parents and then making up.

However, there are some marital fights that are so bitter and protracted that toddlers are not equipped to witness them without having their trust in their parents seriously shaken up. This kind of fight terrifies toddlers.

Not only are they afraid that the parents don't love each other any more, they also see the parents at their worst: immersed in their rage, oblivious to the child, and unavailable to the child's needs. The image of the parents screaming out of control or worse evokes the child's deepest fears of abandonment and loss of love. Many adults remember their parents' loud, uncontrolled fights as the most frightening memories of their childhood.

The child's very existence calls for a commitment by the parents to work out their differences in constructive rather than destructive ways. Divisive fighting, by its very nature, questions this commitment. Conscientious child rearing includes an awareness of how the parents' actions with each other affect the child, and an effort to modulate violent emotions for the sake of the child.

When this effort fails (as it sometimes does) parents need to turn their attention to the aftermath of the fight. Acknowledging the fear, offering reassurance, perhaps even saying "We are sorry" and having a family hug, and trying to do better the next time—all these steps can help to contain the damage from an episode one wishes to but cannot undo.

Discipline: Is It Really Needed?

This is the question asked most often by parents of toddlers. Often it is prompted by a secret wish to hear that if children are loved, understood, and sensitively cared for, they will not need to be disciplined because they will be naturally loving and responsive to their parents' wishes.

Unfortunately, being human is not that simple. Toddlers are not clones of the parents, and they have their own wishes, needs, and plans. Sometimes these do not clash with the larger interests of the family. Many times they do. The toddler needs to learn from the parents' reactions when a particular behavior is not acceptable and cannot be permitted.

At its best, discipline is a form of teaching inner controls. The techniques for doing this vary with the toddler's developmental skills. The preverbal or barely verbal toddler can understand language but is helped best if the parent simultaneously takes action to stop or redirect behavior. The older, verbal toddler has more developed inner controls and can be told what to do and what not to do. However, even senior toddlers (as well as much older children) can test the limits to the point that direct and decisive action is needed to teach them when they have gone too far.

The vignettes that follow illustrate the evolution of different forms of discipline to match the child's developmental needs between 14 and 40 months.

Greg, 14 months, is an active toddler intent on exploring everything that exists at his eye level. He eats the dirt from the living room plants; he sticks his fingers in the electric outlets; he opens the cabinet door below the kitchen sink and rummages in the trash bin; he picks up every little piece of lint or other debris from the floor, looks at it in wonder, and puts it in his mouth.

There is nothing morally wrong in what Greg is doing, but his actions are messy, dangerous, and disruptive. His parents have toddler-proofed the house in every way they could imagine, but Greg always finds something they did not think of. This period is very tiresome for most parents. Again and again they need to say "no" and redirect the child to acceptable pursuits.

Sometimes it looks as if the child is learning nothing, but every bit helps. Soon Greg begins to hesitate before approaching the forbidden goal. He then starts to check the parent's face before proceeding. These behaviors indicate that the memory of the parents' prohibitions and redirection is beginning to compete with Greg's irrepressible impulse to do what he wants.

Although the process will continue for a long time, Greg is beginning to acquire the rudiments of what will eventually become a conscience. He is starting this process by having to obey external directives of right and wrong to guide his behavior.

Joel, 2 years old, bites his parents and friends when he is angry with them. This has caused friction between Joel's parents and the other parents, who do not relish seeing the marks of Joel's teeth on their children's faces and arms. Some children are now reluctant to play with Joel even when he is not angry. Joel's own parents are sometimes uneasy about coming close to him for fear of his bites.

Joel is a little boy who always enjoyed sucking and has given up his mother's breast and the bottle with great reluctance. His anger at having to relinquish these pleasures is expressed in an urge to bite when his feelings become too difficult to control. The mouth, that old receptacle of pleasure, now becomes a handy instrument for revenge.

Understanding Joel does not mean condoning what he is doing. His parents tell him firmly that he cannot bite and remove him from the situation when he does. In response, Joel begins to bite himself. His behavior is telling us that he understands his parents' disapproval and is trying to comply, but his impulses are too powerful for his fledgling mechanisms of inner control.

We can help a barely verbal toddler flooded with emotion by providing him with an alternative way of channeling his urge to bite or to strike out. His parents provided Joel with a teether and told him he could bite that. It took Joel a while to make the transition, but after a week or so he was biting his teether with gusto. It worked: He stopped biting himself as well as others.

The ongoing evolution of his inner controls became clear a year later, when at 36 months the now verbal Joel looked at his newborn brother and said: "Mom, it's true I can *want* to bite, but I cannot bite, right?" Joel's wishes to bite are still ready to resurface, but he can now stop himself from doing something he knows to be wrong. He is beginning to have an internalized sense of right and wrong—namely, a conscience.

Sonya, 2½ years old, is at dinner with her parents and four dinner guests. She begins to sing loudly, making it hard for the adult conversation to continue. Her mother humors her, diverts her attention from the guests, and sings along for a couple of minutes. When the mother goes back to talking with the adults, Sonya shrieks, "Sing with me!" Taken aback, the mother returns to singing. The father says: "Don't sing so loudly," but he listens on. Everybody's attention is on Sonya. This continues for the next 30 minutes. Sonya protests loudly whenever the parents try to go back to adult conversation, and each time the child protests the mother resumes singing with her. The guests finish their dinner with upset stomachs.

What is wrong with this scene? Shouldn't adults yield to little children who want attention? Aren't the dinner guests unreasonable to want adult conversation in the presence of a 2-year-old?

It is never too early to begin teaching children that everybody deserves a turn, and that no one person can monopolize everybody's attention against their will. If the parents had told Sonya at the first loud interruption that she should lower her voice because she was hurting people's ears, and if they had sung along with her for a couple of minutes but then gone back to their guests, this would have taught Sonya that she was one more participant in a social situation, not the only one.

Sonya's protests needed to be met with a firm statement that she had her turn and now it was the turn of others. Later she could have another turn. If she escalated, it would have been appropriate to take her to her room and have a private talk with her about the importance of letting other people talk too. Then she could be asked if she was ready to go back.

Of course, most mothers know that they have to split their attention in many social situations—one ear and one eye for responding to the toddler, the other eye and ear for the social scene. This is one of the most trying aspects of having a toddler. Tiring as it is, this split parental attention is needed to teach toddlers to become partners rather than tyrants in social gatherings.

Cynthia, 40 months, is having a bad afternoon. She has just learned that her parents are going out that night. Although she will be staying with a teenager she knows and likes, Cynthia takes her parents' outing as a personal offense. Instead of using the advance notice to prepare herself for the good-bye, she engages in a full-scale guerilla attack to convince her mother not to go. Every 20 minutes or so, she sobs: "I don't want you to go." Being gifted with an unusual ability to put feelings into words, she elaborates handsomely on her inner experience: "I will miss you too much"; "Why are you going without me?"; "I will be too sad."

Cynthia's mother feels saddened herself by her daughter's experience but also manipulated by the child's precocious ability to make her feel guilty by describing in such detail how badly she feels. Torn between these two sets of feelings, the mother alternates between a cheerful reassurance that Cynthia will be fine, admonishments that the child should get herself together and stop whining, and threats (not pursued) that she will be sent to her room if she continues with her complaints. Cynthia's behavior continues unabated, and it escalates when the baby-sitter arrives and the parents get ready to leave. The child clings to her mother, screaming: "Don't leave!"

Cynthia's mother is unwittingly playing into her daughter's inability to contain her anxiety. Her forbearance and her reluctance to put a drastic stop to her daughter's complaints are interpreted by the child as an agreement that she has the right not just to express her feelings but to badger her mother with them.

Cynthia would be helped by a less patient response. She needs to be told firmly that her behavior is not fair and that she is spoiling the time she and her mother are together. This is a situation when withdrawing affection and approval is called for, to help a child learn to control herself.

One may ask, won't Cynthia feel guilty if she is told she is behaving badly? If she does, her ability to feel guilty will actually speak well for Cynthia's emotional development. As they grow, children (like adults) need to experience remorse when they do something wrong. Guilt is a useful emotion when it is felt in response to specific damaging behavior. It is only unhealthy when it is pervasive, as in the case of children who constantly worry about doing something wrong and become inhibited in their ability to assert themselves.

Peers and older siblings are sometimes better teachers than parents in this regard. They show in no uncertain terms that they do not like what the child is doing, and the child learns from this response. Parents are often too worried about inducing guilt or making the child feel unloved if they express disapproval or withdraw affection. They make themselves act as if they feel equally loving regardless of the child's behavior. This could not be true, and neither the parent nor the child really believes it. The pretense of ongoing benevolence and affection in the face of objectionable behavior is actually quite damaging, because it is not genuine and toddlers can see through it. Real emotion is an important element in helping children understand how their actions affect others and in building inner controls.

In summary, toddlers cannot become socially acceptable and emotionally healthy human beings without their parents' help in modulating, containing, and finding alternative ways of channeling their negative emotions. Preverbal toddlers need to direct their impulses to hit and bite into activities that will not hurt others—hammering on a toy bench instead of on a baby, biting a teether instead of a peer. As the child becomes more verbal, the parental expectations for appropriate behavior can increase. The child can be expected to put feelings into words instead of acting on them, and the parent can express disapproval when the child fails to do so. Even with verbal children, however, energetic action will be needed at times to curtail objectionable behavior. As the case of Cynthia illustrates, a very articulate child can talk about feeling as a form of aggression. When the parent feels verbally battered by the child, it is just as appropriate to stop verbal aggression as it is to stop physical acts.

The good news is that, far from threatening the parent–child partnership, firm limits actually strengthen it. A partnership is based on the ability to encompass a full range of feelings and the knowledge that harmony is not destroyed by a good fight.

CHAPTER NINE

When Parents Divorce

TODDLERS ARE DEEPLY AFFECTED BY FAMILY STRIFE AND BY THEIR PARents' divorce. I remember a little 18-month-old who stood between his parents as they fought, yelling at them to stop. After the parents separated, he called out tearfully for whichever parent was not with him at the time. When his father brought him back to his mother's house, the child clung to him and refused to let him go. After the father managed to leave, this little boy hit his mother, threw himself on the floor crying loudly, and angrily fought off her attempts to console him. This went on for many weeks. His anguish subsided only after much reassurance by both of his parents that they continued to love him and would always come back to him.

Not all toddlers are equally overt in showing their distress. Individual temperament as well as the parents' comfort in allowing expression of negative emotions have a strong influence on each child's particular way of showing pain, anger, and fear. Sometimes the adult needs to glean the toddler's innermost feelings from the subtlest of cues.

Regardless of how readily they express their distress, it is safe to assume that to some degree all toddlers worry about what will happen to them when their parents separate. They miss the absent parent and the family routine. They are afraid that they too are on the verge of being left. They are angry, for different reasons, at both the parent who stays and at the one who leaves.

This need not be a source of crippling guilt for divorcing parents, although some degree of remorse is probably inevitable. In the long run, children may well be better off when they're spared the daily experience of witnessing anger, tension, or aloofness between the parents. Follow-up studies suggest that most children of divorced parents develop in healthy ways when the parents are attuned to the child's responses and remain emotionally available in spite of their own distress.[1,2]

Some of the toddlers' reactions to divorce occur because young children tend to put themselves squarely at the center of whatever happens around them. A happy and well-adjusted little girl, watching a lion roar in the zoo, reflected: "He's roaring because he wants to eat me for breakfast." She could not imagine that the lion had his own private reasons to roar. In her mind, such an impressive display had to involve her in some way. Piaget[3] referred to this feature of early thinking as "egocentrism," not because children are selfish but because they understand an event subjectively, through their own reactions to it. Their understanding of the relation between cause and effect is centered on their own capacity to make things happen. As a result, young children react to an event in terms of how it affects them. In other words, children reason by applying to themselves the real or imagined consequences of an event.

On the basis of this rudimentary form of logic, the toddler's unspoken (and unspeakable) train of associations in cases of divorce goes approximately like this:

- "If daddy left, then people can go away, and if so maybe mommy will leave me too."
- "If mommy stopped loving daddy, maybe she will stop loving me."
- "If mommy and daddy got angry and don't want to live together any more, maybe they won't want to live with me either when they get angry at me."

These inferences are of course inaccurate, but they are emotionally compelling nevertheless. A toddler whose parents are divorcing is discovering, much too prematurely, the bitter truth that human relations can be brittle and that bonds of affection and commitment do not always hold.

Once the toddler's basic trust that mom and dad will always be there is shaken, other anxieties follow. In fact, the toddler's emerging ability to fantasize enables her to imagine scenarios that may frighten her more than the actual reality she is experiencing. A child who was frightened by her parents' fighting fantasized that wild animals would attack her; another child who found himself in the middle of a custody battle developed fears of being kidnapped by a stranger. The challenge for divorcing parents is to convey to their child, in the midst of their personal distress, that they will continue to love her and take care of her, and that moms and dads may leave each other but in their hearts they never leave their child.

A calm explanation that mommy and daddy will no longer live together is the best place to start, together with a simple description of the specific plans the parents have in mind and an assurance that they will continue to take care of the child. Some toddlers ask many questions once given

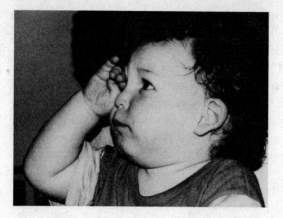

this basic information. Others are too little or too frightened to ask. If the parents are receptive to spoken and unspoken questions, both immediately after the separation and as the questions change in the course of development, the child will learn that this is not a taboo topic and that he is entitled to try to understand it as well as he can.

Divorce as Secure Base Disruption

Divorce can be viewed as the toddler's loss of the secure base represented by the family constellation. This is because toddlers do not use only their individual mother or father as a source of security: they are also acquiring a sense of the family as a unit of care and establishing equally intense but qualitatively different relationships with each family member.

This means that in the normal course of events toddlers are learning to relate to more than one person simultaneously, to share attention, and to relinquish exclusiveness in family interactions. They are not only active participants in the family's dynamics but also watch intently from the sidelines as family members interact with each other. In doing so they learn much about their parents and siblings and begin to make generalizations about human relations. When these complex relationships and interactions are sharply curtailed and modified following marital separation, the toddler and the parents face the task of recreating a secure base that is newly adapted to the changed family conditions.

Like all change, this loss and rebuilding of a secure base seldom proceeds uneventfully. Grief and anger are inseparable components of family dissolution, just as they are inseparable components of any other form of loss. The toddler cannot be spared the experience of witnessing strong emotions in her parents or feeling them herself. She can, however, be helped to go through this difficult situation with relatively little emotional damage if her parents remain emotionally available in spite of their own pain.

Bodily movements often carry strong psychological meanings. With young children in particular, motion conveys emotion more powerfully than words. In the second year of life, motion is centered on the achievement of balance, and the risk of losing this balance becomes a central concern. Physical balance stands as a symbol for emotional balance, in child play as well as in adult imagery. Just as they spend endless hours trying to master the fear of falling, toddlers often set up situations where balance is precarious as a way of expressing uncertainty and mastering the anxiety that goes with it. Two children referred for help during their parents' divorce used this avenue of expression quite graphically.

Barbara is with her parents in the therapist's office playing with some toys. The conversation turns to the parents' conflicting wishes about Barbara's custody. Barbara stops playing and asks her mother to lift her up and place her on the fireplace mantelpiece. Her mother complies and then stands nearby. The child spends the rest of the session on the mantelpiece, clearly afraid of falling but refusing to get down.

Terry's father wants to build a better relationship with his son and hopes that the therapist will help him achieve this goal. However, he is so angry at his wife for leaving him that he cannot stop himself from cursing her even in his son's presence. After listening for a few minutes, Terry walks silently toward the play staircase, climbs up, and perches himself precariously at the top. He seems both afraid of falling and determined to stay where he is. When he finally gets down, he systematically puts all the contents of the doll house (doll house included) upside down.

These two children are showing that they feel off balance, barely able to hold on. They are wordlessly asking the parent to stay very close and to help them feel secure.

Sometimes children become overburdened by the need to keep themselves in balance and long for happier, simpler times. At the end of an intensely emotional therapy session with his father, Terry buries his head on his lap and says: "I am just a baby."

What Do Toddlers Understand?

Divorcing parents often hope that their little ones are barely aware of what is happenign around them, that they do not notice the strife and the dissension and the unexplained absences from the dinner table or the parental bedroom. But toddlers do notice and they form their notions of what is happening much before they are able to speak. The following excerpt from a therapeutic session provides a clear illustration of a mother's wishes to protect her daughter from knowing about her father's departure and the child's own very clear feelings on the matter.

. . . this led into a discussion of Moira's nightmares and (the therapist) asked if Moira had been sleeping better. The mother answered that Moira was still waking up and often cried in her sleep. She then started talking about her husband. The therapist asked what Moira had been told about the separation. The mother answered that she had never spoken to Moira about it because the child was only 18 months at the time. The mother thought Moira was too young to understand it. Moira (now 26 months) was sitting next to her mother during this conversation. The therapist turned to her and said: "Mommy and I are talking about your daddy, Moira." At this, Moira looked directly at the therapist, then at her mother, jumped out of her chair and began to race wildly from the living room to the adjoining kitchen, hall, and back again. The therapist asked the mother how she understood this; the mother replied she had never seen Moira acting so wildly. The therapist asked whether perhaps Moira was scared and needed to feel safe. At this point Moira was running wildly into the bathroom and fell down. The mother picked her up, cuddled her and after a while she asked: "Were you scared because we were talking about your daddy?" Moira looked straight at her mother and said "yes." The mother continued: "Does it hurt you because daddy is gone?" Moira looked down but again said "yes." The mother asked yet again: "Des it make you mad because daddy went away?" Moira again looked directly at her mother and said "yes." She then got up and ran into the bathroom. The mother turned to the therapist and commented: "I didn't think she could ever feel that way. Is it possible for someone 18 months old to understand that? He was hardly around and he paid so little attention to her." She was continuing to talk about her husband when Moira returned and started crawling all over her mother. The mother said: "Do you want me to stop talking about your daddy?" Moira nodded her head in a silent yes. Her mother said: "Moira, listen to me. I want you to know that I love you and I will never leave you. Do you understand?" Moira shook her head and buried it deep into her mother's shoulder. They both rocked each other silently for a while.

This sequence shows clearly that toddlers do notice that a parent has left the home and may grieve without ever saying a word about their loss. Many children harbor secret worries from a very early age, just as Moira did. When not recognized and alleviated by an understanding adult, these worries reappear in disguised form as nightmares, fears of separation, inexplicable terrors, frequent and intense tantrums, negativism, renewed bedwetting, or a myriad other symptoms that can be best understood as the child's cry for help. The symptoms are in effect saying: "Pay attention, Mom and Dad. All is not well with me."

Symptoms may change their appearance. A fearful child may instead become overly aggressive, and nightmares may disappear but be replaced by biting. Symptoms may shift but they do not go away until the underlying problem is relieved. As Reginald Lourie, a wise pediatrician and child psychoanalyst, once put it: "Babies are very patient. They keep on showing us the problem over and over until we understand. The more we understand what children need, the better we will do in helping them."

It is worth nothing that Moira's nightmares did recede when her mother started talking with her about her daddy, empathizing with her anger and sadness about losing him, and reassuring her that mommy would not go away. Moira's mother felt awkward at first speaking about these difficult topics. However, her child's positive response helped her to realize that these issues needed to be addressed, and she became progressively more confident in doing so. This mother also found that, paradoxically, talking about how hard it was that daddy wasn't there actually made his absence more bearable, both for her child and for herself.

Longing for the Way Things Were

Infants and toddlers have well-developed memories. They remember people, events and experiences even when they cannot describe them in words. In fact, the earliest memories are based on perceptual rather than linguistic events. Newborns are able to recognize the smell of their mother's milk and the sound of her voice.[4,5] By 5 to 7 months, infants can store visual memories and retrieve them on cue. For example, babies who watched the photograph of a stranger's face for less than one minute were able to recognize that same face more than a week later.[6] Moreover, at this age babies are already able to recall the specific emotional experience associated with an event. In one study, babies smiled at the mere sight of a silent puppet that had actively "played" with them and made them laugh a week earlier.[7]

If infants can do all this in the first 6 months of life, what can we expect of toddlers? There is much observational evidence that they remember emotionally tinged events many months after their occurrence. At 18 months, Rafi pantomimed the exact sequence of his last medical checkup six months earlier as soon as his mother told him that they were going to the doctor. He did not speak fluently, but he laid down on his mother's lap, pulled at his ear, opened his mouth with gasping sounds, motioned with his hands as if someone was looking into his throat, and said, "No, no." It was clear that he remembered what had happened and did not wish to repeat it.

All this goes to show that out of sight does not meant out of mind for toddlers: they remember clearly and keenly. This continuity of experience exists also when their parents separate. Children hold in their memories the family routines that took place when the family still lived together and may feel an acute sense of longing for the way things were.

Sammy refuses to get out of the car when he and his mother arrive at a favorite restaurant. He puts up a real fight when she

tries to coax him out. It dawns on her that this was a cherished family outing when the parents lived together. She asks: "Does it make you miss daddy when we come here?" Sammy sobs: "Yes."

Tanya clings to a stuffed animal her father gave her, and hugs it tightly when she goes to bed.

Sylvia refuses to listen to her mother's lullaby. She says: "That's daddy's song!" Her father had liked singing that lullaby when he put her to bed.

Cameron puts up a fuss when a dinner guest sits at the table in "daddy's place." He also wants to keep everybody from sitting in "daddy's chair" in the living room.

Gabriel puts the mommy doll and daddy doll in bed together. He says: "All right now."

Marina and her mother go to a summer resort where she had watched her father hunting ducks the year before. Marina says: "Daddy, duck, bang, bang."

These quick glimpses into children's inner lives, their memories and their longings are often missed, or, more sadly, dismissed by people who believe that toddlers cannot remember or feel as intensely and genuinely as adults. Yet it is these glimpses that capture most eloquently the child's experience. Toddlers do not give speeches about their inner lives (or about anything else). They rely on symbols, games, facial expressions, sudden silences, body language, and half-sentences to convey what they remember and how they feel about it. They also rely on adults to decode these messages and to respond to them.

Because of this, it is helpful to talk reassuringly to the child about past experiences. This applies to cherished routines that are no longer viable in the new family composition as well as to the less palatable scenes that tend to precede a divorce—arguments, tears, even physical fights.

Toddlers feel emotionally torn by the parents' separation. On one hand, they may experience relief that the household is calmer and the difficult confrontations have come to an end. On the other hand, they miss the moments of togetherness that did exist, and most of all they miss the parent who left but feel guilty that this longing betrays in some obscure

way the parent who stays. They worry that loving one parent will make the other parent angry at them.

It is confusing to have all these contradictory feelings at the same time, yet this is the very stuff of emotional life. Talking with the child, *while the child is having these feelings,* about missing mommy or daddy, being angry, or being scared enables the toddler to cope with these intense feelings without being overwhelmed by them. Reminiscing about the good times ("Remember when daddy played horsey with you in the park? We laughed and laughed!") and explaining the bad times ("Daddy and I yelled at each other. Sometimes I can't help yelling when I'm angry but I don't like it.") help to integrate the past with the present instead of banishing it to the underground caves of the child's imagination.

While helpful to the child, broaching these topics can be taxing for the parents. They have to make themselves put aside feelings of anger and resentment towards their spouse in order to protect their child's relationship with the other parent. This is difficult to do. It calls for a conscious effort to distinguish between one's ex-spouse and the child's other parent, although both roles are played by the same person. It also calls for an effort to keep in mind the positive attributes of the other parent, and to remember that those attributes can help the child even if the marriage is doomed.

In the section below we will examine some of the factors that interfere with the parents' ability to protect their child from the anger and bitterness they may feel toward each other.

The Divorced Mother's Situation

Although every woman's situation is different and uniquely personal, most women's experiences are influenced in some way by the demographics of divorce. The figures are sobering:

- Divorce affects the finances of men and women differently. Women's income declines while men's income increases at least in the years immediately following the breakup of the marriage. The estimates vary, but according to one study women's income decreases by 30 percent while men's income rises by 15 percent.[8]
- As a general rule, women's economic situations improve more slowly if they do not remarry.[8,10]
- Over 95 percent of children from divorced families live with their mothers, a figure that has not changed since 1960. Currently, more than 10 million American children live in families headed by a single mother who is either separated or divorced.[9]
- Forty percent of families headed by women have incomes below the poverty level.[12]
- Divorced fathers often lose contact with their children, a situation that places sole responsibility for raising the children on the mother. In a survey of 1,423 children from divorced families funded by the National Institutes of Mental Health, 52 percent had not heard from their fathers in the past year, and 35 percent of children in this group had had no contact with their fathers for five years.[5]

These interlocking sets of facts have a profound influence on the everyday life and emotional experience of divorced mothers, regardless of their children's age. Financial worries, major changes in life-style as the result of reduced economic resources, and primary responsibility for the children put serious stresses on the lives of divorced mothers.

Women with babies and toddlers may have an even more difficult time because child-rearing habits and routines are not yet fully established, because alternative child care is scarce and expensive, and because very young children place high demands on their mothers' energy and emotional resources. In spite of these difficulties, many women successfully meet the challenges of being a single mother to their young children.[1]

The Divorced Father's Situation

Fathers' feelings about their divorce tend to center around two major issues: the financial burden of support payments and the psychological burden of limited access to the child. These issues are often intertwined in conflict situations. Many fathers believe that the mother withholds visitation to enforce support payments and that the children are used as ransom to achieve financial aims. A common complaint is that fathers have to work longer hours or even take an additional job to meet their court obligations for child and spousal support. Some men argue that the increased financial burden leaves them with less time and energy to remain active in their children's lives.[13]

The census data do not support these perceptions of the impact of divorce on men as a group. However, a subset of divorced fathers is certainly faced with these predicaments. They may find themselves having to support two households on a single income. Their access to the children may be restricted or closely regulated by the mother, either as a form of pressure or because of disagreements about child-rearing styles. The father may be rebuked or criticized by the mother in front of the child for failing to fulfill financial or parental responsibilities.

Regardless of the legitimacy of the mutual complaints, the bitterness between the parents can set up volatile situations where conflict escalates, often without warning. This is not difficult to understand. Divorce touches parents at their very core, making them feel alone, vulnerable, and unprotected. These are the very conditions that trigger tantrums in toddlers, and it is these same conditions that lead to angry battles between adults.

Divorce can bring out the worst in us, and it usually does. Feelings of resentment, victimization, and rage often gain the upper hand, leading to a desire for revenge and to efforts at settling old scores. These impulses can easily override the parents' best efforts at retaining self-control. Sometimes the only hope for containing punitive action is remembering that the children are the first to suffer from parental strife, both within the marriage and after the divorce.

"Divide the Living Child"

"And the king said, Divide the living child in two, and give half to one and half to the other."
                                                        —Kings, III, 24

Could King Solomon foresee that his predicament in deciding the fate of a contested child would one day become a commonplace event, as parents sue each other for the right to their child? We will never know, but it is sobering to consider how often we face this biblical dilemma in modern garb.

In fact, we may think that the great king's quandary was trivial when compared to present-day legal conflicts. Solomon could count on the rapacious self-interest of the false mother, who was blinded by her own desire to the point that she acquiesced to a verdict that would destroy the child. Today's custody battles are less clear-cut; both parties sincerely believe that they are trying to protect the best interests of the child.

Perhaps the most useful way of applying the wisdom of Solomon to current circumstances is to think of the biblical drama in psychological terms. Every parent fighting for his or her child's custody personifies the three characters of the story at one and the same time. Each parent carries within the potential to become the false mother, who cannot distinguish between the child's welfare and her own needs and who would rather see the child destroyed than renounce her claim. Similarly, each parent can embody the loving true mother, whose wish to protect her child overrides her own self-interest.

Each parent also has available within him- or herself the wisdom of Solomon, who represents the point of balance between two extremes: the readiness on one hand to sacrifice the child to one's own needs, and the willingness on the other hand to renounce a legitimate personal claim for the child's sake. By transforming a clash of petty personal wills into a test of the mothers' deepest motivations, Solomon could find a solution that was based not on the right to possess but on the willingness to protect and love.

Children do best when they have access to a mother and a father who can put aside their personal grievances to work together on behalf of their child. This need not mean becoming friends or remaining lovers. It does not mean brushing aside legitimate demands. It does entail recognizing that each parent has a unique part to play in the child's life, that neither parent can fill the role of the other in the child's development, and that neither parent can replace the other in the child's affection.

The child's relationship with each parent needs to be kept separate from the relationship of the former spouses to each other. A toddler should not become one parent's ally against the other, and should not have to bear witness to the parents' mutual complaints and recriminations.

In spite of this, putting each other down in front of the child is the most common mistake made by divorcing parents. They often find fault with every detail of the former spouse's parenting, and berate each other for feeding the child junk food, not keeping her clean, overstimulating her, not having a predictable schedule, being overly permissive or harshly restrictive. They also complain that the other parent does not provide a thorough account of what transpired while the child was in his or her care—what they did, who they saw, where they went.

Those problems often lead to active efforts to curtail or restrict visitation. In most cases, this is a serious mistake. In the long run, eating one or even four cookies too many or missing a nap are far less important for a toddler's welfare than being allowed to establish comfortable relationships with both parents.

Parents who criticize each other are seldom arguing specifically about the child's diet or daily routine. They are actually struggling for sole control over the child's life. They are unconsciously setting themselves up as the ideal parent, the one that the child should love the best.

In accepting the value of their child's separate relationship with the former spouse, parents must come to grips with the sad realization that they will have no access to a major part of the toddler's life. They will not be able to watch as the child forms a relationship with the other parent and with a new and different circle of that parent's friends. They will not share the child's developmental milestones and daily joys and tribulations with a partner who is just as passionately committed to the child. There will be large areas of the child's experience that they will neither understand nor oversee.

These are some of the enduringly painful consequences of divorce. In an effort to avoid them, many parents try to make themselves the one and only center of their child's life and to push the other parent to a peripheral role. When they do this, parents unwittingly impoverish their child's emotional development and deprive themselves of a valuable source of support—the other parent's emotional investment in the child.

Toddlers are immeasurably relieved when they can watch their parents join forces on their behalf. A mother who greets her child back by saying, "My goodness, your boots are all muddy! You and your daddy must have had quite an adventure!" is contributing to her child's peace of mind much more profoundly than a mother who greets him with a worried or angry comment about his father's negligence in issues of cleanliness. A father who can say sympathetically to his daughter, "Mommy takes a long time saying good-bye because she loves you so much" is protecting his child's mental health much more thoroughly than another who responds to the identical situation by snarling at the mother: "Stop clinging to her."

Even when one parent infuriates the other, it is possible to frame the situation in a way that supports the child's self-esteem. One mother, seriously inconvenienced by the father's tardiness in picking up the child for the weekend, was able to respond to the toddler's clear worry and discomfort by saying, "Don't worry, honey. Sometimes your daddy has to work late. I am sure he is trying to get here soon because he wants to see you." (Later, she discussed the situation with the father when the child could not hear.) Another mother responded to a similar situation in a less constructive way. She blurted out, "He only cares about himself. He doesn't care that you and I are waiting!"

The first mother kept herself focused on her child's need to be reassured about the father's continuing (if imperfect) love. The second mother could not contain her anger at feeling abandoned and exploited by her child's father. She was unable to allow her daughter to develop a different and more positive relationship, and coached her to feel as exploited and unloved by him as she did.

Toddlers need their parents' assistance to restore some confidence that in spite of the divorce, each parent can continue serving as a secure base in the absence of the other. If the parents support each other, the child will be able to integrate their separate contributions into a cohesive sense of himself as reliably cherished and protected by the two people most important to him.

If, on the contrary, the parents undermine each other, the child will internalize each parent's mistrust of the other, and will become anxious about her own well-being while in their care. She will also worry about betraying one parent when she is having a good time with the other.

These anxieties are much too burdensome for a young child. Each parent needs to reassure him, and mean it, that it is OK to love and enjoy being with the other, and that both his mother and his father love him and will help each other to take care of him.

Missing the Father

Most children of divorced families live with their mother[7] and have varying degrees of contact with their father. Because of this, missing the father and waiting for him to call or visit are major components of their divorce experience.

While ideally children of all ages would profit from regular and frequent access to their fathers, toddlers are in special need of a reliable visitation pattern because of their unique cognitive and emotional needs.

The toddler's relationships are still in the process of evolution and highly influenced by external circumstances such as changes in the parents' physical and emotional availability. A relationship that had been comfortable and secure may become tinged with anxiety if the parent withdraws from the child. Conversely, an anxious relationship can improve significantly if the parent becomes more emotionally attuned.[14,15]

A few days of no contact with the parent can be far more unsettling for a toddler than for an older child, who has a better internalized image of the parent, more sophisticated coping mechanisms (including language, symbolic play, and capacity to delay gratification) and a broader network of relationships and activities to help in withstanding the separation. Toddlers respond strongly to broken promises and failed visitations. The day before Terry and his father were at a scheduled therapist's session, the father had failed to show up for a visit with the boy. At the session, Terry expressed his feelings about his disappointment. This is what the therapist reported:

Terry and his father came a few minutes late. It was immediately clear that there was a great deal of tension between them. Terry was not looking at his father and Mr. F. in turn seemed angry with his son. Mr. F. started the session by complaining that Terry had put up a fuss when he picked him up to come to the session. The therapist asked what might make Terry put up such a fuss. After much digression, it emerged that Mr. F. had missed his regular visit with Terry the previous day. While Mr. F. talked to the therapist, but not to his son, about the reasons for this, Terry went about overturning every chair in the room and then began to lightly kick every one of them. As his father continued to talk without paying attention to him, Terry muttered very quietly, as if to himself: 'Motherfucker!'

Most toddlers do not have Terry's opportunity to express how they feel in the safety of a therapeutic session, where their behavior can be observed and understood and where they can be helped to experience and cope with their feelings. Even in these favorable circumstances, it was ultimately Terry's father who could best help his son, by becoming more aware of his importance to the child and by arranging his schedule so that visits were given the priority they deserved.

Toddlers who miss their father and have no consistent access to him may develop a longing for him that manifests itself in sleep disturbances and other symptoms. The child psychiatrist James Herzog reports that in a six-month period, he saw 12 little boys, ranging in age from 18 to 28 months, who were brought to the clinic because of night terrors. The children would wake up at night screaming and calling for their father. In each one of the cases, the parents had separated or divorced in the previous four months. Herzog found that the mother alone was unable to help the child, but the assistance of the father or another male figure did bring about a decrease in the child's fears. He concluded that these toddlers were responding to a developmental need for a father figure with whom they could identify and who could serve as a model as they moved from the mother-oriented world of infancy to finding a gender-specific identity as boys.[16]

Girls, too, are in need of a father as they learn about their femininity and practice how to relate to the opposite sex. Their longing for their father may be expressed in less dramatic ways than the boys studied by Herzog. It may also be more easily overlooked, because girls as a group are more likely than boys to internalize negative feelings and to make often superhuman efforts to be "good" (which they identify with being undemanding). They may manage their longing for their father by developing an idealized fantasy of an imaginary father who is perfect and unfailingly loving. They may also insist that another male figure in their life is their real father.

Antonia, a bright 30-month-old, had not seen her father or heard from him for two months. She knew that he lived far away and often kissed his picture, which she had placed carefully by her bed. At the same time, she developed an ongoing dialogue with an imaginary father who lived in the garden just outside of her room and who knew all her secrets. She also insisted that either her loving maternal grandfather or her uncle were her real fathers. She was able to maintain all these contradictory beliefs at the same time. It seemed as if her efforts to find another daddy

helped her to compensate for the loss of her father, because when her mother spoke to her about "your daddy" the child knew exactly who was being talked about. When the father finally called Antonia, she refused to speak to him on the phone but later asked to send him a Valentine's Day card. She needed to gain some control over his comings and goings. Taking the initiative in refusing or accepting contact enabled her to do so.

Antonia's grief over her father's elusive role in her life was apparent in other areas as well. She cried inconsolably over minor incidents at nursery school and became overly anxious when she could not immediately find an object that she was looking for. The anger inherent in her grief was expressed in stubborn defiance of her mother and in her gleefulness when she killed the ants that abounded in her garden. Like the little boys described by Herzog, Antonia also woke up crying at night, complaining of monsters that threatened to attack her.

Blaming the Mother

Antonia's defiance of her mother illustrates a common phenomenon among toddlers: they automatically blame their mothers for whatever goes wrong in their experience.

This unpalatable tendency is a logical by-product of the mother's centrality in the young child's emotional life. She is all-powerful in the baby's and toddler's eyes simply by virtue of her ability to evoke good and bad feelings. She can make a hurt go away with a kiss, and she can make one's world crumble with a glare. Her absence brings sadness and worry, and her presence restores buoyancy and joy. This is understandable. For as long as the toddler can remember, mommy has been the one who most often feeds and diapers, holds and cuddles, praises and admonishes, ministers and punishes. She is inextricably bounded with the child's sense of who he is. Who else could possibly be responsible for all that happens in his world? Some telling examples:

Mark's aunt, an old-fashioned type, is shocked when she finds him naked on the beach, covering his penis with sand and triumphantly retrieving it again. Like a classical witch from the annals of psychoanalysis, the aunt hisses: "Your penis will fall off if you keep playing with it." Mark's mother shrieks: "That is not true,

Mark. Aunt Helen is just being silly." But it is too late. For the next few hours Mark repeatedly pulls at his penis, as if testing his aunt's prophesy. His mother tells him: "Mark, I think you are still worried about what Aunt Helen told you." "What did she tell me?" asks Mark. "That your penis will fall off," stammers the mother. With utter conviction, Mark replies: "It wasn't Aunt Helen. You told me that." His chagrined mother cannot make him change his mind. For Mark, only his mother could be the origin of such dramatic news, and he changed the facts to fit this perception.

Lisa is severely injured by her father when he suffers a psychotic break. When she recovers consciousness and sees her mother next to her, she screams: "Why did you hurt me like that?"

Mina is clumsy in her efforts to climb a wooden structure and falls on the ground. When her mother rushes to rescue her, Mina hits her, yelling: "Bad mommy!"

Mothers are also seen as the culprits when it comes to divorce. Not only are they all-powerful, they are also most often the ones who stay and are therefore ready targets for the child's anger and grief. When that happens, mothers need to be careful. Their own guilt over the divorce can trick them into accepting the child's blame. They need to find within themselves the calm conviction to say: "I know you are angry at me, but it is not my fault."

Protecting the Mother

Sometimes the reverse happens. The toddler is keenly aware of the mother's pain and depression and feels compelled to protect her. A child may dry her mother's tears, or may try to cajole her out of her sadness by being artificially jolly or extraordinarily good. When a child responds like this, a role reversal takes place. It is the child who attempts to protect and nurture the parent, and the parent may take on the role of a needy and vulnerable child. When this role reversal colors the whole relationship, toddlers become precociously competent and overly mature at the expense of their own age-appropriate emotional spontaneity in asking for help or expressing their needs. The most common expression of precocious competence is the toddlers' worry about the mother's welfare or their excessively solicitousness. A toddler may tell the mother not to worry or ask her if she is all right.

When these behaviors occur repeatedly, it is worthwhile to reflect on their meaning and to assure a child that the mother can and will take care of herself and that it is not the child's responsibility to take care of her. This can be done in simple ways: telling a child what one did while he was gone ("When you were with your daddy I went for a nice walk and saw a very cute puppy"), commenting on pleasant plans or even telling a child not to worry ("I am big and strong and it's my job to be the mommy. It is not your job to take care of me").

When a Parent Is Unfit to Care for the Child

There are, of course, situations where one of the parents turns out to be a reprehensible individual in whose care the child is at substantial risk for physical or psychological harm.

These situations are invariably extremely complex and call for thoughtful evaluation of all the factors involved in a particular case before devising a long-term plan that is appropriately protective of the child. No two situations are alike and it would be inappropriate to search for a single formula that would magically do away with the anguish, hard work, and painful compromises that are usually called for.

The services of an infant mental health professional (a child psychologist, psychiatrist, pediatrician, social worker, or other professional specializing in the emotional issues of the first three years of life) can be most useful and are often crucial in these situations. Talking with an experienced and sympathetic professional can help a frightened parent sort out his or her worries about the spouse's liabilities as a parent from the strong emotions associated with the divorce process itself.

Even when fitness to parent is not at stake, many parents engage in thoughtless, uncaring, or even objectionable actions in the course of a failing marriage. Other parents suffer from chronic character flaws that were manifest even in the happier times of the family. For aggrieved spouses, it is often difficult to watch their toddler adore and admire a mommy or a daddy they know to be undeserving of such uncritical love. They may experience a wish to set the child straight, to tell the child what mommy or daddy are "really like." Often this impulse is experienced as a wish to protect the child from disappointment later on. However, this is hardly ever a task that parents should take upon themselves. Children learn to discern the weaknesses of their parents as they grow older and as they are readier to see the parents with more objective eyes. A toddler needs to idealize her parents because through their perceived strength and goodness she learns to find those qualities in herself.

Introducing a New Partner

Sometimes the divorce is intertwined with the presence of new partners in the parents' lives. These partners may have children of their own who are of the same or different gender and the same age or older or younger than the toddler. Circumstances vary greatly and each situation has its own rewards and challenges for the toddler.

In spite of the diversity, general rules are worth keeping in mind:

It is best not to rush toddlers into making a close emotional connection with a new partner and his or her children. Particularly if the adults' relationship is new and still tentative, the pressure of bringing children into it too fast can strain it in unhealthy ways. Sometimes divorcing parents long to reconstitute a family and move too swiftly into a new commitment, bringing the toddler into it. A gradual deepening of the connections is preferable because it protects the toddler from yet another loss if the new relationship does not work out.

Sometimes a new partner wants to become the child's emotional parent. If the toddler's own mother or father are not involved, this willingness to serve a parental role is of course a wonderful opportunity for the toddler. If, on the other hand, both parents are active in the child's life, it is not a good idea to try to replace them. The stepparent does not need to compete with the same-sex parent, or vice versa. Each has a valuable part to play in the child's life.

Toddlers in divorced families fare best when the adults respect each other's importance for the child. Toddlers are not confused by their relation to more than two parenting figures if the adults themselves are confident of their roles. Stepparents and their children can enrich the toddler's lives directly and by being a source of emotional support and stability to the parents.

Is There an Ideal Custody Arrangement?

The search for a perfect custody arrangement is like the search for the perfect mate or the perfect diet—elusive, ultimately futile, but also most tantalizing.

Custody arrangements go through fashions. It used to be taken for granted that mother care was the best and that the children should stay with the mother and have periodic visitations with the father. Then joint custody became the arrangement of choice, until it became clear that the various schedules often called for more cooperation and flexible negotiation than the parents could muster even while married.

There is no "quick fix" for custody arrangements. All of them call for hard work, flexibility, willingness to accommodate, and ability to negotiate. It is even possible that one type of arrangement may work better at one time and a different type may be desirable later, as the child's needs and family circumstances change.

Following are some factors that are useful to consider in arriving at arrangements consistent with a toddler's needs.

- What is the child's temperament? Is she easily upset by changes in routine, or does she adjust to comings and goings relatively easily? Are separations and reunions emotionally draining for her, so that her responses to transitions affect her general functioning?
- Does the child markedly prefer one parent over the other?
- How verbal is the child? Can she understand verbal explanations of who will pick her up and when? Can she ask questions about what will happen and when?
- Is one parent much better able to provide quality time than the other?
- Can the parents cooperate with each other in setting up transitions and helping the child through them?

In general, joint custody arrangements are likely to work best with relatively flexible children whose distress during transitions can be contained through the parents' help, who can understand verbal explanations and ask even rudimentary questions, who are clearly emotionally invested in both the mother and the father, and whose parents can cooperate with each other so that the separations and reunions occur in a supportive emotional climate.

If these conditions do not exist or if well-intentioned trials show that the child does not fare well in a split custody arrangement, it might be best to consider a single home arrangement with liberal opportunities for access to the noncustodial parent.

It is quite possible that the actual custody arrangement is less important than the spirit in which the agreement is carried out. Custody can be a fertile ground for acting out the unfinished business of the failed marriage. If this is the case, no custody arrangement will serve the child well. If, on the other hand, custody is understood as what it should be—a reasonable arrangement to protect and preserve the child's relationships with both parents—many different arrangements can work basically well.

Helping the Toddler with Transitions

Transitions from mother to father and back again epitomize what is most difficult about divorce: the lost togetherness of the family unit. As the spouses face each other to exchange their child, each of them is confronted most clearly with their mutual resentments and recriminations as well as with their grief over the parting of ways. They are immersed in their own emotions, and hardly at their best to attend to their toddler's own urgent need for support as he is asked to say good-bye to one parent and get ready to adjust to the other.

Separations and reunions can be difficult for toddlers in the best of circumstances. When they take place in a tense emotional climate, the burden on the child increases and she often falls apart. The scenes that ensue can be heartrending, as the toddler clings first to one parent and then to the other, crying and unable to stay or go.

The child's distress is often paralyzing to the parents. Unable to help, they may resort to blaming each other for the child's difficulties. The father may suspect that the mother is influencing the child against him. The mother may see the child's distress as evidence of the father's negligent care or worse.

Transitions from one home to another may always remain a painful time for children. If the parents feel confident that the transitions are necessary, that contact with the other is valuable, this conviction will be transmitted to the toddler and separation distress greatly reduced. Some suggestions that may help:

- Find a private time to speak with your former spouse about the transitions. Explain that you believe the child needs to spend time with each of you and profits from it, and that you would like the transitions to be as free of stress as possible for all concerned. Try to identify the sources of problems, and offer constructive suggestions that apply to both of you. Do not lose your temper or your willingness to continue trying if this approach is not immediately welcomed by your former spouse.
- Before a transition, prepare yourself for it. Try to get in touch with your emotions about the child's departure or return. Are you relieved? Anxious? Angry? Overburdened?
- Prepare your child for the transition. Tell her that mommy or daddy will pick her up for their time together. Whenever possible, spend some quiet time with the child before she is due to leave. However, do not start an engrossing pastime that will be interrupted by the other parent's arrival.
- Use a confident and supportive tone of voice when you talk to the child about going with the other parent. Be ready to acknowledge that it is sad to say good-bye, but be equally ready to remind her that she also has a good time with the other parent.
- Make use of transitional objects—a favorite toy or blanket that the child can take along and bring back.
- Agree with your former spouse that phone calls will not be restricted. Offer to the child the chance to call the other parent when she is with you.
- Speak positively to the child about the other parent and their relationship.

Parents who live apart represent for the child a split in the secure base of an undivided home. The child needs to bring together the split halves to form a cohesive secure base that is internalized and becomes a reliable part of him. In actions and in words, the parents can help in this endeavor by remaining partners in child rearing on behalf of their child.

The Toddler in Child Care

Damian is sitting at a table in his day-care center, slowly moving his jaws and mouth while staring into space. "What are you chewing, Damian?" asks his caregiver. "I'm chewing Mommy," replies Damian dreamily.[1]

DAMIAN'S ANSWER TELLS US WITH HAIKU-LIKE CONCISENESS ABOUT A major aspect of the toddler's child-care experience: missing mommy, yet holding on to her through a combination of memory, hope, and imagination. By chewing on his mother's image, Damian is carrying her in the most reliable place of all—inside himself.

Damian is reminding us that child care is first and foremost about relationships. It is about how to separate from the parents with trust that they will come back. It is also about forming new relationships with the caregiver and with the other children that will be enriching and sustaining in the course of the day.

These two sets of experiences—learning to say bye-bye and enjoying the new hellos—are closely intertwined. When toddlers can separate from the parents with a sadness that is manageable, they are more able to engage with other people than if they are overcome by distress. Conversely, enjoying the child-care setting can help to relieve the toddler's apprehension when the parent leaves.

For the parents, and particularly for mothers, child care is also about relationships. It is about how to let go of their little one with the trust that they are not hurting the child by not being together full-time. It is about going through the day with confidence that the child is well cared for and having a good time, so that this knowledge can compensate for the waves of longing and guilt that are a regular part of the working mother's routine. It is about developing ways of communicating with the child's caregiver that lead to a solid partnership on behalf of the child.

A successful child-care experience calls for careful attention to three major aspects of nonparental care: the daily transitions of departing and reuniting, the quality of the child's emotional experiences in the course of the day, and the quality of the parents' relationship with the caregivers. These three factors remain important regardless of where the child-care arrangements takes place: in the child's home, in the caregiver's home, or in a day-care center.

Making the Transition: Saying Good-bye

Let's examine two contrasting scenes that illustrate some of the pressures of parting for the day.

On Monday Charlie and his mother enjoy a lovely early morning together. The whole family had spent a relaxed weekend. The chores were disposed of without tension between mother and father and there was time to go to the park, play games, and watch a family movie together. This particular Monday morning everybody woke up easily and father took the older children to school in time and without the need for admonishments to hurry up. Charlie's mother is feeling that family harmony is possible

after all, even when both parents work. She dresses Charlie for the day in a playful manner, tells him she will miss him during the day, and chats with him about what they will have for dinner that evening. They sing silly songs on the way to Charlie's child care. When they get there, Charlie's mother lingers a while, telling the caregiver about the pleasant weekend. She then tells Charlie, who had drifted off toward the other children, that she needs to leave. She approaches him, hugs and kisses him, tells him she will see him that evening, and leaves. Charlie looks at the door for a few seconds as she disappears. He sighs with a brief expression of sadness and then rejoins the other children in their play.

On Thursday morning things do not go so smoothly. The whole family is tired from a week of work, school, chores, and nightly homework for the older children, and the weekend seems a long way off. Tempers are short. To compound matters, Charlie puts up a fuss while getting dressed because he wants to wear his green overalls, which are in the laundry. Later he spills his bowl of cereal on the floor. (Fortunately, the dog, a good friend, laps it up.) The mother yells at Charlie and he, not to be outdone, yells back. On the way to the car he trips and falls and cries inconsolably, as if this small accident gives him the chance to release the accumulated tension of the morning. His mother picks him up and cuddles him, but she is keenly aware of the time. They are already 15 minutes late. On the way to child care, she drives fast, changes lanes frequently, and goes through every yellow light. She is totally focused on getting to work as soon as possible and cannot pay attention to Charlie, who is sulking in the back seat. The good-bye at child care is rushed and per-functory. Charlie's mother spends the day with a feeling of guilt and longing for her little boy. She finds herself having trouble concentrating on her work. Images of Charlie's sad face as they said good-bye keep crossing her mind, and she wishes she had spoken with Charlie about the difficult time they had. She wishes she had told him she still loved him and was no longer mad at him. At his child care setting, Charlie mirrors those feelings in his own way. An assertive child with a strong will, today he is particularly prone to get into struggles with his peers. He fights taking a nap and cries bitterly when the caregiver lets another child rather than him sit on her lap. Fortunately, his mother calls him on the phone and tells him she loves him. The mood of both of them picks up a great deal as a result.

These two vignettes illustrate how the same parent–child pair can have different kinds of separation experiences at different times depending on their mood and the circumstances involved. The vignettes also show that a separation begins long before the actual event takes place, and its effects may linger for a prolonged period of time afterwards. The good news is that being conscious of this process can improve things considerably for both parent and child.

Separation has at least two developmental meanings for toddlers. First and foremost, it triggers the fear of losing the parent that is so prevalent at this age. Closely connected with this fear is the fantasy that something they did is prompting the parent to go away; in other words, that they are to blame for this loss because of their bad behavior. A long day away from the parent gives the toddler plenty of time to embroider on these fears, and to worry that mommy or daddy will not pick her up today because she bit the baby or did not go potty or spit out her cereal or refused to wear the dress mom picked out for her.

Acknowledging separation feelings directly and sympathetically is the best way of coping with them. It is actually helpful to tell a toddler "I'll miss you," or "I will think of you during the day," or "It is hard to say good-bye," or "I can't wait to see you at the end of the day." These messages tell the child that he is important to the parent even when they are not together and that out of sight need not mean out of mind. Making up after an early morning conflict is also an important way of reassuring the child that daily conflicts have no bearing on the enduring emotional connection between parent and child.

When parents try not to experience the feelings aroused by separation, they tend to avoid the experience altogether. The parents may sneak out while the child is not paying attention, or say that they are going to the bathroom and coming right back, when, in fact, they are leaving for the day.

Lying to a toddler is usually done to protect the adult's feelings rather than the child's. There is nothing a toddler cannot hear and assimilate if it is age-appropriate and explained in a calm and supportive way, leaving plenty of room for the child's reaction and the questions that he might have as he assimilates the news over time.

Toddlers who are lied to about separations cannot trust what their parents tell them. Some become hypervigilant and clingy because they never know when they will be left. They need to monitor the environment for signs of abandonment because they cannot trust the adults to be forthright about what will happen and when. Other toddlers become dismissive of the importance of relationships. They avoid close emotional ties and adopt an indifferent "Who cares" attitude as a way of coping with the uncertainty of the parents' comings and goings.

Parents who have trouble leaving may do the opposite of sneaking out. They may be unable to leave at all, and linger around the child postponing the moment of saying good-bye. They are persuaded again and again by their child's pleas to stay "a little longer," all the while telling the toddler that they really need to leave. This contrast between what they say and what they do can be quite confusing to their child, who keeps asking them to stay because this strategy is so clearly successful in getting what he wants.

Staying a little longer can certainly be a sensitive response to the child's need if the parent uses this time to talk about the separation and to help the child make the transition to the caregiver, to a peer, or to a favorite activity. If, on the other hand, the parents become trapped in an indecisive sequence of efforts to leave followed by half-hearted decisions to stay longer, the effect is actually counterproductive because children get the message that separations are as emotionally unmanageable as they fear them to be.

Spending the Day in Child Care

The act of saying good-bye is the most noticeable aspect of the parent's departure, but it only marks the beginning of the separation process. The child is now faced with a long day away from the parent. Being apart arouses anxiety and taxes the child's coping resources, but there are ways of keeping the parents' reassuring image alive in the toddler's heart and mind.

Bridging the Parent's Absence

Within the toddler period there are developmental differences in the ease with which the child can adapt to being away from their primary caregiver—most often the mother. Between 12 and 18 months there is an increase in the child's distress over separation. After 24 months, most toddlers have an easier time being away from the mother, and this ease becomes more pronounced after the middle of the second year. The toddler's sustained progress in the areas of memory, language, and symbolic play means that she can bring more sophisticated cognitive and emotional skills to the task of coping with the parent's absence.

This developmental trajectory can guide parental considerations about when to start child care for a toddler. The later it begins the more likely it is that the child will adjust to it more smoothly.

Regardless of when it begins, full-time child care is more taxing to the child than shorter daily separations. There is good observational documentation that part-time child care puts less strain on the child's resources for adaptation than a full eight- or ten-hour day away from home. For most toddlers, their parents are their first and best love, and they experience a sense of relief (even if they do not show it) when they are reunited at the end of the day.

This situation makes it particularly important to build bridges between the child care setting and the home. When the child-care setting is the home—that is, when the caregiver comes to the child's home—the child is surrounded by familiar and reassuring reminders of the parents' presence and of their life together. When child care occurs outside the home, the bridges need to be consciously and conscientiously built and maintained.

Sally Provence and her colleagues pioneered the use of many simple yet effective means of helping the young child with separations in a day-care center called Children's House, which they opened in New Haven in 1967 with a grant from the U.S. Children's Bureau.[2] To this day, their work remains a model of what developmentally oriented, family-focused child care can provide for infants and toddlers and their families. Clinicians, child-care workers and researchers have built upon this model to apply, expand, and adapt the techniques to a variety of child-care settings.[3] How many of these measures are feasible will depend on each family's circumstances, but the following is an outline of optimal efforts to ease the transition between home and child care.

1. Make yourself familiar with the child-care setting and with the daily routine. This will enable you to talk about the routine with your child. It will also help you understand your child better when she talks about what happened during the day.

2. Try to acquaint your child with the caregivers and the new setting before child care actually begins. How intensive and extensive this period of familiarization needs to be depends in part on the child's temperament, previous experience, and ease of adjustment to new situations. Your own child's responses are the best barometer of this.

3. Discuss with the caregiver your child's individual preferences, her areas of strength and vulnerability, and your child-rearing values, including your approach to discipline. This will enable the caregiver to use the knowledge in her own relationship with your child. Tell the caregiver about any special events when they occur so that she can talk about them with your child in the course of the day. (Are Grandma and Grandpa visiting? Did the dog run away? Did you watch a special movie last night?)

4. If at all possible, start out with briefer separations that become progressively longer as the child adjusts to the new setting. How brief the initial separations need to be depends on many factors, including your child's prior experience with separations and ease of adjustment to the new setting.

5. Avoid dropping the child off and leaving right away. Try to stay for a while until your child has settled in.

6. Try to establish contact with your child in the course of the day. This may mean dropping in at lunchtime or making a phone call. Telephone contact is particularly useful with toddlers over two, but it can be helpful as early as 18 months to provide a sense of

continuity. Even if your child does not speak very much, he can recognize your voice and cherish the connection with you.

7. Encourage the caregiver to let the child call you on the phone at times of unusually intense distress. Many caregivers feel that this takes away from their own role as a substitute parent, or that it disrupts the child-care routine. This may call for a talk with the caregiver in which you can acknowledge her importance in the child's life without relinquishing yours.

8. Give your child something from home to take to the child-care setting. It may be a toy, a security blanket, or something that belongs to the parent. Such a transitional object serves as a concrete representation of the parent and helps the child to remember that his home has not disappeared from his life.

9. Give your child a photograph of yourself. This photograph can be kept in the child's locker, with ready access to it in the course of the day. Toddlers know just how to use this precious resource. They go to it at times of stress and may not look at it for weeks at a time when things are going well.

10. Talk with your child about what it is like to be apart and about the pleasures of being together. This will help to make separation feelings a legitimate area for parent–child communication.

11. Play games that build on the mastery of separation experiences, such as hide-and-seek, the hiding and recovery of objects, and play with dolls around themes of going away and coming back. These games strengthen the child's sense of object permanence—the knowledge that people and things continue to exist when they are out of sight.

Different parents will find some of these suggestions more compatible with their own style than others. Similarly, different caregivers and child-care settings may lend themselves more easily than others to some of these efforts to build connections with the child's home. The specific configuration of what is done matters less than the spirit of partnership between parent and caregiver in arriving at workable ways of helping the child feel at home even while away from home.

The Child–Caregiver Relationship

Child care represents the toddler's home away from home for a major portion of the day. Most of the major developmental milestones take place while the toddler is in child care—new motor skills like jumping and running; toilet training; learning about objects through play and manipulation, and learning about the larger environment through exploring and roaming about.

All of these developments occur in the context of human relationships. Just as children raised full-time by a parent, the toddler in child care needs a secure base from which to explore the surroundings. In the home, this secure base is the parent; in child care, it should be the caregiver.

The toddler's relationship with the caregiver is the single most important component of the child-care experience. Young children internalize the quality of their interactions not only with their parents but with other important people as well. The relationship with the caregiver becomes an important model of what human connections outside the family have to offer.

If the child–caregiver relationship is nurturing, reliable and often even joyous, the child's confidence in human relationships as a source of comfort and reciprocity will be strengthened and expanded in spite of the parent's absence. The child will learn that not only are the parents to be trusted but that other people are trustworthy as well.

If, on the contrary, the child feels emotionally lost in the child-care relationship, with no reliable adult to turn to when he needs help or when he wants to share a discovery, this experience will mar the toddler's emotional investment in himself, in others, and in the world at large.

Different children respond to inadequate conditions in different ways.

At best, the more competent and resilient toddlers fall back on their own budding coping resources and make the most of whatever the environment has to offer. They may become precociously self-reliant or form an intense relationship with a peer to help them find challenge and interest in the course of the day. They may also develop a single-minded pursuit of something they can do on their own, such as fantasy play or building structures. These activities are constructive and growth-promoting in themselves, but they can result in emotional isolation when the child uses them as a defense against anxiety.

Other toddlers cope less creatively with the absence of an invested and available caregiver. They may roam about listlessly, becoming fleetingly interested in one or another feature of the environment but unable to sustain this interest through the supportive presence of a caring adult. Such children spend the day marking time until the parents return. It is as if they put their hearts, souls, and minds in storage until "real" life begins again. Some toddlers can regain a relatively intact sense of themselves at the end of a long and emotionally depleting day in child care. Others carry the losses into other settings as well, in the form of mistrust, aggression, or emotional withdrawal.

This should not do. Jeree Pawl puts it succinctly: "As parents, we can allow our child in day care to miss us, but she should not miss herself."[4] The child needs ongoing access to her sense of being emotionally alive in order to flourish as a human being.

It behooves parents to assess the child-care setting for its ability to provide meaningful human relationships. First and foremost, this means finding a caregiver or small set of caregivers who can get along with toddlers for a major portion of the day.

This is probably easier said than done. Provence and her colleagues[2] acknowledge that they found it harder to create a program geared to the developmental needs of toddlers between 15 and 30 months than to devise a program for younger or older children. They elaborate on this difficulty as follows:

> To live exclusively with a group of toddlers is not easy. They tend to impinge sharply and more or less continuously upon adults and upon each other. Their rapid shifts from helplessness to independent behavior, from negativism to angelic compliance, from adamant holding on to explosive casting out, from wishing to be as one with the adult to insisting on separateness and standing alone, from tenderness towards others to hostility, from taking initiatives to acting passively—

this radically varying behavior is physically and psychologically taxing to adults (p. 104).

All parents will recognize this catalogue of the toddler's inner states and outer behaviors. If parents (who love their child with all their hearts) have trouble coping with these swiftly changing and often contradictory moods, what could we expect of the caregiver, who even under optimal conditions may be very fond of the child but does not hold him at the very core of her being as do the parents?

It is difficult to find adults (parents included!) who can derive a sense of fun from being with toddlers all day and who can negotiate the developmental challenges of the toddler's newfound mobility, genital curiosity, toilet-training requirements, separation anxiety, and experimentation with self-assertion. Still, such adults do exist.[5] In searching for them, it is good to remember that caregivers (like parents) need not be omnipotent or omniscient. They do need to know and empathize with the needs of toddlers and be able and willing to give of themselves in relating to the children in their charge.

Things to Do

Relationships do not unfold in a vacuum. They are most rewarding when they become a vehicle for learning about oneself, about each other, and about the world. For toddlers, having things to do is a prerequisite for all these kinds of learning.

Child care arrangements vary a great deal in their structure. Some settings offer a highly structured curriculum with emphasis on academic topics such as learning to recognize and use numbers and letters. Others have no organized program and rely largely on free play and spontaneous activities.

Similarly, individual caregivers vary greatly in their ability to stimulate and entertain a child when she is cared for in the home. Some caregivers are wonderfully resourceful in coming up with interesting projects; others are so lackadaisical that the child can become quite bored as the hours go by.

The specific structure of the day matters less than the spirit with which it is carried out. An academic focus can challenge a toddler's intellect but carries the risk of becoming overly structured at an age when spontaneity is a key factor in developing a love for learning. Conversely, a totally unstructured atmosphere that emphasizes spontaneity can degenerate into chaos and anarchy if the caregivers lose touch with what is happening around them.

It is likely that different toddlers will do best in different settings. Some toddlers crave the safety of a predictable schedule; others are brimming with the impetus for doing what most fascinates them at any give time.

The optimal toddler child-care environments combine structured activities with plenty of attention to the child's individual needs.[6] Toddlers are unlikely to spend an inordinately long period of time at any activity, no matter how entranced with it they may be at first. A child-care schedule organized around the idea that toddlers may spend about 15 minutes in any one pursuit is realistically geared to the attention span of this age. Of course, even within this time frame there should be flexibility to enable one toddler to finish "putting the baby to sleep" or give more time to another toddler for putting the last touches to his block structure.

This means that the child-care setting should provide opportunities both for free play and for mastery of the environment through the development of new skills. The following materials and activities help toddlers to become engaged in different kinds of discoveries and accomplishments.

- Construction toys and puzzles that allow for fine motor manipulation and for visual–motor coordination
- Housekeeping utensils that encourage reenactment of the daily home routines and imaginative variations on domestic chores
- Dolls and play furniture to stimulate play around themes of caregiving and nurturance
- Playdough, painting equipment, and other "messy" materials and water-play toys that represent the bodily processes the toddler is struggling to master
- Musical instruments to encourage singing and dancing as a form of esthetics expression through the body
- Dress-up clothes to allow the child symbolic experimentation with other ways of being
- Playground equipment for outdoor play to enable the child to release energy and to acquire, expand, and refine gross motor skills.

A child-care setting that provides at least a sizable proportion of these opportunities for play and exploration is likely to have a good understanding of toddlers' developmental needs. When child care takes place in the home, outings to the park, to community centers, or to play groups can add variety to the daily routine.

The physical safety of the child-care setting is an essential ingredient. Without it nothing else can work well. Physical safety is important in itself, but it also serves as an index of the quality of the setting. Carollee Howes, whose research on child care has set a standard in the field, found that physical safety is related to the caregiver's attitude toward the children. Safer settings allow the caregiver to be less restrictive of the toddlers' activities and to give them more freedom to explore. When the setting is safe, caregivers are also more physically affectionate with the children in their charge, perhaps because they feel less need to be vigilant and can be more relaxed and spontaneous as a result.[7]

Relationship with Peers

Toddlers in child care form stable, reciprocal, and meaningful relationships with other children. In fact, friendships with other children alleviate the distress caused by the day-long separation from the parents.

Furthermore, toddlers in child care interact more with each other and learn each other's names at an earlier age than toddlers who are raised full-time by their mothers. They also engage in more sophisticated pretend play.[8,9] This greater cognitive and social complexity of peer play in toddlers who attend child care suggests that friendships with other children enable the toddler to cope more effectively with the daily stresses of separation from the parents.

The stability of these friendships is helpful. Toddlers who have long-term relationships with the same group of peers tend to be more popular and more socially interactive in the child-care setting.[10] Just like adults, toddlers feel more comfortable with friends they have known for a long time. Similarly, losing a friend in toddlerhood has noticeable effects on the child's sociability. Toddlers whose friends left the child-care setting tended to be less socially involved one year later.[10]

These findings highlight the importance of striving to provide the child with stable child care. Although parents cannot control the departure of their child's friends, they can try to minimize the number of changes that they themselves initiate. Toddlers, like adults, miss their friends, and may become more self-protective after losing a cherished relationship.

The child's relationship with the mother and with the caregiver has a significant effect on the ability to form friendships with other children.

Toddlers who have secure, nurturing, mutually satisfying relationships with both their mother and their caregiver are much more sociable with peers than children who feel insecure in their relationships with both women.[11] This finding highlights the continuing importance of the mother as well as the centrality of the caregiver in enabling toddlers to expand their social horizons. The secure base provided by emotionally available parents and parent surrogates sustains the child's confidence in exploring relationships with peers.

Saying Hello: The Joys and Stresses of Reunion

Coming together again after a long day apart can be an experience where joy, relief, anger, and fatigue are all present in different degrees both for the parent and for the child. Because of their importance in marking the resumption of direct contact, reunions deserve as much attention and care as separations to enhance the relationship between parent and child.

Reunions can be eagerly anticipated and still be something of a letdown when they finally occur. The parent and the child may be in different moods. One may be exuberantly active, the other tired and low-keyed. Worse yet, they might both be grumpy and needy and with few emotional resources left to share.

Toddlers often do not show pleasure on being picked up at the end of the day. They may be involved in play and figure that the parent can wait for them for a change. They may be angry at the separation and show it through a "cold shoulder" or through outright aggression. They may have intense positive and negative emotions raging inside them and try to cope with these feelings by keeping some distance from the parents until they can offer a genuinely warm hello.

For a parent who is looking forward to a loving reunion, these responses can feel like a dismal welcome indeed. Feeling unneeded and unappreciated, the parent may withdraw emotionally in return. This sequence of child reaction and parental counterreaction may set the tone for an evening of emotional distance between parent and child.

A reunion is colored by the emotional baggage of the separation experience, and some ambivalence is inevitably attached to it. Because of this, it is a good idea not to overinvest the reunion with the hope for instant and complete emotional reconnection. It takes some time to process the reality of the separation, to let go of the coping mechanisms one used for dealing with it, and to relax into being together again.

Parents can help themselves and their toddlers in this process by becoming aware of the range of feelings that come up during reunions and accepting them without guilt or blame. Lingering a while in the child-care setting, greeting the child warmly but giving her space to wind up an activity while staying near, chatting with the caregiver and the other children—these small but meaningful gestures can go a long way in creating an atmosphere where both parent and child feel permission for taking their time in being together and enjoying each other again.

The Parent–Caregiver Relationship

Child-care providers report that their relationships with children and co-workers are the most satisfying aspect of their work.[23] This response is yet another reminder that child care is primarily about relationships.

Parents are potentially valuable partners of the child-care circle, yet their relationship with the caregiver does not receive the attention it deserves. For example, parents spend an average of seven minutes a day in the child-care setting, and 10 percent of parents do not even go in. When parents are so minimally involved with their child's caregiver, they are losing an opportunity for partnership on behalf of their child.

There are concrete factors that account for this perfunctory contact. The parents are in a rush in the morning, and everybody is tired and wanting to go home by the end of the day. However, there are also built-in tensions in the relationship between parent and caregiver that contribute to the lack of communication between them.

Perhaps the most salient source of tension is a certain unease over who "owns" the child. When the toddler is at home, the parents' values and child-care routines are clearly the order of the day. In the child-care setting, the provider's own guidelines take over. There are multiple opportunities for conflicting attitudes and practices about the appropriate age to give up the bottle, when and how to begin toilet training, how to respond to the child's curiosity about bodily matters, how to mediate conflicts between peers—the list could go on and on.

Areas of disagreement can easily become sources of tension and even enmity between parent and caregiver, with feelings of disapproval and defensiveness experienced simultaneously by both sides. If these feelings are not modulated by a certain amount of good will, each party might come to feel that the child should be raised in a particular way (the way she favors) and that the child does best while in her care.

It is easy for caregivers to feel exploited by the parents, who often have better salaries and a more sophisticated life-style. The caregiver might feel that she is expected to take care of the child but is not given the respect and deference that such a responsibility should command. This experience is heightened if the parent is late in the payments or in picking up the child at the end of the day.

It is also easy for parents to feel criticized by the child-care provider, particularly if they are already feeling guilty or insecure. Mutual dissatisfaction often leads to mutual avoidance in an effort to prevent a fight that could end the child-care arrangement.

Enhancing the parent–provider relationship improves the quality of life for all involved: the parent, the caregiver, and, most of all, the child. The suggestions that follow can be helpful in facilitating this process.

• Set up an interview with the caregiver before you decide on a child-care arrangement. Elicit her views on the areas of child development and child rearing that are important to you. Ask her how she handles particular situations that are likely to occur, such as the child's refusal to obey or the child's calling for you. Ask also about her expectations regarding contact with you. For example, will you be able to drop in unannounced while your child is in her care? If you feel satisfied and reassured by her responses and by her affective style during this talk, this is a good sign that the two of you can form an effective working partnership with each other.

• Try to set up regular times to talk with the caregiver and exchange views about your child. The frequency and length of these talks may vary depending on circumstances and how smoothly things are going. It is imperative, however, that you keep an ongoing sense of being able to talk to each other whenever an issue of importance arises.

• Remember that the caregiver is a stable presence in your family life. Do not restrict your interaction with her to child-care events. Allow yourself to be friendly and open with her. Chat with her. If she looks tired, make a kind comment about that. If she was sick, ask her how she is feeling now. Inquire after her children. Feel free to explore the limits of what is feasible and appropriate between the two of you. The warmer your relationship, the greater the continuity your toddler will experience between child care and home.

• If your child tells you something about the caregiver's behavior that seems unusual or worrisome, do not dismiss it as a figment of a toddler's imagination. Toddlers can be amazingly accurate observers and reporters. On the other hand, remember that young children can misinterpret events: a caregiver who is trying to dislodge a piece of food stuck in a child's throat might be perceived by a young observer as hitting the child. Try to get a sense of the context in which the event reported took place. Then bring it up with the care provider in a calm, nonaccusing manner.

• If a conflict emerges, give some thought to strategy before you attempt to deal with it. If you can buy some time, let off steam by talking with the trusted people in your life and taking time to sort out your feelings. When you discuss it with the caregiver, try to frame the problem in a positive context. If at all possible, start out with the things that you value about her caregiving style, and work your way gradually to the area of concern. People (caregivers and parents included) respond much better when they are reassured that their areas of strength are noticed and appreciated.

Signs of Trouble

There are times when a toddler is not doing well in child care. How can we tell? The signs can be as varied as the children's personalities, but some recurrent warning signals are listed below.

- Sudden changes for the worse in the child's behavior that persist for longer than a few days and that cannot be attributed to increased stresses at home. For example, the toddler might become unusually aggressive, clingy, fearful, defiant, or negativistic. An increase in the symptoms of anxiety described in chapter 6 should alert the parents to look more closely at what is happening in child care.
- Avoidance or fear of a particular child-care provider.
- Persistent and sustained refusal to go to child care, particularly when the onset of this refusal is sudden and occurred after the child had settled into the child-care arrangement.
- Loss of zest for learning and exploring, sadness, and emotional withdrawal.
- Repeated statements about not liking a caregiver or another child, or reports that somebody did something scary such as yelling or spanking.

Children might misinterpret adult behavior, but more often they report accurately what they see. It is always important to pay attention to the child's verbal reports and behavioral changes. The two examples that follow make this point even more strongly.

Kerri, 36 months, says to her mother: "My teacher lies on top of us to make us take a nap." The mother believes Kerri is exaggerating. Two weeks later, she comes in at naptime and finds the assistant caregiver "containing" a struggling child by placing her body on top of his.

Trim, 2 years old, struggles every morning on being taken to his grandmother's house. "No hit, no hit," he cries. When his mother finds a bruise on his leg, she realizes the grandmother has been hitting him.

Children's distress in child care is not necessarily the result of abuse. One child refused to go to her day-care center for a week after listening to a story that frightened her. Another one developed nightmares as the result of daily confrontations with an older, stronger, and more aggressive child who bullied him. A third child relapsed in toilet training and became clingy and whiny after her favorite caregiver left suddenly without notice.

Signs of distress need to alert parents to look more closely at the child's experience of child care. This is when the efforts at building a relationship with the caregiver really pay off. The more parents and caregivers can cooperate with each other in tracing the reasons for the child's distress and in working toward a solution, the more effective they will be in making the child-care situation a secure base that sustains the child's emotional growth.

The Emotional Effects of Child Care

Does child care affect the toddler's attachment to the mother? There is a lively debate among child development specialists about the effects of child care on the young child's development. Some experts worry that long daily separations may create anxiety in the infant and toddler over the mother's availability. Other experts counter that young children acquire important social skills in the expanded social context of child care.[12,13]

The debate revolves around disagreements over theoretical and methodological issues, but two decades of research have failed to yield reliable findings that early child care has substantially negative effects on the relationship between mother and child. The majority of infants and toddlers with early day-care experience are securely attached to their toddlers.[14]

These findings make sense from many theoretical perspectives, including that of attachment theory. As Alan Sroufe remarked, one would expect infants to do well when they can learn over time that separations are predictable and lead equally predictably to reunions, that caregivers are emotionally available, and that parents and caregivers are accepting of the child's ambivalence about separations.[15]

Under normal circumstances, the emotional connection between parent and child is too powerful to be dampened by a family's need for two incomes or by the mother's desire to pursue other interests in addition to motherhood. Even when they cannot be always available, the parents' fierce, unique love for their child makes them different in the child's heart and mind from all other caregivers. In spite of a long working day, a parent's passion for his or her child retains its many nuances of emotional intensity, ranging from rapture and delight to impatience and even rage, that no other relationship in the child's life can match. Even very young infants are smart enough to recognize this passionate commitment and to reciprocate it in kind. Researchers may argue, but young children know best.

The question, "Is early child care detrimental to the child's relationship with the parents?" should be turned on its head. The question should become: "What are the emotional costs to the child of not providing adequate substitute care when both parents work out of the home?"

Fifty percent of American mothers return to work within their baby's first year.[16] In this context, it is high time to transform the debate on the effects of early child care on attachment into a debate about the human costs of not providing good substitute care to a young child when both parents need or choose to work. This leads us to the question of what constitutes good substitute care.

Choosing Good-Quality Child Care

It is difficult to determine exactly what constitutes good child care because this care comes in many forms. The child-care provider may be a cherished relative (an aunt, a grandmother) or someone hired especially for this purpose. The child might receive individual or group care. The setting may be the child's home, the child-care provider's home or a day-care center. There might be one or several child-care providers. The setting might be licensed or unlicensed, and it might be for-profit or sponsored by nonprofit organizations such as churches and community centers.

Within this diversity, quality criteria that apply to one setting may not be relevant to a different type of care. The most obvious example is group size, which is not an issue when the child is the single charge of a single caregiver but becomes an important factor in judging the quality of group care.

Some settings are easier to study than others. Day-care centers are more open to systematic research because they are formal settings at least nominally accountable to state standards. Private providers and family day-care homes are less likely to be licensed and more likely to argue that they are providing informal, homelike care not amenable to systematic evaluation research. For these reasons, most of the research on quality indicators has been conducted and validated in day-care centers, in spite of the fact that only 18 percent of children in child care receive this kind of care.[17] Recently there has also been research on the quality of family day care.[7]

The following factors have emerged as reliable indicators of quality group care.[18,19]

1.   *Stability of care.* The ongoing availability of the same caregiver or a small number of caregivers is a requisite to establish trusting emotional relationships that are not marred by a continuous process of loss and replacement. In addition, caregivers who are committed to their jobs for the long term relate to children in more stimulating and developmentally appropriate ways than those who see child care as a temporary job.[20]

For these two major reasons, the stability of the child-care provider is a pivotal factor in the quality of care. Optimal group care settings assign a primary caregiver to a small group of toddlers in order to maximize the child's use of a specific caregiver as a secure base. Clearly, caregiver stability is just as important in individual care as it is in group situations.

2.   *Caregiver training.* Childcare providers are better able to give quality care when they have specific training in child development. Knowledge of age-specific issues enables the caregiver to keep a broad perspective on the child's behavior. A toddler's negativism or temper tantrums, for example, can be handled with greater sensitivity by a caregiver who is aware of the autonomy strivings and intense emotions of this age.

Training is particularly important when the caregiver must attend to several toddlers with competing individual needs and demands. If she does not have specific knowledge about child development, the caregiver can only rely on her personal experience, which might not equip her well for the challenges of her task. A well-trained provider is also better qualified to identify early signs of behavioral problems and to share her perceptions constructively with the parents.

3. *The child:adult ratio.* Each caregiver can interact frequently and harmoniously with only a small number of toddlers. When they are asked about their work, caregivers report that being responsible for too many children is a major source of job-related stress. They cope with this situation by putting more emphasis on routine and cutting down on spontaneous, individualized exchanges. A ratio of three to five toddlers per adult allows for playfulness as well as ready attention to child distress before it becomes unmanageable. The higher this ratio becomes, the more difficult it is for the caregiver to maintain individualized care.

4. *Group size.* Even with an adequate number of children in the care of each adult, a large group of toddlers can easily become draining and unmanageable. There is too much noise, too many simultaneous demands, too much distraction. A group size no larger than eight or ten toddlers allows the caregivers to focus on playfulness and emotional availability and diminishes the need for rigid group management.

5. *The presence of another adult.* Individual caregivers are supported both concretely and emotionally by another adult who can pitch in, help out, and provide some companionship. The presence of a second caregiver can also reduce the likelihood of child abuse both because there is a potential witness and because each caregiver is less likely to lose control if she can delegate responsibility before she is pressed to her limits and events get out of hand.

Does the Quality of Child Care Matter?

The shortest and most accurate answer is: yes, quality matters very much. Good child care enhances the child's well-being, and poor quality child care is damaging to it. At least a dozen recent research studies document this conclusion. Infants, toddlers, and preschoolers have more advanced social and cognitive skills when they attend good-quality child care.[19]

One study is of particular interest because it chose to investigate reports that the early beginning of child care is associated with later aggression and noncompliance. The authors found that this was indeed the case when the children were enrolled in low-quality settings. These toddlers had a higher incidence of temper tantrums and refusals to comply with adult requests. On the contrary, toddlers enrolled in high-quality day-care centers were better able to modulate their behavior when compared to children with no child-care experience and to children in poor quality day care.[21]

The quality of child care matters a great deal, but so does the family's input on the selection of child care. Parents whose lives are stressful are more likely to place their children in centers of poor quality, regardless of their income and of tuition costs.[23] This is not hard to understand. Overburdened parents are less likely to do extensive research before choosing a setting.

While understandable, this is unfortunate because children raised in high-stress families are even more in need of high-quality care than other toddlers in order to compensate for the difficulties they face in their homes. Since there is a greater abundance of mediocre care than of high-quality care, parents need help in sorting out the different factors they should consider. In addition to the information in this chapter, there are some very readable publications to assist parents in this task.[5,22]

The Social Realities of Current Child Care

As a society we know what constitutes good child care, but we have not yet learned how to provide it to all our children. The criteria for quality care, painstakingly gleaned from extensive and expensive research, are routinely overridden because there is no national mandate to follow up the money for research with money for service delivery.

As a result, we acquire more and more academic information that remains unused, because we are eager to collect it but not to apply it. The knowledge stays in books and journals without fulfilling its potential value in enhancing the lives of millions of children and their families.

The effectiveness of the different states in setting and enforcing standards of quality is a case in point. Licensing is under state control, and it provides a primary means for regulating the quality of care. Those states that do have guidelines frame them in terms of such minimum standards that the goal is simply to prevent physical harm to the child rather than to assure a developmentally appropriate environment. In this sense, the research findings regarding quality of child care have not been systematically incorporated into state regulations. For example, 27 states have no requirements for the education or training for child-care teachers as a condition of employment.[23]

This situation has a direct effect on quality of care. A major index of quality, the stability of caregivers, tells the story. Although frequent changes in care providers is detrimental to the child, staff turnover in child-care settings approaches or exceeds 50 percent in some areas of the country. This is more than double the average replacement rate for all occupations, which is about 20 percent.[23]

The strikingly high rate of turnover in child-care workers reflects the low pay, lack of benefits, and stressful working conditions inherent in the child-care field. The National Committee on Pay Equity reported that child-care providers are the second most underpaid workers in the nation. Only the clergy earn less.[24] Translated into dollars and cents, this means that the median annual income of child-care workers is actually below the official poverty level for a family of four, which in 1986 was $11,200. The low salary is not offset by the incentive of good benefits. Paid vacation averages nine days a year and about half of day-care center staff receives no medical insurance.

This dismal situation cannot be excused as the natural consequence of lack of training. The education of child-care providers reflects the national profile for all occupations. However, caregivers who can earn more money elsewhere tend to leave the field, with the result that there might be a net decline in the availability of highly trained child-care providers.

What accounts for this state of affairs? Most likely a combination of factors involving deeply rooted societal attitudes about "women's work." Child care was traditionally provided by mothers at no cost before they had to join the work force in droves as a result of changing economic and social conditions. We have been slow to relinquish our idealized image of caring for children as a nonprofit activity deeply rooted in the maternal instinct and unrelated to economic concerns.

This stereotype is reinforced by the fact that women, particularly minority women, are overrepresented in the field of child care. The most recent available data show that between 95 percent and 98 percent of all child-care providers are women. Of these, approximately 35 percent of child-care staff and 60 percent of family child-care providers belong to ethnic minorities.[23] Women and minorities are traditionally underpaid, a factor that compounds the built-in tendency to regard child care as an occupation untouched by the market forces of supply and demand.

These considerations provide the background for understanding the child-care provider's daily experience. Caregivers who are underpaid and overworked are less able to provide quality care because these stresses detract from their energy and emotional availability. On the contrary, caregivers who are at ease with their working conditions are more likely to provide appropriate care.

In summary, good child care results from an effective partnership between society as a whole, caregivers, and parents on behalf of our children. A national commitment to finance and uphold the standards of good child care is an essential framework to provide the stability and continuity that all children need to become well-functioning adults. Such a framework in turn promotes and sustains the day-to-day and moment-to-moment efforts of parents and caregivers to be physically available and emotionally responsive to the children's needs.

Conclusion:
Staying Close and Letting Go

As babies become toddlers and begin to assert their need to build an autonomous sphere of action, parents learn to face their own limitations in nurturing and protecting their child. The fantasy that the parent's physical and emotional presence is enough to keep the child safe and content gives way to the realization that there are disappointments, challenges, and even dangers that we are helpless to wish away.

The desire to do well by our child goes hand in hand with the inevitability, even the desirability, of failing our child sometimes.

Many a knowledgeable and well-meaning parent has tried to anticipate every sorrow and put into words each nuance of what the child is thinking and feeling in the belief that this would prevent loneliness and fear. In the process, the parents may rob their child of the experience of struggling with inner uncertainties and coming up triumphantly with very personal insights and solutions. By injecting themselves excessively into their children's inner life, parents may deprive them of the opportunity to develop a self of their own.

Not until adolescence will parents face as many dilemmas in raising their children as they do in the toddler years. In fact, the second and third years of life are excellent practice for the challenges posed by a teenager. Toddlerhood resembles adolescence because of the rapidity of physical growth and because of the impulse to break loose of parental boundaries. At both ages, the struggle for independence exists hand in hand with the often hidden wish to be contained and protected while striving to move forward in the world. How parents and toddlers negotiate their differences sets the stage for their ability to remain partners during childhood and through the rebellions of the teenage years.

Toddlers, just like adolescents, need to forge an identity that integrates a solid sense of personal initiative with a reliable feeling of communal belonging. Parents are faced in both periods with the task of deciding when to respect aloneness, when to offer companionship, and when to exercise firm authority. When the parents' choice is responsive to the child's needs, the negativism of toddlers becomes the self-assured assertiveness of the preschool years, just as the emotional storms of adolescence resolve themselves in the self-worth of young adulthood.

Communication is important in growing up, but so is the chance to think and feel on one's own. Letting the child be is at times just as important as being with the child. The lifelong lesson of the toddler years involves learning that sometimes letting go—within limits—is the surest way of staying close.

References

Chapter 2: Who Is the Toddler?

1. Kierkegaard, S. (1983). *Purity of heart is to will one thing* (p. 85). New York: Harper & Row.
2. Ainsworth, M. D. S., Blehar, M. C., Waters, E., & Wall, S. (1978). *Patterns of attachment: A psychological study of the strange situation.* Hillsdale, NJ: Erlbaum.
3. Bowlby, J. (1982). *Attachment and loss: Vol. 1. Attachment* (2nd ed.). New York: Basic Books.
4. Bowlby, J. (1973). *Attachment and loss: Vol. 2. Separation: anxiety and anger.* New York: Basic Books.
5. Smart, M. S. & Smart, M. C. (1967). Children: Development and relationships (p. 146). New York: Macmillan.
6. Anderson, J. W. (1972). Attachment behavior out of doors. In N. Blurton Jones (Ed.), *Ethological studies of child behavior* (pp. 199–217). Cambridge, England: Cambridge University Press.
7. Erikson, E. (1950). *Childhood and society* (p. 227). New York: Norton.
8. Mahler, M. S., Pine, F., & Bergman, A. (1975). *The psychological birth of the human infant.* New York: Basic Books.
9. Marvin, R. S. (1977). An ethological-cognitive model for the attenuation of mother-child attachment behavior. In T. Alloway, L. Kramer, & P. Pliner (Eds.), *Advances in the study of communication and affect: Vol. 3. Attachment behavior* (pp. 25–60). New York: Plenum.
10. Brazelton, T. B. (1989). *Toddlers and parents: A declaration of independence.* New York: Delta/Seymour Lawrence.
11. Lewis, M. & Brooks-Gunn, J. (1979). *Social cognition and the acquisition of self.* New York: Plenum.

Chapter 3: The Challenges of Being (and Raising) a Toddler

1. Patterson, G. R. (1980). Mothers: the unacknowledged victims. *Monographs of the Society for Research in Child Development, 45,*(5).
2. Fawl, C. L. (1963). Disturbances experienced by children in their natural habitat. In R. Barker (Ed.), *The stream of behavior.* New York: Appleton-Century-Crofts.
3. Minton, C., Kagan, J., & Levine, J. (1971). Maternal control and obedience in the two-year-old. *Child Development, 42,* 1873–1894.

4. Forehand, R., King, H. E., Peed, S., & Yoder, P. (1975). Mother-child interactions: comparison of a noncompliant clinic group and a nonclinic group. *Behavior Research and Therapy, 13,* 79–84.

5. Rexroat, C. & Shehan, C. (1987). The family life cycle and spouses' time in housework. *Journal of Marriage and the Family 49,* 737–750.

6. Lamb, M. E. (Ed.) (1976). *The role of the father in child development.* New York: Wiley.

7. Fraiberg, S. (1959). *The magic years.* New York: Scribner's.

8. Bowlby, J. (1982). *Attachment and loss: Vol. 1. Attachment* (2nd ed.). New York: Basic Books.

9. Greenspan, S. (1989). *The essential partnership.* New York: Viking Books.

10. Stern, D. (1985). *The interpersonal world of the infant.* New York: Basic Books.

11. Letter from Kevin Frank, quoted by Murphy, L. B. (1988). When a child is inconsolable: Staying near. *Zero to three. Bulletin of the National Center for Clinical Infant Programs, 9*(2), 15.

Chapter 4: The Question of Temperament

1. Brazelton, T. B. (1969). *Infants and mothers: Differences in development.* New York: Delacorte Press/Seymour Lawrence, 1969.

2. Brazelton, T. B. (1973). The neonatal behavioral assessment scale. *Clinics in Developmental Medicine, 50.*

3. Thomas, A., Chess, S., & Birch, H. (1968). *Temperament and behavior disorders in children.* New York: New York Universities Press.

4. Stern, D. (1985). *The interpersonal world of the infant.* New York: Basic Books.

5. Goldsmith, H., Buss, A., Plomin, R., Rothbart, M., Thomas, A., Chess, S., Hinde, R., & McCall, R. (1987). Roundtable: What is temperament? *Child Development, 58,* 505–529.

6. Thomas, A. & Chess, S. (1977). *Temperament and development.* New York: Brunner/Mazel.

7. Thomas, A. & Chess, S. (1980). *The dynamics of psychological development.* New York: Brunner/Mazel.

8. Chess, S. & Thomas, A. (1984). *Origins and evolution of behavior disorders: From infancy to early adult life.* New York: Brunner/Mazel.

9. Escalona, S. (1968). *The roots of individuality.* Chicago: Aldine.

10. Greenspan, S. (1989). *The essential partnership.* New York: Viking.

11. Erikson, E. (1950). *Childhood and society* (p. 64). New York: Norton.

12. Crockenberg, S. B. (1981). Infant irritability, mother responsiveness

and social support influences on the security of infant–mother attachment. *Child Development, 52,* 857–869.

13. Gandour, M. J. (1989). Activity level as a dimension of temperament in toddlers: Its relevance for the organismic specificity hypothesis. *Child Development, 60,* 1092–1098.

Chapter 5: The Active Toddler

1. Provence, S. & Lipton, R. C. (1962). *Infants in institutions.* New York: International Universities Press.
2. Lieberman, A. F. & Pawl, J. H. (1988). Clinical applications of attachment. In J. Belsky & T. Nezworski (Eds.), *Clinical implications of attachment* (pp. 327–351). New York: Lawrence Erlbaum.
3. Fraiberg, S. (1959). *The magic years.* New York: Scribner's.
4. "Flexible, fearful or feisty: The different temperaments of infants and toddlers" (Video). (1979). Sausalito, CA: Far West Laboratories Center for Child and Family Studies for California State Department of Education.
5. Parens, H. (1979). *The development of aggression in early childhood.* New York: Aronson.

Chapter 6: The Shy Toddler

1. Kagan, J. & Snidman, N. (1991). Temperamental factors in human development. *American Psychologist, 46*(8), 856–862.
1a. Ibid.
2. Kagan, J., Reznick, J. S., & Snidman, N. (1987). The physiology and psychology of behavioral inhibition in children. *Child Development, 58,* 1459–1473.
3. Kagan, J. & Moss, H. A. (1962). *Birth to maturity,* New York: Wiley.
4. Kagan, J., Reznick, J. S., Snidman, N., Gibbons, J., & Johnson, M. D. (1988). Childhood derivatives of inhibition and lack of inhibition to the unfamiliar. *Child Development, 59,* 1580–1589.
5. Kagan, J. & Snidman, N. (1991). Infant predictors of inhibited and uninhibited profiles. *Psychological Science, 2,* 40–44.
6. Kagan, J. (1991). The shy and the sociable. *Harvard Alumni Magazine,* Winter.
7. "Flexible, fearful, or feisty: The different temperaments of infants and toddlers" (Video) (1979). Sausalito, CA: Far West Laboratories Center for Child and Family Studies for California State Department of Education.

Chapter 7: Early Anxieties

1. Bowlby, J. (1973). *Attachment and loss: Vol. 2. Separation: anxiety and anger.* New York: Basic Books.

2. Humphrey, T. (1970). The development of human fetal activity and its relation to postnatal behavior. In H. W. Reese and L. P. Lipsitt (Eds.), *Advances in child development and behavior* (Vol. 2, pp. 1–57). New York: Academic Press.

3. Field, T. (1990). *Infancy.* Cambridge, Mass.: Harvard University Press.

4. Stern, D. N. (1971). A micro-analysis of mother–infant interaction: Behavior regulating social contact between a mother and her 3 ½-month-old twins. *Journal of the American Academy of Child Psychiatry, 10,* 501–516.

5. Ainsworth, M. D. S., Blehar, M. C., Waters, E., & Wall, S. (1978). *Patterns of attachment: A psychological study of the strange situation.* Hillsdale, NJ: Erlbaum.

6. Graves, P. (1980). The functioning fetus. In S. I. Greenspan and G. H. Pollock (Eds.), *The course of life: Psychoanalytic contributions toward understanding personality development: Vol. 1. Infancy and early childhood* (pp. 235–256). Washington, DC: U.S. Government Printing Office.

7. DeCasper, A. J., & Fifer, W. P. (1980). Of human bonding: Newborns prefer their mothers' voices. *Science, 208,* 1174–1176.

8. McFarlane, J. (1975). Olfaction in the development of social preferences in the human neonate. In H. Hofer (Ed.), *Parent-infant interaction.* Amsterdam: Elsevier.

9. Sander, L. (1962). Issues in early mother–child interaction. *Journal of the American Academy of Child Psychiatry, 1,* 141–166.

10. Greenspan, S. I., & Greenspan, N. T. (1989). *First feelings: Milestones in the emotional development of your baby and child.* New York: Penguin.

11. Bell, S. M. & Ainsworth, M. D. S. (1972). Infant crying and maternal responsiveness. *Child Development, 43,* 1171–1190.

12. Winnicott, D. W. (1965). *The maturational process and the facilitating environment.* New York: International Universities Press.

13. Pruett, K. D. (1987). *The nurturing father: Journey toward the complete man.* New York: Warner Books.

14. Dixon, S., Yogman, M. W., Tronick, E., Als, H., Adamson, L., & Brazelton, T. B. (1981). Early social interaction of infants with parents and strangers. *Journal of the American Academy of Child Psychiatry, 20,* 32.

15. Main, M., & Weston, D. R. (1981). The quality of the toddler's relationship to mother and to father: Related to conflict behavior and the readiness to establish new relationships. *Child Development, 52,* 932–940.

16. Main, M., Kaplan, N., & Cassidy, J. (1985). Security in infancy, childhood, and adulthood: A move to the level of representation. In I. Bretherton & E. Waters (Eds.), Growing points of attachment theory and research. *Monographs of the Society for Research in Child Development, 50,* (Nos. 1-2, Serial No. 209), 66–104.

17. Roiphe, H. & Galensau, E. (1981). *Infantile origins of sexual identity.* New York: International Universities Press.

18. Lozoff, B., Brittenham, G., Trause, M., Kennell, J., & Klaus, M. (1977). The mother–newborn relationship: Limits of adaptability. *Journal of Pediatrics, 91*(1), 1–12.

19. Erikson, Erik H. (1963). *Childhood and society.* New York: Norton.

20. Fraiberg, S. (1982). Pathological defenses in infancy. *Psychoanalytic Quarterly, 51,* 612–635.

21. Lieberman, A. F. (1985). Infant mental health: A model for service delivery. *Journal of Clinical Child Psychology 14*(3), 196–201.

22. Lieberman, A. F., Weston, D. R., & Pawl, J. H. (1991). Preventive intervention and outcome with anxiously attached dyads. *Child Development, 62,* 199–209.

23. Matas, L., Arend, R., & Sroufe, L. A. (1978). Continuity of adaptation in the second year: The relationship between quality of attachment and later competence. *Child Development, 49,* 547–556.

24. Sroufe, L. A. (1983). Infant–caregiver attachment and patterns of adaptation in preschool: The roots of maladaptation and competence. In M. Perlmutter (Ed.), *Minnesota Symposium in Child Psychology* (Vol. 16). Hillsdale, NJ: Erlbaum.

25. Arend, R., Grove, F., & Sroufe, L. A. (1979). Continuity of individual adaptation from infancy to kindergarten: A predictive study of ego-resiliency. *Child Development, 50,* 950–959.

26. Lewis, M., Feiring, C., McGoffog, C., & Jaskir, J. (1984). Predicting psychopathology in six-year-olds from early social relations. *Child Development, 55,* 123–126.

Chapter 8: Issues to Negotiate

1. Bowlby, J. (1973). *Attachment and loss: Vol. 2. Separation: anxiety and anger.* New York: Basic Books.

2. Fraiberg, S. (1959). *The magic years.* New York: Schribner's.

3. Brazelton, T. B. (1977). *Toddlers and parents: A declaration of independence.* New York: Bantam/Doubleday.

4. Kagan, J. (1981). *The second year.* Cambridge: Harvard University Press.

5. Richman, N. (1981). A community survey of the characteristics of the 1–2 year olds with sleep disruptions. *Journal of the American Academy of Child & Adolescent Psychiatry, 20,* 281–291.

6. Keener, M., Zeanah, C., & Anders, T. (1988). Infant temperament, sleep organization, and nighttime parental interventions. *Pediatrics, 81,* 762–771.

7. Minde, K., Popiel, K., Leos, N., Falkner, S., Parker, K., & Handley-Derry, M. (1993). The evaluation and treatment of sleep disturbances in young children. *Journal of Child Psychology & Psychiatry, 34.*

8. Guilleminault, C. (1987). Disorders of arousal in children: somnambulism and night terrors. In C. Guilleminault (Ed.), *Sleep and its disorders in children* (pp. 243–252). New York: Raven Press.

Chapter 9: When Parents Divorce

1. Hetherington, E. M. (1989). Coping with family transitions: Winners, losers and survivors. *Child Development, 60,* 1–14.

2. Wallerstein, J. (1989). *Second chances: Men, women and children a decade after divorce.* New York: Ticknor & Fields.

3. Piaget, J. (1959). *The language and thought of the child.* London: Routledge & Kegan Paul.

4. MacFarlane, J. (1975). Olfaction in the development of social preferences in the human neonate. In H. Hofer (Ed.), *Parent-infant interaction.* Amsterdam: Elsevier.

5. DeCasper, A. J., and Fifer, W. P. (1980). Of human bonding: Newborns prefer their mothers' voices. *Science, 208,* 1174–76.

6. Fagan, J. F. (1973). Infant's delayed recognition necessary and forgetting. *Journal of Experimental Child Psychology, 16,* 424–50.

7. Nachman, P., & Stern, D. (1983). Recall memory for emotional experience in pre-linguistic infants. Paper presented at the National Clinical Infancy Fellows Conference, Yale University, New Haven, CT.

8. Duncan, G. J., & Hoffman, S. D. (1985). A reconsideration of the economic consequences of marital dissolution. *Demography, 22*(5), 480–485.

9. Arendell, T. (1986). *Mothers and divorce: Legal, economic and social dilemmas.* Berkeley: University of California Press.

10. Weitzman, L. (1985). *The divorce revolution: The unexpected social and economic consequences for women and children in America.* New York: Free Press.

11. National Center for Health Statistics (1984). *Monthly Vital Statistics Report.* Supplement, *32*(3). Washington, DC: U.S. Department of Health and Human Services.

12. U.S. Bureau of the Census (1985). Statistical abstract of the United States. *National Data Board and Guide to Sources.* Washington, DC: U.S. Government Printing Office.

13. Gatley, R. & Koulack, D. (1979). *Single father's handbook: A guide for separated and divorced fathers.* New York: Anchor Books.

14. Thompson, R., Lamp, M. E., & Estes, D. (1982). Stability of infant–mother attachment and its relationship to changing life circumstances in an unselected middle class sample. *Child Development, 53,* 144–148.

15. Lieberman, A. F., Weston, D., & Pawl, J. H. (1991). Preventive intervention and outcome with anxiously attached dyads. *Child Development, 62,* 199–209.

16. Herzog, J. (1980). Sleep disturbance and father hunger in 19-to 28-month-old boys: The Erlkoning syndrome. *The Psychoanalytic Study of the Child, 35,* 219–236.

Chapter 10: The Toddler in Childcare

1. Provence, S. (1986). Presentation made at the Symposium on Early Infant and Toddler Care, San Francisco Psychoanalytic Institute Extension Division, San Francisco, CA.

2. Provence, S., Naylor, A., & Patterson, J. (1977). *The challenge of daycare.* New Haven: Yale University Press.

3. Kalmanson, B. (1990). Understanding's responses to separation. In S. Chehrazi (Ed.), *Psychological issues in day care* (pp. 159–175). Washington, DC: American Psychiatric Press.

4. Pawl, J. H. (1990). Infants in daycare: Reflections on experiences, expectations and relationships. *Zero to Three: Bulletin of the National Center for Clinical Infant Programs,* February, 1–6.

5. Roemer, J. (1989). *Two to four from 9–5: The adventures of a daycare provider.* New York: Harper & Row.

6. Lally, R. (1990). *A guide to social-emotional growth and socialization.* Sacramento: California Department of Education.

7. Howes, C. (1983). Caregiver behavior in center and family day care. *Journal of Applied Developmental Psychology, 4,* 99–107.

8. Howes, C. (1985). Sharing fantasy: Social pretend play in toddlers. *Child Development, 56,* 1253–1258.

9. Nachman, P. A. (1990). A companion study of toddlers cared for by mother or by substitute caregivers. In S. Chehrazi (Ed.), *Psychosocial issues in day care* (pp. 147–158). Washington, DC: American Psychiatric Press.

10. Howes, C. (1987). Social competence with peers in young children: development sequences. *Developmental Review, 7,* 252–272.

11. Howes, C., Rodning, C., Galluzzo, D. C., & Myers, L. (1990). Attachment and child care: Relationships with mother and caregiver. In N. Fox & G. G. Fein (Eds.), *Infant day care: The current debate* (pp. 169–182). New Jersey: Ablex.

12. Belsky, J. (1990). The "effects" of infant day care reconsidered. In N. Fox & G. G. Fein (Eds.), *Infant day care: The current debate* (pp. 3–40). New Jersey: Ablex.

13. Clarke-Steward, K. A. (1990). "The effects of infant day care reconsidered": Risks for parents, children and researchers. In N. Fox & G. G. Fein (Eds.), *Infant day care: The current debate* (pp. 61–86). New Jersey: Ablex.

14. Thompson, R. A. (1990). The effects of infant day care through the prism of attachment theory: A critical appraisal. In N. Fox & G. G. Fein (Eds.), *Infant day care: The current debate* (pp. 41–50). New Jersey: Ablex.

15. Sroufe, A. (1990). A developmental perspective on day care. In N. Fox & G. G. Fein (Eds.), *Infant day care: The current debate* (pp. 51–59). New Jersey: Ablex.

16. House Select Committee on Children, U.S. Congress. (1984). Youth and Families: Families and child care: Improving the options. Washington, DC: U.S. Government Printing Office.

17. Zigler, E., & Hall, N. (1988). Day care and its effects on children: An overview for pediatric health professionals. *Journal of Developmental and Behavioral Pediatrics, 9,* 38–46.

18. Ruopp, R., Travers, J., Cornell, D., & Goodrich, R. (1979). *Children at the Center.* Summary findings and implications of the National Day Care Study. Cambridge, MA: Abt Books.

19. Howes, C. (1990). Current research on early day care. In S. Chehrazi (Ed.), *Psychological issues in day care* (pp. 21–36). Washington, DC: American Psychiatric Press.

20. Berk, L. (1985). Relationships of educational attainments, child oriented attitudes, job satisfaction, and career commitment to caregiver behavior toward children. *Child Care Quarterly, 14,* 103–129.

21. Howes, C. & Olenick, M. (1986). Family and child care influences on toddler compliance. *Child Development, 57,* 206–216.

22. Katzner, A. R. & Bragdon, N. H. (1990). *Childcare solutions: A parents' guide to finding childcare you can trust.* New York: Avon Books.

23. Phillips, D. & Whitebook, M. (1990). The child care provider: pivotal player in the child's world. In S. Chehrazi (Ed.), *Psychological issues in day care* (pp. 129–146). Washington, DC: American Psychiatric Press.

24. National Committee on Pay Equity. (1987). Pay equity: An issue of race, ethnicity and sex. Washington, DC: NCPE.

Index